Brian Arbour
Unhyphenated America in Transition

The De Gruyter Series in American Political Geography

Edited by
Nicholas F. Jacobs and B. Kal Munis

Volume 1

Brian Arbour

Unhyphenated America in Transition

Political Geography, Ethnic Identity, and the Unique Partisan Realignment of Appalachia and the Upper South

DE GRUYTER

ISBN (Paperback) 978-3-11-161545-5
ISBN (Hardcover) 978-3-11-161618-6
e-ISBN (PDF) 978-3-11-161570-7
e-ISBN (EPUB) 978-3-11-161589-9
ISSN 3052-2552

Library of Congress Control Number: 2025940717

Bibliographic information published by the Deutsche Nationalbibliothek
The Deutsche Nationalbibliothek lists this publication in the Deutsche Nationalbibliografie;
detailed bibliographic data are available on the internet at http://dnb.dnb.de.

© 2025 Walter de Gruyter GmbH, Berlin/Boston, Genthiner Straße 13, 10785 Berlin
Cover image: iStock/Getty Images Plus/omersukrugoksu
Typesetting: Integra Software Services Pvt. Ltd.

www.degruyter.com
Questions about General Product Safety Regulation:
productsafety@degruyterbrill.com

Preface

When I teach my Introduction to American Government class, I begin the course with a lecture titled "Who are Americans?" This is a vexing question in the United States because there is no obvious and clear definition. In fact, if you look at something like the House Un-*American* Activities Committee, one can see that who are Americans is a contested question throughout American history. At one level, to be an American is a birthright of all born inside the borders of the United States or born to an American citizen. The Declaration of Independence argues that citizens are "endowed by their creator with certain unalienable rights," which presumes that these rights are bestowed at birth and cannot be taken away by the government. Americans are born into being Americans.

But being an American is not limited to "natural born citizens." Throughout its history, the United States has welcomed immigrants from every corner of the globe and allowed them to become Americans. That statement is not fully accurate. Immigrants are not just allowed to become Americans; they assimilate into being Americans. They adapt to American customs and democratic norms while also contributing their own customs, foods, and traditions into what an American is. Thus, American has taken a large number of immigrants from a wide variety of nationalities, religions, customs and practices and made them and their descendants Americans. Anyone can be an American if they choose to be.

In this vision of what it means to be an American, unity is created not by family ties, ethnicity, or even a shared history. What is central to being an American is the broad acceptance of a shared sense of democratic values, mostly succinctly expressed in the Declaration of Independence's proclamation that "all men are created equal," each individual possesses unalienable rights to "life, liberty, and the pursuit of happiness" and that governments derive their "just powers from the consent of the governed." In these words, the American founders established the key principle of American government and political culture—equality, liberty, and democracy.

The answer to the question of who is an American has thus expanded well beyond the original conception of America's Founders. It has expanded fully to women, to the descendants of slaves, and to generations of immigrants and their descendants. America is thus an idea and an ideal and as an idea, being an American is available to all.

In this book, I explore a distinctly different idea of "who is an American." The Americans I examine in this book are those who identify their own ethnic heritage as American. A change in the Census questionnaire in 1980 allowed individuals to describe their own heritage in an open-ended question, and since then, about 8% of respondents have written "American" as the answer to this question.

https://doi.org/10.1515/9783111615707-202

Sociologists have examined this group in detail, finding that the choice for an individual to describe his or her heritage as American was not made from ignorance of one's European roots. Instead, it reflected the long-term process of shifting one's ethnic identity. Just as Celts became Angles who became English, so too do others transform their ethnic heritage over generations of intermarriage, immigration, and settlement. The sociologists also gave this group the name "unhyphenated Americans." The unhyphenated Americans—that is white Americans who see their own ethnic heritage as distinctly American—are not randomly scattered across the United States. Instead they are concentrated in the Appalachias and the Upper South.

It is unclear what these individuals mean when they write "American" as their ethnic heritage. But the conclusion of sociologists is that it is not a statement of patriotic intent. They are not declaring themselves Americans with no divided loyalty. A large number of unhyphenated Americans are the children whose parents write a more complicated answer to their own ethnic heritage and simplify it for their children. As such, it is not a statement of loyalty to America and the natural rights it grants citizens upon birth. Nor is it a statement of adherence to the set of democratic ideals spelled out in the Declaration of Independence. Few naturalized Americans define their heritage as American despite having to pass a citizenship test and swear allegiance to their new country. It is a different vision of being an American than I discuss in the first lecture in my American Government class.

I think it is this contrast between my classroom version of being an American and the one expressed by American ethnic identifiers that drew me to this project. I learned about American ethnic identifiers in the 2008 Democratic nomination contest, when a model of vote choice found it to be a significant predictor of voting for Hillary Clinton over Barack Obama. I explored the negative reaction to Obama in regions with concentrations of unhyphenated Americans in an article I wrote in 2010 with Jeremy Teigen. But my thoughts about about the importance of unhyphenated America to vote choice did not go away. It strengthened as I watched subsequent elections and the Appalachias and the upper South moved further and further away from the Democrats.

In the definition of who is an American I use in my classroom, being an American is a set of ideals endowed within the national creed and passed on from generation to generation through the teaching of history, citizenship and the continual practice of patriotic rituals—the Pledge at the start of the school day, the Anthem at the start of a baseball game, and the playing of "Stars and Stripes Forever" at the conclusion of a Fourth of July fireworks extravaganza. In the ethnic version, America is an individual's ethnic heritage. That it is concentrated among whites and among those in a particular geographic region indicates it is limited version of what it means to be an American. It seems rooted in the lack of distinctiveness of the communities of the Appalachias and the upper South from the idealized view of what America is—small towns, low levels of immigrants, names and heritage from the British Isles, and lots of churches and guns. It is not a definition of being American that is truly open to all.

I am also a political scientist and a scholar of American elections. My interest in unhyphenated America also stems from my own interest in elections that changing patterns of vote results. The combination of geography and ethnicity in regions with large concentrations of unhyphenated Americans is also associated with large gains for Republicans in presidential and congressional elections since the middle of the 1990s. I argue that the timing of this realignment makes it different from the well-studied Southern Republican realignment, which happened earlier in time.

I also examine why the shift in unhyphenated America happened, and find it is primarily caused by an increase in issue salience for social issues such as abortion and environmental issues such as climate change. Unhyphenated America has distinctly conservative attitudes on these issues. Unhyphenated America's conservative attitudes on racial issues were activated by the nationalization of racial issues prompted by the inauguration of Barack Obama and the backlash to his administration embodied by Donald Trump's racially resentful rhetoric.

This book tells the story of the rapid shift of unhyphenated America from a politically mixed region in the 1980s to a landslide Republican region in the 2010s and 2020s. I use ethnicity to identify a broad but demographically similar region and its particular political journey to the right. It is a version of who is American different from what I teach in my classroom, but possibly one that I should. What it means to be an American has become intimately connected to vote choice for people in the Appalachias and the upper South. And in American politics, that is a vitally important story.

* * *

My book is solo authored, which means I am responsible for every word that is written, every table and figure contained between these covers, and every omission, bad edit, and bit of faulty analysis that you can find here.

Yet, no solo authored project is the creation of one person. I am indebted to a large number of friends and colleagues who assisted me along the way. I have presented versions of this work at academic conferences for over a decade at this point. This provided a needed opportunity for deadlines to move the project along, but also for feedback from a host of panel discussants. In particular, I have presented this work many times at the biennial Citadel Symposium on Southern Politics. My thanks to Dubose Kapeluk, Scott Buchanan, and Mark Owens for continuing the long tradition of this conference to the benefit of myself and so many others. My discussants at the Citadel have included distinguished southern politics scholars such as Keith Gaddie, Joe Aistrup, Trey Hood and Bruce Ransom. I am thankful to each for their careful reading of earlier versions of this work.

Seth McKee is the person who introduced me to the Citadel Symposium and the host of other Southern politics scholars I have met there. But more importantly, he read chapters of this book and offered helpful and encouraging feedback. I appreciate him as a friend. Another friend I appreciate and who made a specific contribution to this book is Jeremy Teigen, who patiently guided me to making the maps presented in this book. I literally could not have done that without him.

I am fortunate to be on the faculty at John Jay College, CUNY. My research was supported by a grant from the Professional Staff Congress—City University of New York Research Award Program administered by the Research Fund of the CUNY. In addition, a sabbatical semester in Fall 2024 allowed me to finish the book project after too many years of working on it. More importantly, I am fortunate to be John Jay because I am surrounded by a boatload of supportive colleagues. My four most recent Department chairs—Jim Cauthen, Andrew Sidman, Susan Kang, and Max Mak—have ably served their colleagues. More important, each is a friend who has supported by work on both an administrative and a personal level. They have my deep thanks.

I wrote most of this book at local coffee shops because I find going somewhere else more conducive to writing than staying in my office at home or at my College. I would especially like to thank 23 Skiddoo in Bloomfield, NJ and Trend in Montclair, NJ for the free wifi and well-brewed cafe au laits.

My deepest thanks go to my family. My parents—Alice and Peter Arbour—have offered me unflinching love and support throughout my life. My sister Megan Long and brother-in-law Wesley Long are not just relatives but close friends. Marriage and fatherhood have shown me how much I have in common with my brother Blake, and we have grown closer as a result. His best decision was marrying my sister-in-law, Lindsay.

As noted, I am married and a father, and that is the best thing in my life. I continue to be amazed how fortunate I am to have I found a woman to love and support me as much as Erin Ackerman has. My son Joshua is a delight, and I have learned so much about music, opera, and musical theater from him. He has occasionally learned something about baseball from me, whether he needed to or not. This book would not have been possible without Erin and Joshua.

Contents

Chapter 1
Who and What are the Unhyphenated?

Little went well in the 1988 campaign for Michael Dukakis. An early lead over Vice President George H. W. Bush eroded against an aggressive and patriotic Bush campaign, and the Dukakis campaign is remembered primarily for its gaffes—the "iceman" response to Bernard Shaw's debate question about the death penalty, the disastrous photo-op in the tank, and the campaign's ineffectual response to the Willie Horton attack. Dukakis limped home nearly nine points behind Bush in the popular vote. As a result, Dukakis won only the most loyal Democratic states in the Pacific Northwest, the upper Midwest, in New England, and, of course, West Virginia.

To contemporary political observers, Dukakis's 52–47 victory in West Virginia seems peculiar. In 2024, Donald Trump was the seventh straight Republican nominee to win the Mountain State, and he did so by a landslide margin of forty-two points. The only good news for Democrats about their result in West Virginia in 2024 was that it was slightly better than their result in 2020 and in 2016. In 2016, Hillary Clinton ran twenty-three points below her national popular vote total in the Mountain State. Joe Biden ran only twenty-two points behind, and Kamala Harris was only twenty points behind in West Virginia in 2024.

The reality of that good news is that it is hardly good news at all for Democrats. From 1988 to 2016, each Democratic presidential nominee won a smaller share of West Virginia's popular vote compared to their national two-party vote share than his or her predecessor. Bill Clinton ran worse in West Virginia in 1992 than Michael Dukakis, and then ran worse when he ran for re-election in 1996. Al Gore did even worse in 2000; for only the second time since the New Deal Realignment, the Democratic presidential nominee ran behind his national vote share in the Mountain State. That trend continued: John Kerry ran 5.2% behind his national vote share. Barack Obama ran 10.4% behind his national vote share in 2008 and a 15.6% behind in 2012. The trend reached its zenith in 2016, as Hillary Clinton ran 23.3% behind her national vote share in West Virginia.

Figure 1.1 shows the Democratic vote trend in West Virginia across the entire Arbour_0925_EFArbour_0925_EF history of the state. This provides a long-term perspective on the Republican shift in the Mountain State in recent years. Throughout most of its history, West Virginia has been a state that has trended Democrat at the national level. The trend was less strong during the final quarter of the nineteenth century and was more favorable to Republicans in the early twentieth century, with the exception of the 1924 election, when the Progressive

https://doi.org/10.1515/9783111615707-001

Robert LaFollette cut into the Democratic vote share in many places nationally, but not in West Virginia.[1]

Figure 1.1: Democratic Two-Party Presidential Vote Trend, West Virginia, 1864–2024.
Note: Values are Democratic two-party presidential vote share in West Virginia subtracted from the national Democratic two-party presidential vote share.

One can then see the rise of Democrats in West Virginia starting in the 1930s as labor unions grew in strength. The Democratic trend in the state held except for the landslide defeat of George McGovern in 1972. But then the trend starts moving to the Republicans. Initially it is slight, as Clinton in 1996 lost only three points from Dukakis's vote share eight years earlier. The big move starts in 2000, when Gore ran 3.5% worse in West Virginia than he did nationally and begins the process of the bottom falling out of Democrats' vote share in the state. Biden finally ended the slide but did so during a landslide margin for Republicans in the Mountain State. Over the twenty-first century, West Virginia has become a solidly red state at the national level.

Of course, West Virginia is not alone in its shift toward the national Republican Party over the last political generation. In both 1992 and 1996, Bill Clinton won not only West Virginia, but also Kentucky, Tennessee, and his home state of

---

1 LaFollette won 16% of the vote nationally, but only 6% in West Virginia.

Arkansas. But in none of these upper Southern states have Democratic presidential nominees been competitive in the twenty-first century.

There are similar trends in congressional races. In Tennessee, Democrats held both Senate seats when Al Gore resigned to take the vice presidency. In the subsequent Senate elections of 1994, Democrats lost both of Tennessee's Senate seats and have not won either one since. In Kentucky, Democrats have not won a Senate seat since 1998. Democrats also used to be able to handily win Appalachian seats in the US House of Representatives (hereafter House) seats like those in West Virginia. But Democrats lost their monopoly on West Virginia seats when they lost the 2nd District in 2000. They then lost the 1st District in 2010 and the 3rd District in 2014. Republicans have held these seats (usually in landslide fashion) ever since.[2] A similar story emerged in Virginia's 9th District, which is centered in the state's southwestern panhandle—the most Appalachian part of the state. In 2010, Republican Morgan Griffin defeated long-time incumbent Democrat Rich Boucher and has held the seat easily ever since. Republicans currently hold five of the six US House seats in Kentucky, lacking only the district centered in Louisville. A similar path was followed in Tennessee. At present, Democrats hold only the African American majority district in Memphis; Republicans hold the other eight Volunteer State seats. In Arkansas, Democrats held three of the state's four US House seats up through the 2010 election. In 2010, they lost the 1st and 2nd Districts and in 2012, Democrats lost the 4th District. Since then, Republicans have held all four of Arkansas's US House seats by landslide margins. In short, the trend in West Virginia is a trend across the broader region of the upper South. The region moved strongly towards the Republicans and there is no evidence that the trend will reverse any time soon.

Voting patterns in states across the Appalachian Mountains and the upper South such as West Virginia, Kentucky, Tennessee, and Arkansas very closely follow the punctuated equilibrium model of political realignment (Burnham 1999). One equilibrium existed for a long time, then it was "punctured" and shifted quickly. The similarity of the 2020 and 2024 presidential election results in West Virginia to those of 2016 suggest that a new equilibrium has been established, one in which Republicans are the dominant party of the upper South, and one that wins the region by landslide margins.

In this book, I examine the partisan transformation of this part of the country to a landslide Republican region. I try to assess how and why the upper South moved to the right, identifying a shift in the issue agenda away from economic

---

2 West Virginia lost a congressional district in reapportionment after the 2020 Census, but its two districts have remained resolutely Republican in House elections this decade.

concerns and toward non-material issues centered on sexuality and the environment as one key. I also find that partisan polarization over issues of race as well as its increased salience in the national politics of the twenty-first century also helped push the region toward the Republicans.

The partisan shift on race provides an important explanation for the well-studied Southern Republican realignment. But I argue that these transformations are distinct from each other. The biggest reason for this is timing. Both deep and Rim South states moved toward the Republican Party at the presidential level in the 1960s and the 1970s (Black and Black 1987, 2002; see also Glaser 1996, 2005; Hood et al. 2012; Lublin 2004). At the congressional level, the shift grew slowly but surely from the 1960s to the 1980s and reached it apotheosis with the 1994 Republican wave election (McKee 2010; Hayes and McKee 2008).

The timing is very different in the highland South that I study in this book. That area moved towards the Republicans primarily in the period between 1994 and 2010, and continued at a less rapid but still clear pace thereafter (Arbour 2018). The timing indicates that factors that are responsible for the shift in the upper South are different to those that caused the shift in other parts of the South.

What is different in the upper South that would have political relevance and help to explain its Republican shift? One key difference I identify is ethnicity. The upper South is home to the nation's largest concentrations of what sociologists call unhyphenated Americans—whites who identify their ancestry not with a European country, but with the United States. The region is home to a group of whites whose immigrant stories are so far in the past that they no longer identify their own heritage with their immigrant ancestors, but with the generations of their families that have lived in and been fully assimilated into a culture they identify as American.

The core of the argument of this book is that the combination of geography and ethnicity—that is, the presence of a large share of unhyphenated Americans in a geographic region—has important political meaning. It builds on previous research I have done which shows that these concentrations of American ethnic identifiers are a significant mark of reduced vote share for Barack Obama, Hillary Clinton, and other contemporary Democrats (Arbour and Teigen 2011; Arbour 2011, 2018). This book expands on those arguments, detailing the long-term yet sharp move of unhyphenated America toward the Republicans over the last political generation. I leverage temporal variation and public opinion to try to explain why those who live in regions with large concentrations of unhyphenated Americans have been attracted to Republican candidates—and repelled by Democratic candidates—in twenty-first century elections.

1 Who and What are the Unhyphenated?

Who are these "unhyphenated Americans" who are concentrated in the Appalachian Mountains and other parts of the upper South? They are what sociologists consider a "new ethnic population" of white Americans who have "a recognition of being white but lack any clear-cut identification with and/or knowledge of a specific European origin" (Lieberson 1985, 159). In other words, they are whites who identify their ethnic heritage not with the European home of their ancestors, and thus are not Scottish Americans or German Americans or any combination of European origins. Instead, these individuals who see themselves as ethnically American.

How did these unhyphenated Americans start to emerge as a "new ethnic population?" To answer this question, it is important to understand that sociologists reject the belief that ethnicity is a fixed trait, established at birth (Farley 1991). Contemporary scholars find that race and ethnicity are created by social construction, a belief so strong that it is regarded as axiomatic (Omi 2001; Omi and Winant 2014; Farley 1991). The social construction of ethnicity is "mediated by a number of factors, including ethnic admixture (blending), the awareness and preservation of knowledge about ancestral origins, prevailing ideologies about race and racial divisions, and the number of generations removed from the arrival of immigrant ancestors" (Perez and Hirschman 2009, 3–4). For example, Angles and Saxons were once distinct groups who clashed and warred in medieval Britain, until they intermarried to the point that we long ago acknowledged their descendants as English.

Ethnicity, thus, can change over time, especially in a country like the United States where immigration from a wide number of countries, religions, and cultures erodes ethnic distinctions. This is particularly true for descendants of old immigrant stocks of northern and western Europe, whose ties to their European roots have eroded (Alba 1990; Alba and Nee 1997). Each generation is further and further removed from the values, norms, and traditions that European immigrants brought with them. In response to this distance from their ethnic roots, and the need to blend together disparate and large numbers of ancestors, individuals simplify their ethnic identities, often with little acknowledgment of the complexity of their full ancestry (Perez and Hirschman 2009).

As whites have simplified their ancestry, scholars today find that white Americans regard their ethnic origins as "symbolic" (Gans 1979) or "optional" (Waters 1990). As a result, ethnicity among whites has "Americanized," which is "the replacement of detailed ethnic origins with simplified panethnic . . . categories" and the growing use of "New World" ancestries, rather than European ones (Perez and Hirschman 2009, 4, 30).

Unhyphenated Americans are one of these emerging "New World" ethnic groups. Over time, this group has emerged as whites in the United States have identified themselves more with the country of their birth than the country from which their ancestors migrated to the United States. And while sociologists identify this group as "new," the process of adjusting one's ethnic identity is not—it takes generations to occur.

Sociologists began studying unhyphenated Americans due to a change in a US Census question for the 1980 Census. Previously, the Census had asked respondents in which country their father and mother were born. In 1980, the Census eliminated that question and asked a new one: "What is this person's ancestry or ethnic origin?" (Figure 1.2) The question is supposed to elicit answers of countries other than the United States; below the question on Census forms is a note that reads: "For example: Italian, Jamaican, African American, Cambodian, Cape Verdean, Norwegian, Dominican, French Canadian, Haitian, Korean, Lebanese, Polish, Nigerian, and so on." Yet, about 7% of all respondents to the Census question write in the answer "America," "American," or "United States."[3] In the 2022 American Community Survey, they comprised the fourth largest ancestry group in the country (US Census Bureau 2023).[4]

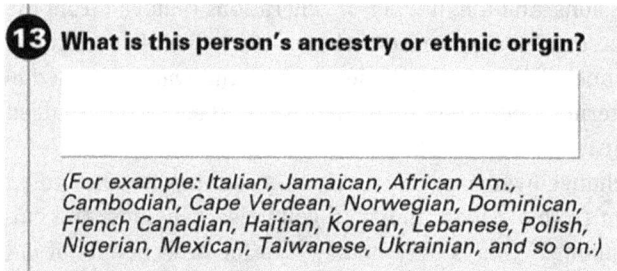

13 **What is this person's ancestry or ethnic origin?**

(For example: Italian, Jamaican, African Am., Cambodian, Cape Verdean, Norwegian, Dominican, French Canadian, Haitian, Korean, Lebanese, Polish, Nigerian, Mexican, Taiwanese, Ukrainian, and so on.)

Figure 1.2: The Census Ancestry Question.
Note: For more on the Census Ancestry Question, including the screenshot above, see Census Reporter n.d.; US Census Bureau n.d.

It is worth noting that this is almost certainly an undercount of the share of Americans who identify their ancestry as American. The Census counts the first two countries that an individual lists in their Census form as part of their ancestry. If an individual writes French and German as their answer to the ethnic ori-

---

3 Among all respondents, 80% give an ethnicity in response to this question.
4 The ancestry question was asked as part of the decennial Census in 1980, 1990, and 2000. Since then, the question has moved to the American Community Survey.

gin question, they will count as both a French American and a German American. But the Census does not apply this same method to those who write that their heritage is "American." Only this ethnicity is counted if it is listed as the *only* ancestry an individual writes on their Census form. Which means that if an individual writes that her ancestry is American and Irish, the Census will only count her as an Irish American.

Why do these individuals regard themselves as Americans, rather than reporting a European ancestry? The literature suggests several rationales. First, some respondents may write American for political or patriotic reasons. Their identification as Americans shows that they are "true-blue citizens of the United States, being neither sojourners nor of questionable loyalty" (Lieberson 1985, 172). Second, those with lower educational achievement are less likely to report multiple ancestries (Alba 1990; Lieberson and Waters 1986), which may mean that less-educated people are less aware of their own immigration story.

Yet, the dominant explanation in the sociology literature for why individuals report their nationality as American is that they do not see their heritage connected to a European country. When asked to think about their heritage, they see themselves as Americans.

Individuals who trace their origin to countries that experienced most of their immigration to the United States before the Civil War—English, Dutch, Germans, and others of northern European ancestors—are most likely to include "American" as one of their countries of origin, or to record their children as having American ancestry (Farley 1991). As a result, the "American" ancestry "tends to absorb a very large number of the children in families . . . of mixed parents in which one parent is American and the other is of some specific ancestry" (Lieberson and Waters 1993, 443–444). Lieberson and Waters (1993) show that even controlling for education levels, writing "American" on Census forms represents a clear choice made by respondents. Thus, they conclude that writing "American" on Census forms is not caused by technical errors made by those who design or fill out Census forms but represents "true substantive changes in the determination of ancestry and ethnicity for later generation Americans" (1993, 423). Thus, unhyphenated whites have not only assimilated but have Americanized themselves.

These American ethnic identifiers are not randomly spread out through the national population. Instead, the Americanization process leads to a distinct set of demographic, sociological, and psychographic characteristics which provide many reasons to believe that these American ethnic identifiers may hold distinctive political opinions as well. Unhyphenated Americans are heavily concentrated in the South as defined by the US Census (Farley 1991; Lieberson 1985) and in rural areas (Neidert and Farley 1985), are heavily Protestant (Lieberson 1985; Lieberson and Waters 1989), and are less likely to have graduated from college (Neidert and Farley 1985). One study reports that "the individuals who were most prone to write 'American' were young native whites living in the South who had dropped out of high school" (Farley 1991, 417).

Figure 1.3 shows where these American ethnic identifiers are concentrated using county-level Census data. I define the shaded counties on the map as *unhyphenated concentrated*—which are counties in which the percentage of people who identify their ethnicity as American is more than one standard deviation greater than the national mean; that is, 19.4% (mean = 11.9%; standard deviation = 7.5%). Throughout this book, I will refer to these counties with concentrations of unhyphenated Americans as "unhyphenated America." It is also worth noting that while there is a connection between unhyphenated concentrated areas and Appalachia, it is not an exact match, in large part because unhyphenated America is much larger than the Appalachian Mountain range. To help demonstrate this, I also included the counties that make up the Appalachian Regional Commission, a federal agency; in Figure 1.3 these counties are outlined in black.

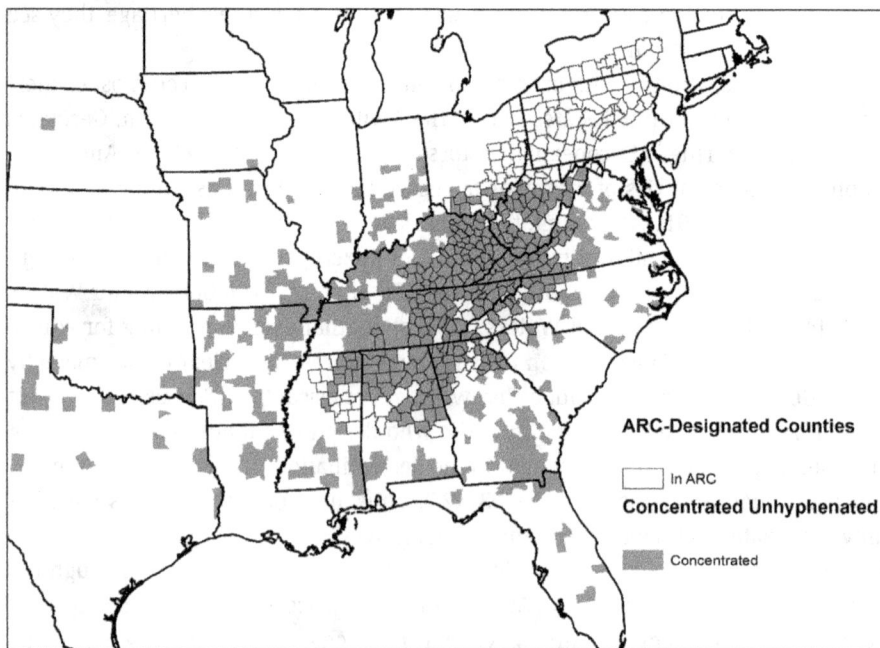

Figure 1.3: Unhyphenated Concentrated Counties.
Note: Unhyphenated concentrated counties are defined as those where 12.5% of residents or more identify their ethnic origin as "American." ARC represents the counties that belong to the Appalachian Regional Commission.

Unhyphenated America certainly begins in the Appalachian Mountains, the most eastern point of the region. Then it follows a line of pre-Civil War western migration of highland southerners, the farmers of the hardscrabble Southern hills who never had enough money to buy land in the fertile Deep South and who moved from the Appalachian highlands across the upper South and into the near Southwest. These backwoodsmen and women often descended from later immigrants to the American colonies who often came from Scotland or the English borderlands (Fischer 1989).

Unhyphenated concentrated regions are centered in the Appalachian Mountains, especially in the southern portions of the Appalachias. There are no unhyphenated concentrated counties north of the Mason-Dixon line in Pennsylvania or New York, even in those states' counties that are part of the ARC. Unhyphenated concentrated areas also spread out from the Appalachias themselves. There are counties in central Virginia and North Carolina that have concentrations of American ethnic identifiers, in addition to a set of counties in southern Georgia and scattered across rural Florida. Unhyphenated America also stretches west from the Appalachias, as a majority of the counties in both Kentucky and Tennessee are unhyphenated concentrated. Unhyphenated America does cross the Ohio River, as a handful of rural counties in southern Ohio, Indiana, and Illinois have concentrations of unhyphenated Americans. One can also see a handful of unhyphenated concentrated counties across the Mississippi River in Arkansas in particular, and spreading into Missouri, northern Louisiana, Oklahoma, and in eastern and northern Texas. Thus, from a geographic standpoint, unhyphenated Americans are highly concentrated in the Appalachian Mountains and in the upper South.

Another notable facet of unhyphenated America is its small-town and rural character. If one looks closely at Tennessee on the map, one can see that the unhyphenated concentrated counties do not include the state's largest county—Shelby in the southwestern corner; home of Memphis. It does not include the state's second largest county—Davidson (Nashville), or even its third (Knox County—Knoxville), fourth (Hamilton County—Chattanooga), fifth (Rutherford County—Murfreesboro), or sixth (Williamson County—suburban Nashville) largest counties in the state. But of the state's ninety smallest counties, seventy-six of them have a concentration of American ethnic identifiers.

A similar story is told in Kentucky. Jefferson County, the state's largest county and home to Louisville, is not unhyphenated concentrated. Neither is Fayette County, the state's second largest and home to Lexington and the University of Kentucky. The most populous unhyphenated concentrated county in Kentucky is Daviess, home of Owensboro. Its population is 103,312.

That is the basic story across unhyphenated America. Of the 531 unhyphenated concentrated counties I have identified, only twenty-three of them have a population of over 100,000. The largest unhyphenated concentrated county in the country is Denton County, Texas, which is a suburban county of a large metropolitan area (Dallas). But in that, it is an outlier. Many of the largest unhyphenated concentrated counties are centered on small towns—Springfield, IL; Lafayette, LA; Bristol, TN. Others of the largest counties are exurban counties of bigger metropolitan areas—Paulding County, GA; Sumner County, TN; Rankin County, MS—where suburban growth may have increased the population slightly, but whose rural character still dominates. Another demonstration of the rural character of unhyphenated concentrated regions is provided by the state of Virginia. Virginia's 1870 constitution made its incorporated cities at the time "free" or "independent" from the state's counties. Of Virginia's thirty-seven independent cities, only five are unhyphenated concentrated. Among the state's ninety-five counties, forty of them—that is 42%—have a concentration of unhyphenated Americans.

Overall, unhyphenated concentrated counties have a population of 17,130,076 according to the 2020 Census. These counties thus make up 5.2% of the nation's population. As such, they are quite small, but, as I argue here, their political impact has been stark and meaningful over the most recent political generation.

2 The Characteristics of the Unhyphenated

The previous section outlines the geography and population size of areas with concentrations of unhyphenated Americans. But it tells us little about what these communities are like. What characteristics are present in unhyphenated America, especially ones that might tell us why the region has moved toward the Republicans in recent political generations?

To answer that question, I turn to Census data. The Census not only counts every single American once every ten years, but it also provides important demographic data about each of those Americans. One challenge of studying unhyphenated America is that it is such a small portion of the American population. The comprehensiveness of Census data helps to alleviate the issues caused by the region's small population size.

Table 1.1 shows the data for many of the characteristics of the unhyphenated concentrated counties from the 2020 Census. To provide context, the table also includes the national share of the population for each of these measures. One of the most important data points in the table is the measure of population growth. Nationally, the population of the mean county grew 7.4% between 2010 and 2020. In unhyphenated America, the population growth rate was nearly half that, at 3.9%. Population is stagnating more in unhyphenated America than in the average place in the United States. This has important political implications. In his book

Movers and Stayers, Irwin Morris finds that counties with low population growth and disproportionately white populations in the Old Confederacy are moving toward the Republicans as locals blame economic and social stagnation on national factors, such as the policies of the national Democratic Party. Morris's conclusions fit squarely with my own about the Republican shift of unhyphenated America.

Table 1.1: Census Data.

	Unhyphenated Concentrated Counties (%)	All US (%)
Total Population	17,130,076 (5.2%)	330,715,890
Population Growth		
2010 to 2020 (mean by county)	3.9	7.4
Race		
White Not Hispanic	80.0	57.8
Black Not Hispanic	8.6	12.1
Hispanic	5.8	18.8
Asian Not Hispanic	1.3	5.9
Two or More Races	5.5	10.2
Age		
Children (17 and under)	22.1	21.1
Senior Citizens	18.9	16.8
Household Status		
Married Couples with Children	16.6	17.5
Single Males (No Spouse)	18.1	18.8
Single Females (No Spouse)	27.1	28.1
Housing Units		
Vacant	11.5	9.8
Owner Occupied	62.9	57.0
Renter Occupied	25.6	33.2

Source: 2020 US Census data. All calculations done by author.
Note: Unhyphenated concentrated counties are defined as those where 12.5% of residents or more identify their ethnic origin as "American."

Of course, important to conclusions Morris draws is that a region must be disproportionately white, which certainly describes the racial composition of unhyphenated America. Here, 80% of the population identifies themselves as white, while only 57.8% of the US population does. There is a smaller share of each minority group in unhyphenated concentrated regions than in the country as a whole. Unhyphenated America is 8.6% Black, as compared to 12.1% of the national population. Unhyphenated America has notably fewer Hispanics (5.8%), Asian Americans (1.3%) and people who identify themselves as being of two or more races (5.5%) as compared to the national population (18.8% Hispanic, 5.9% Asian, 10.2% two or more races). In short, one big difference between unhyphenated America and the rest of the country is that it is whiter. In America's racialized democracy, this has important political consequences.

The other measures in Table 1.1 show smaller, but notable differences between unhyphenated America and the country as a whole. The region has a slightly larger share of both children and seniors than the nation as a whole. As a result, there are 3.1% fewer working-age people (18–64) in unhyphenated America than America as a whole. There are slightly fewer married couples with children, single males, and single females in unhyphenated America than the national share. These differences are relatively small but do suggest a slightly different set of family arrangements in unhyphenated America. One area where there are clear differences between unhyphenated America and the rest of the country is in home ownership. A larger share of homes in unhyphenated concentrated counties are owner-occupied and a smaller share are renter-occupied. At one level, home ownership is a salutary benefit, but some of this benefit is cut by the fact that home values are lower in the region, a reflection of the lack of demand for housing stock. This is also reflected in the higher rate of vacant housing stock in unhyphenated America.

Table 1.2 provides a number of economic variables in unhyphenated America. The results show relatively few differences in the employment status and the type of jobs in the region. The share of people in the labor force in unhyphenated concentrated areas is less than 1% higher than the share nationally. The share that is employed and unemployed look very similar to the national numbers. The job category numbers also show very little difference between unhyphenated America and the national numbers. Slightly fewer people in unhyphenated America work in management and business jobs and slightly more work in natural resources and transportation. But these differences are at the margins. Similarly, the share without health insurance is only slightly higher in unhyphenated America than the nation as a whole, mostly due to slightly fewer residents of unhyphenated America having public health insurance.

Where there is a clear difference between unhyphenated America and America as a whole is in income. Unhyphenated America has a greater share of individuals who make less than $50,000 a year (37.2% compared to 33.9% nationally) and

Table 1.2: Economic Data.

	Unhyphenated Concentrated Counties (%)	All US (%)
Employment Status		
In Labor Force	63.4	62.6
Employed	59.6	59.0
Unemployed	3.4	3.1
Job Category		
Management, Business, Science & Art	39.7	41.0
Service	15.8	16.8
Sales and Office Jobs	21.0	20.5
Natural Resources, Transportation, and	8.7	8.7
Material Moving	14.8	13.1
Income		
Under $25,000	17.3	15.7
Under $50,000	37.2	33.9
Over $100,000	33.0	37.2
Health Insurance		
Private Health Insurance	67.3	67.6
Public Health Insurance	34.9	35.8
No Health Insurance	9.8	8.7

Source: 2020 US Census data.
Note: Unhyphenated concentrated counties are defined as those where 12.5% of residents or more identify their ethnic origin as "American."

a smaller share who report an income above $100,000 (33.0% compared to 37.2% nationally). Residents of unhyphenated America are as likely to work and do similar jobs as their counterparts around the country, with the major difference being that they receive less compensation for their work.

The modern Census only asks respondents a handful of questions, and many other questions have been moved to the American Community Survey (ACS). The ACS is a detailed representative sample survey of the American population conducted by the US Census Bureau. Its large size allows for big enough subsample analysis of small geographic units such as unhyphenated concentrated counties and its detailed questionnaire makes it possible to learn more information than provided by the decennial Census data.

The questions asked by the ACS reveal some important differences between unhyphenated America and the country as a whole (see Table 1.3). For example, there is a much smaller share of foreign-born residents in unhyphenated America (4.3%) than in the country as a whole (13.7%). Similarly, only 6.8% of residents of unhyphenated America report speaking a language other than English at home, as compared to 21.7% of all Americans. Immigration is much less common in unhyphenated America than in the rest of the country. This helps explain why the region is so much whiter than the rest of the country, but also why whites have less interaction with people from other nationalities and ethnicities than in the rest of the country.

Table 1.3: American Community Survey Data.

	Unhyphenated Concentrated Counties (%)	All US (%)
Immigration		
Foreign Born	4.3	13.7
Speaks a Language Other Than English at Home	6.8	21.7
Life Experience		
Military Veteran	8.1	6.8
Earned Bachelor's Degree	21.6	33.8
Graduate or Professional Degree	7.6	13.1
Has Broadband Internet	81.0	87.1
Marital Status (Women)		
Never Married	24.0	31.0
Divorced/Separated	15.9	14.2

Source: 2021 American Community Survey.
Note: Unhyphenated concentrated counties are defined as those where 12.5% of residents or more identify their ethnic origin as "American."

Furthermore, a much smaller share of residents of unhyphenated America have earned a bachelor's degree than in the national sample—21.6% compared to 33.8%—and a smaller share have earned a graduate or professional degree—7.6% compared to 13.1%. In recent years, education levels have become more correlated with partisan voting behavior, as Democrats have made gains among college graduates and Republicans made gains among those without a college degree (Grossman and Hopkins 2024; Zingher 2022a). Unhyphenated America fits quite well with this national pattern.

The results also show a slightly higher share of residents of unhyphenated America are veterans of America's military. A higher share of veterans in the region might be expected given its long tradition of supporting America's military efforts (Trubowitz 1992; Webb 2004). Unhyphenated America has a lower share of people with broadband internet in their home than across the nation as a whole, though adoption of this technology is quite high in unhyphenated America. Also, the share of individuals who have never been married is much lower in unhyphenated concentrated counties (24.0% compared to 31.0% nationally). The divorce rate is slightly higher.

The Census data tell us that unhyphenated America is primarily distinct from the rest of the country when it comes to the region's racial makeup and its educational achievement. The lack of immigration into the region—in addition to its small African American population—make it whiter than the rest of the country. It also has a smaller share of residents with a college degree than the nation as whole. In contemporary politics, these are quite meaningful demographic characteristics.

On the other hand, it is notable that there are fewer differences observed in the other Census and ACS measures. In particular, on measures of employment and household status, unhyphenated America looks like the rest of the country. People in the region work at similar jobs to their counterparts across the country. And they live in similar family arrangements, despite fewer people in unhyphenated America having never been married. The biggest difference in this sphere is in income—those who live in unhyphenated America make less than the average American. Yet, they are more likely to own their own home.

2.1 Public Opinion Data

Census data gives us some perspective on the unhyphenated concentrated regions of the country. But details are of course limited by the questions asked on Census forms. To expand understanding of the characteristics of unhyphenated America, I turn to the Cooperative Election Study (CES), an online survey conducted by YouGov/Polimetrix.[5] Because unhyphenated concentrated areas represent such a small share of the American population, it is difficult to study them through survey research. The CES addresses this problem by having large samples of respondents (up to 64,000 each year) and asking the same demographic questions across multiple years of the survey. The CES Cumulative File (Kuriwaki 2022) includes responses from surveys taken from 2006 through 2021, with larger samples in even-numbered (i.e. election) years. There are 557,455 respondents in the cumulative file, and 30,040 of those respondents are from unhyphenated concentrated counties—that is, 5.4% of the sample. The large sample reduces the level of uncertainty in analysis of the subsample population.

---

5 I discuss in more detail the methodology and representativeness of the CES in Chapter 5.

The results shown in Table 1.4 often mirror those found in the Census data. For example, there is a higher share of white respondents in unhyphenated concentrated counties than in the country as a whole—nearly 86% of residents of unhyphenated America are white, compared to 72% across the country. In addition, the family income of respondents from unhyphenated concentrated counties is lower than the national sample by over $10,000 on average.

That last finding fits with several others that show different socioeconomic characteristics of unhyphenated America. A much smaller share of residents have college degrees (17% compared to 28% of the national sample) and nearly twice as many residents of unhyphenated America report that they are "permanently disabled" (11% compared to 6% of the national sample).

Lieberson and Waters (1989) found that unhyphenated Americans were disproportionately Protestant, and the survey data supports that conclusion. The results show that about 56% of residents of unhyphenated concentrated regions are Protestant, greater than the 38% share found in the national sample. But the survey results show another area where the religious makeup of unhyphenated America differs from the national sample. Only about half as many respondents—6% compared to 10% nationally—say that they are agnostics or atheists. The distribution of religious preferences is quite distinct in unhyphenated America.

Overall, these responses show that unhyphenated America is disproportionately white and disproportionately Protestant with high levels of religiosity. They also reveal that the region's socioeconomic indicators are low on the scale—lower levels of income, education, and health outcomes. As such, it is a demographically distinct region of the country, set apart from the trends of ethnic and racial diversification and increasing educational achievement that are a big part of the nation's demographic trends in recent decades.

These distinctions have important political implications as well. As discussed in the opening to this chapter, this region has experienced an increase in Republican vote share in the twenty-first century. The political section of Table 1.4 indicates that these voting results are reflected in the individual political preferences of residents of unhyphenated America. The national sample finds that about 34% of respondents identify as Democrats and about 27% as Republicans.[6] Those numbers are basically flipped in unhyphenated concentrated counties; in these areas, about 34% of respondents identify as Republicans while 26% identify as Democrats. One can see a similar pattern with ideology. Nationally, about 34% of respondents say they are conservatives and about 24% say they are liberals. In un-

---

6 Results here are from a three-way measure of party identification. They do not take into account the strength of partisanship, nor whether the independents lean to one party or the other.

Table 1.4: Demographic Characteristics of Unhyphened Concentrated Counties.

	Unhyphenated Concentrated Counties (%)	All Respondents (%)
Demographics		
White	86	72
Married	56	51
Single/Never Married	27	21
Age (mean)	48	47
Socio-economic Status		
College Degree	17	28
Family Income (mean)	$45,714	$56,238
Employed Full Time	39	32
Permanently Disabled	11	6
Does Not Have Health Insurance	18	13
Owns House	67	60
Religion		
Protestant	56	38
Atheist/Agnostic	6	10
Life Experience		
No Military Service	43	45
Union Member	18	25
Parent of Young Child	27	30
Political		
Democrat	26	34
Republican	34	27
Liberal	14	24
Conservative	43	34
Follows News Most of the Time	44	48

Source: Results calculated by author from CES Cumulative File (Kuriwaki 2022).
Note: Unhyphenated concentrated counties are defined as those where 12.5% of residents or more identify their ethnic heritage as "American" according to US Census Bureau data.

hyphenated America, a greater share (43%) say they are conservatives, and a smaller share (14%) say they are liberals.[7]

---

7 Respondents were given five response options for their ideology. "Conservative" and "very conservative" responses were combined to calculate the "Conservative" percentage in the table. "Liberal" and "very liberal" were combined to calculate the "Liberal" percentage.

Thus, just as unhyphenated America has a distinct set of demographic characteristics, it also has a distinct set of political characteristics, with higher levels of Republican partisanship and conservative ideology than the country as a whole.

3 A Study of Geography, Not Identity

So far, we have learned that the unhyphenated are a group geographically concentrated in rural and small-town areas of the Appalachian Mountains and upper South. They are also demographically concentrated, not just based on their race (white), but also by having lower levels of income, educational achievement, and foreign in-migration. The survey data also showed that higher levels of conservatism and identification as Republican are found in unhyphenated America.

This book provides an exploration of the geographic and demographic links between unhyphenated Americans and support for Republican candidates. The region has shifted strongly toward the Republicans over the last political generation, and the correlation suggests that an important factor in this shift is the presence of concentrations of people who have an American ethnic identity.

My previous research has found a close connection between the presence of unhyphenated Americans in a county and reduced vote share for Barack Obama (Arbour and Teigen 2011), and for Democratic congressional candidates in the 2010 election (Arbour 2011), In addition, scholars find that increased shares of unhyphenated Americans are associated with increased vote share for Donald Trump both in the 2016 Republican primary (Arbour and Teigen 2016) and general election (Arbour 2018). This book tries to expand on those findings to identify not only when the region's strong Republican shift began, but also why it happened.

In making this argument, I have a very clear limitation. The data available to me as a researcher do not allow me to make conclusions about the role that identity plays in the political behavior of unhyphenated Americans. This is because political science surveys do not ask individuals to discuss their ethnic identity. Such a question is not offered on major political science surveys such as the American National Election Study (ANES) or the Cooperative Election Study (CES). And although the question is asked on the General Social Survey (GSS), the response options do not include "American." One can infer American ethnic identity from whites that choose the "Other" option, but inferential data are not conducive to studying identity. Further, "unhyphenated Americans" make up a relatively small portion of the American population. The 2022 American Community Survey (ACS) estimates that 18 million out of an estimated 335 million Americans identify their ethnicity as American—that is, 5.3% of the population (US Census Bureau 2023).[8] Thus, the size of such a subsample population on all but the largest surveys would be quite small, increasing confidence intervals and margins of error.

Because of these limitations, this is a study of geography, not identity. I can use Census data at the county and congressional district level to identify places with concentrations of unhyphenated Americans (as I did in Figure 1.3) and use that to make conclusions about the voting behavior of the region. Further, I can also use those definitions of unhyphenated concentrated regions to assess the opinions of people who live in the region. And thanks to the large size of the CES, a substantial enough subsample population of respondents from these areas allows confidence in the results presented here.

Even if I did have the proper survey instrument to oversample those who see their ethnicity as American, I would still hypothesize that such an ethnicity does not have the characteristics of a social identity. They may well identify as Appalachian or Southern; they have lots of characteristics that would give them a white identity (Jardina 2019). They may well identify as a Christian or as a Kentuckian or an Arkansan, but they are not as likely to identify with their ethnicity.

Certainly, I think many people in the Appalachias and upper South identify themselves as Americans, but that is a national—not an ethnic—identity. As such, it would not be *that* different from how individuals across the country—whether urban or rural, Northern or Southern, white or person of color—would identify themselves as American (Garand et al. 2022; Schildkraut 2003). My hypothesis would be that these people identify themselves as American in answer to the ethnicity question on the Census because they do not have a strong sense of a specific ethnic identity. Answering the question may be the first time they have had to think about what their ethnic identity is.

People in the Appalachias and the upper South tend to pick American as the answer to the ethnic identity question because they see themselves as indistinct in lots of ways. They are white—like the majority of the county—and Christian—like the majority of the country. Their Christianity is Protestant, which is the majority form of American Christianity, both historically and in modern America. While most of the population is not from a small-town or a rural area, such regions are valorized as representative of the true America. The lack of distinctiveness is exacerbated by the fact that the story of the immigration of the ancestors of residents of Appalachia and the upper South is so far in the past that it is not remembered. Further, the lack of immigration into the region keeps people

---

8 The precise numbers are 18,027,452 estimated American ethnic identifiers out of an estimated US population of 334,914,896.

from comparing their own ethnicity to that of new arrivals who have stronger ethnic connections to their native countries.

As such, ethnic identity among unhyphenated Americans works differently than it does in studies of ethnic voting. These studies—highlighted by the seminal book *Beyond the Melting Pot* (Glazer and Moynihan 1963)—have demonstrated that ethnic ties did not die out after a generation or two, as previously assumed (cf. Dahl 1961). Instead, the shared immigrant experience and socialization into the United States shapes the political behavior of members of an immigrant community (Greeley 1972; Wilson and Banfield 1964), not just shortly after immigration (Portes and Mozo 1985) but for generations (Wolfinger 1965), something that can been seen among various communities such as white New Englanders (Gimpel and Tam Cho 2004), Jews in Los Angeles (Sonenshein and Valentino 2000), and Cuban immigrants in Miami (Bishin and Klofstad 2012). In unhyphenated America, there may be a shared experience, but that experience is not likely filtered through an ethnic lens and certainly does not reflect a shared immigrant experience.

I would argue instead that the claim of American ethnicity is almost an anti-identity. People who assert such an ethnicity likely do not have a specific ethnic identity at all and writing "American" serves as a top-of-the-head response to a question they have possibly never thought about. Is the response meaningful then? It may not be as a matter of identity, but as a matter of geography, it most certainly is. I have identified a specific region of the country that, while not fully contiguous, shares both the demographic characteristics identified earlier in this chapter and a political behavior—shifting toward the Republicans over the last political generation.

4 Polarization and Contemporary Politics

The shift of unhyphenated America toward the Republicans is a component of two broader trends in contemporary American politics—geographic polarization and affective polarization. Both trends include the word polarization, which reflects that as elites in the two parties have sorted themselves into parties that are more internally homogenous and externally heterogeneous than their mid-twentieth-century predecessors, voters have followed these cues (Hetherington 2001; Zingher 2022b). As a result, voters tend to be more consistent in voting straight tickets for one party and a greater number of geographic regions are won by one or other party with landslide margins (Abramowitz 2022; Abramowitz and Webster 2016). As the parties have become more distant from each other—both in their ideology and in election results in specific jurisdictions—individuals feel more distant from those who identify with the other party.

4.1 Geographic Polarization

Unhyphenated America's shift toward the Republican Party is also a component of the geographic polarization of the country. Some regions are moving sharply toward the Democrats, and others, like unhyphenated America, are moving toward the Republicans. In particular, rural and small-town areas are moving toward the Republicans, and urban areas toward the Democrats (Brown and Mettler 2024).

The evidence for geographic polarization is robust. A number of studies have addressed the question and all come to an affirmative answer, regardless of whether they study election results at a regional (Johnston et al. 2016), state (Myers 2013), metropolitan (Kinsella et al. 2015), county (Lang and Pearson-Markowitz 2015; Wing and Walker 2010), or precinct (Rohla et al. 2018) level. Others studies have focused on voter registration data (Brown and Enos 2021; McGhee and Krim 2009), and they too find strong evidence for geographic polarization.

Geographic polarization is also a relatively recent phenomenon. Elections were more competitive in smaller geographic regions in the 1970s and 1980s, but evidence of the partisan split between large and small towns started to emerge by the 1996 election (Aistrup et al. 2023; Lang and Pearson-Merkowitz 2015). It has continued nearly unabated since then.

Another key question addressed by the literature on geographic polarization is whether individuals are relocating with the intention of living with fellow partisans, in a pattern that journalist Bill Bishop coined *The Big Sort* (Bishop and Cushing 2008). Researchers tend to find that these claims are exaggerated at best, and do not show up in the data of where people move (Mummolo and Nall 2017). Instead, scholars find "that location must have some influence on political preference, rather than the other way around" (Martin and Webster 2020, 215). That is, individuals are adapting their political preferences to those of their neighbors (cf. Morris 2021), as discussed in Chapter 2.

If place is having an effect on the political behavior of individuals, the implications for unhyphenated America are profound. Individuals are thus being affected by the dominant set of thoughts they encounter on a daily basis at work, at church, and in conversations with neighbors and friends. If the political mood of a place is moving in one direction, then more and more people in that place will follow that mood. I present strong evidence for such a dynamic in unhyphenated America.

4.2 Rural Voting

The growth of geographic polarization means that Democrats are gaining votes in urban and suburban areas and that Republicans are gaining in rural areas. At one level, this analysis is overly simplistic, as rural America has a great amount of diversity, including in vote patterns; not every part of rural America has moved toward the Republicans, nor has all of it moved in lockstep to the right (Scala et al. 2015; Scala and Johnson 2017). With that noted, rural areas have generally moved strongly toward the Republicans since the 1996 election (Brown and Mettler 2024; Lang and Pearson-Merkowitz 2015).

This broader rural shift toward the Republicans has confounded materialistic assumptions about voting patterns because rural areas feature large cohorts of working-class voters, yet they are moving away from the party that supports redistributive policies in favor of the party whose major policy focus in recent presidential administrations is regressive tax cuts.[9] This has led to political scientists trying to re-examine how and why rural voters have moved toward the Republicans. Daniel Shea and Nicolas F. Jacobs (2024, 13) offer the most comprehensive explanation arguing this move reflects "a remarkable and unflinching sense of place. That sense of place helps rural Americans form a collective, group identity. They identify with their place, and their place is rural. And, for these Americans, this sense of place is foundational to how they understand politics." Scholars find that all sorts of Americans can develop an identity centered on their type of community (Jacobs and Munis 2019), but that rural identities are the strongest of these (Lyons and Utych 2023)

Shea and Jacobs build on the importance of place from the idea of rural consciousness, developed by Katherine Cramer (2016). Cramer's deep qualitative study of rural Wisconsinites found that their politics are shaped primarily by resentments that developed from perceptions that rural areas are underrepresented in decision making, that residents of urban and suburban areas have different values and lifestyles than themselves, and that rural areas do not get their fair share of public resources. In particular, perceptions of differences in the way of life in rural and urban places—the idea that there are different values, lifestyles, and work ethics in the two places—most strongly affects vote choice among rural voters (Trujillo and Crowley 2022). These perceptions produce feelings that rural communities are under threat, which unites voters of all socioeconomic statuses to

---

9 One can obviously make the opposite argument about how the well-heeled suburbs are moving toward the party that wants to redistribute resources away from them.

see themselves as "a group on the defensive, ready to come together and preserve what makes their rural community special" (Shea and Jacobs 2024, 12).

The rural trend toward the Republicans has occurred in part because "rural Americans have developed a nationalized sense of place" (Shea and Jacobs 2024, 16). One can see the broad trend as Democrats have not only become a party led by urbanites, but one that has become more urbane and cosmopolitan. Democrats have tended to move positions on issues such as abortion, gay rights, and climate change to appeal to feminist, gay, and environmental voters. Republicans have maintained conservative positions on these issues, while embracing more conservative stances on issues such as gun control and immigration. One can see why this would appeal to rural areas where ideas of moral traditionalism run so strongly (Knuckey 2005a; Trujillo and Crowley 2022).

Yet, despite the broad national trends in rural areas, there is still strong reason to believe that unhyphenated America continues to have a distinct effect on the politics of its citizens. As shown above, the region is demographically distinct in its socioeconomic status and its low levels of immigration and mobility. The lack of economic or demographic changes helps to propel the conservatism of the region. Further, unhyphenated America is known for its economic dependence on extractive industries, and counties that are home to such industries of have moved toward Republicans more than other types of rural counties (Albrecht 2019; Goetz et al. 2019; Sutton 2009). In addition, the region's concentration of evangelical and Protestant churches make it religiously distinct, which explains its conservatism on abortion (see Chapter 5). That stands in contrast to the national opinion on abortion, which shows little difference based on community size (Kaufman 2021a, 2021b).

In short, unhyphenated America is part of the trend of rural areas moving to the right and thus nationalized geographic polarization. Some of the reasons for this shift are similar to those in other rural parts of the county. But some are distinct to unhyphenated America. And those distinctions are important.

4.3 Affective Polarization

Geographic polarization is both reinforced by and contributes to affective polarization. Iyengar and his co-authors (2019) define affective polarization as a "phenomenon of animosity between the two parties." In that definition, one can see echoes of Shea and Jacobs's contention that rural Americans see themselves as "a group on the defensive" from changes happening in the rest of the country. Individuals have grown to hold more negative views of not just the well-known politicians from the other party, but also individuals who identify with that party.

They are less willing to socialize or to partner with members of the other party. As the share of Republican voters increases in unhyphenated America, there are fewer and fewer Democrats to socialize with.

Affective polarization grows out of a sense of a connection between one's social identity and one's partisan identity. In recent years, a variety of social identities—including race, ideology, geography, religion, and education—have grown to more clearly and distinctly line up with partisan divisions. Lilliana Mason (2018) argues that this shift in alignment—which also includes a reduction in cross-cutting social ties—has turned partisanship into a "mega identity." As polarization continued over time, so continued and grew the dislike and distrust that those who identify as Republicans felt about Democrats, and vice versa (Levendusky and Malhotra 2016a).

The social identity basis of affective polarization also means that it is distinct from ideological divisions (Iyengar et al. 2012; Mason 2015; Levendusky and Malhotra 2016b). Thus, it is more deep-seated than a reaction to the issue position and ideological maneuverings of specific politicians. And as affective polarization increases, individuals are less likely to encounter conflicting political ideas and identities in their everyday life (Roccas and Brewer 2002). This serves to reinforce the distance individuals feel in relation to members of the opposing camp.

In unhyphenated America, like in other parts of the country, affective polarization has pushed one party to the fore and the other party to the background. As identities such as religion (e.g. evangelical Christian) and region (i.e. rural or small town) have mapped more clearly on to partisan identity, the region has pushed more toward the Republicans, and away from the Democrats.

The trends of affective and geographic polarization are also reinforcing. Individuals who support the other political party become more distant in both a geographic and a psychological sense. This seems particularly relevant in unhyphenated concentrated areas, where population growth and immigration is low, reducing the share of people with different experiences. As a consequence, in one's daily life one encounters fewer people with different experiences and fewer members of the opposing party, and one learns less about the complexities of why individuals choose to identify with that party. Stereotypes and exaggerations of the out-party grow, reinforcing the apparent strangeness of that party. The growing Republican trend in unhyphenated America reflects this reinforcing pattern of identification.

5 The Argument of the Book

This book examines these reinforcing patterns of polarization and geography in one specific region of the country—unhyphenated America. This is the region that begins in the Appalachian Mountains and then spills out to the west across the highland areas of the broader South, though it has branches that extend into the Midwest and across the Mississippi River. In examining this region, I reach several clear conclusions.

1. The region has shifted strongly toward the Republicans in the last political generation, driven by both the geographic and affective polarization discussed in the previous section and the demographic distinctiveness of the region.

2. This shift is apparent at different levels of elections. In this book I present clear and strong evidence for the shift in both presidential and US House elections. As such, it is a phenomenon that is broader than any individual candidate and their strengths and weaknesses.

3. The partisan shift seems durable and should last well into the next political generation, if not beyond. For example, when Republicans take unhyphenated concentrated congressional districts from Democrats, the Republicans have continued to hold those seats and usually face very little partisan competition for them in future elections.

4. The regional shift I identify is driven primarily by a change in issue salience. Unhyphenated America moved toward the Republican Party less because residents there changed their opinions on key issues. Rather, the region shifted because what are often called social issues—abortion, gay rights, gun policy—became more salient not only to the national political discussion but to the divides between the two parties.

The empirical portions of the book are of course dedicated to providing the evidentiary basis for these conclusions. I use detailed election and public opinion data—focusing on the unhyphenated concentrated counties identified in Figure 1.3—to reach these conclusions.

6 A Southern Realignment, but Not *the* Southern Realignment

Another conclusion that I reach from my data is that the partisan shift in unhyphenated America is distinct from other partisan shifts in recent American politics. Obviously, there has been a counter shift in unhyphenated America in the nation's suburbs, as they have drifted to the Democrats over the course of the same time period (Schaffner and Gaus 2023; Hacker et al. 2024). Similar factors matter here, as the social liberalism of the suburbs played a key role in pushing them left, but so to has the increasing share of minority voters there (McGowen 2017; Rastogi and Jones-Correa 2023).

As discussed above, there was a shift in small-town rural voters—especially in the Midwest—toward the Republicans that culminated with Donald Trump's 2016 victory. The origins of both of these shifts can be traced back to 1996, when the rural/urban split started to grow (Aistrup et al. 2023; Lang and Pearson-Markowitz 2015). Yet, there is still a distinct timeline to the shift in unhyphenated America, which moved most strongly toward the Republicans between 1994 and 2010, as opposed to the rural Midwest, which shifted more from 2016 to 2024.

But the partisan shift that most readers are likely to have in mind as I discuss the shift in unhyphenated America is the Republican realignment of the American South. The similarities are clear—unhyphenated America is concentrated heavily in the South and it moved toward the Republicans. This observation prompts the question, hasn't this been covered already?

At one level, yes: the Southern Republican realignment is one of the most well-studied phenomena in recent American politics, with seemingly an entire branch of American political science dedicated to tracing in minute detail the South's move from a region of "yellow dog Democrats" to one dominated by conservative Republicans to a more competitive if Republican-leaning region in recent years.

On another level, I will argue in this book that the shift in unyphenated America is a different political shift than the more traditional Southern Republican realignment. There are several reasons for this. For one, the mountains of Appalachia were never as solidly Democratic as the rest of the South. V. O. Key identified a strain of "Mountain Republicans" in the Appalachias that provided much greater two-party competition than in the rest of the South. Unhyphenated America also includes places outside of the eleven states of the Confederacy that Key studied and thus includes areas that had robust two-party competition before the Southern Republican realignment.

I also argue that the shift in unhyphenated America happened at a different time than the Southern Republican realignment. The shift in unhyphenated America happened most sharply between 1994 and 2010 and then moved more gradually but still towards the Republican Party after that. The Southern Republican realignment took place primarily from the 1970s to the 1990s. That the two Republican shifts happened in different time periods suggests there are different reasons why the two regions changed.

Thus, Chapter 2 lays out in full how and why the Southern Republican realignment happened, but also how and why the shift in unhyphenated America is happening. The chapter provides a detailed explanation not just of the issues that propelled the Southern Republican realignment, but also the different set of issues that I believe have pushed unhyphenated America to the right. In the process of providing this explication the chapter also sets up how the data will be used to prove my hypotheses throughout the book.

This chapter began by discussing election results from West Virginia, where Republicans have made spectacular gains over a generation, turning it into one of the nation's most reliably Republican states at the presidential level. West Virginia is notable for several reasons, most particularly for having large concentrations of unhyphenated Americans and for its shift to the right over the past ten presidential elections. But it is also notably not Southern, carved out of the Confederacy by its opposition to secession and loyalty to the United States. One can see this in the results of the 1988 presidential election. That year, the eleven states of the Confederacy all voted for Republican George H. W. Bush, as part of his solid national popular vote victory. Only the most loyally Democratic states cast their electoral votes for Michael Dukakis, including West Virginia, the bastion of the New Deal Democratic coalition.

This book shows how that coalition broke down in West Virginia, but not just in West Virginia—also across lots of other regions that share the large concentrations of American ethnic identifiers present in much of the Mountain State. The forces that prompted the Southern Republican realignment were not present in West Virginia. A different process unfolded in West Virginia, and I argue that this process is a similar to that observed in the rest of the Appalachias and the upper South. This is a region that was never as loyal to the Democrats as the Deep South during the one-party South era, and did not move as strongly to the Republicans from the 1960s to the early 1990s, as did the other parts of the South. Instead, the region began moving toward the Republicans starting in the mid-1990s, a movement that continued for over two decades up to the election and presidency of Donald Trump. This book tells how and why that happened.

Chapter 2
A Tale of Two Republican Realignments: Why the Realignment of Unhyphenated America is Different from the Southern Realignment

It was big news when, on March 3, 1994, William Natcher (D-KY) was too sick to show up to cast his vote in the US House. Natcher had voted on every single piece of legislation in the US House for over forty straight years—a total of 18,401 consecutive votes. Colleagues described Natcher as a "true icon" and said his vote record would "never be equaled in the universe" (Seelye 1994). Missing a vote for the first time in forty years showed how sick Natcher was, and by the end of March, he passed away.

Forty years in Congress requires a member to win re-election many times, and Natcher did that. After first winning a special election in August 1953, he won re-election twenty times in Kentucky's 2nd District. Natcher's vote streak reflected his "hard-working and conscientious" home style (Barone and Ujifusa 1995). Natcher "generally campaigned by placing a few newspaper advertisements and driving from town to town in his own automobile" (Wines 1994). He refused to take campaign contributions and would spend only a few thousand dollars of his own money to campaign. But it worked. Natcher always won re-election and usually by landslide margins. One of his Republican opponents said that facing off with Natcher was like "running against God" (Wines 1994).

Natcher's death created a special election for the seat, but this east-central Kentucky district had been in Democratic hands not just for Natcher's forty-one years in Congress, but for generations before that. Thus, the expectation was that the Democratic nominee, Joe Prather, a former state Senator, would win. Indeed, Republicans "seemed resigned . . . to the prospect of continued" Democratic control of the seat (Cross 1994a). The Republicans nominated Ron Lewis, who had initially filed to run as just another sacrificial lamb against Natcher. Lewis was an ordained minister who ran a Christian bookstore. In contrast to Prather, who local reporters described as a political "fixture" (Cross 1994a), Lewis was "the opposite of a political insider" (Barone and Ujifusa 1999, 549).

Being the opposite of a political insider was an asset in 1994. Political scientist Gary Jacobson noted that the Democrats—after the inauguration of Bill Clinton—"were now the party of government. And the party to blame if voters want to send a message of unhappiness" (quoted in Berke 1994). Lewis's campaign themes were based on the idea that voters wanted to send a message of unhappiness to the party of government. Lewis's ads attacked "Prather as a professional

https://doi.org/10.1515/9783111615707-002

politician who cut deals and raised taxes" (Cross 1994b). Prather was not the only professional politician the Lewis campaign attacked. Lewis's ads attacked Bill Clinton for seeking to raise taxes (National Journal 1994a). In his ads, Lewis also portrayed himself as the more conservative candidate, and that appealed to a district that had voted for Republicans in US Senate and presidential elections (Cross 1994b). In addition, Lewis was boosted by mobilization in Christian churches, where his status as a minister and his opposition to abortion were big plusses.

The national Republican Party sensed they could win, and the National Republican Congressional Campaign funded ads that nationalized the race, attacking not just Prather but also Clinton (Cross 1994c). Bob Dole, the Senate majority leader, campaigned with Lewis on the eve of election day (National Journal 1994b). These efforts worked. Lewis beat Prather by 55% to 45%.

Lewis had to run again in the general election in November, and once again the Democrats ran an experienced elected official, the mayor of Owensboro. Nevertheless, Lewis won by an even larger margin—60% to 40%—showing that his win in the special election was not a low-turnout fluke. Lewis then turned away another Democratic political insider in 1996, winning by sixteen points. By 1998, he had full control of the district, winning 64%-35% over a Democrat who had never won office before (Barone and Ujifusa 1999, 678). Lewis won re-election for another decade before finally retiring in 2008, winning consistently by landslide margins. He was succeeded by another Republican in Brett Guthrie, who has held the seat easily for the GOP since then.

Lewis's win in the special election was not just a signal that Kentucky's 2nd District was different now that William Natcher was not on the ballot. It also "signaled the Republican landslide to come that November" (Sabato 2006). Themes from the Lewis-Prather race remained important in November, including voter anger at political insiders, unhappiness with Bill Clinton's tax and health care policies, and the success of Republican candidates at tying local Democrats to their liberal national party. That fall, Republicans won a majority in the US House for the first time in forty years, thanks in large part to their gains in rural and small-town districts like the Kentucky 2nd (McKee 2010).

The 1994 election reflects the fulfillment of the Southern Republican realignment. From the 1950s through the early 1990s, Republicans made gains at the presidential level, winning an increasing share of votes over time, especially after the political success of the Reagan Administration (Black and Black 1992). Republican gains were more limited down the ballot, as Democratic candidates were able to successfully separate themselves from the liberalizing national party among white voters while attaching themselves to the pro-civil rights national party to win over Black voters (see Glaser 1996). As a result, Southern Democrats were able to build biracial coalitions to hold off the growing Republican Party and maintain Democratic majorities in Southern House and Senate seats throughout the 1970s and 1980s (Black and Black 2002).

The 1994 election ended the Democratic majority in Southern congressional elections. Republicans won a majority of seats in both US House and Senate elections for the first time since Reconstruction (Black and Black 2002). Southern Republicans have not conceded their Southern congressional majority in the thirty years since. GOP gains across the South followed in state legislatures (McKee and Yoshinaka 2015) and local offices (Hood et al. 2012, 25–37). The Republican shift in the South had profound consequences nationally. From the Great Depression to 1994, Democrats had won a majority of the US House on all but two occasions, thanks in large part to the surplus of seats they won in the South. After 1994, that surplus ended, leading to the long period of close and highly contested congressional politics we have seen since then (Lee 2016).

However, the election of Ron Lewis in 1994, both in his special election victory in May and his general election victory in November, are part of a different trend. The Kentucky 2nd is not part of the Old Confederacy, and thus, not part of the regional studies in the classic tracts on Southern politics (see Key 1949 and the progeny of that book).[10] But it does fit in the definitions used in this book, as fourteen of the seventeen counties in the district in the 1990s, meet the definition of unhyphenated concentrated used in Chapter 1.[11] The Kentucky 2nd is an unhyphenated concentrated district, and in 1994, districts like it began moving toward the Republicans, both strongly and durably.

The Southern Republican realignment, the one that begun at the presidential level in the 1950s and climaxed at the congressional level in the 1990s, is an exceedingly well-studied phenomenon. In this chapter, I will argue that the Republican shift in unhyphenated America that I detail throughout the course of this book is distinct from the Southern Republican realignment. To do this, I will discuss the explanations for the Southern Republican realignment in the voluminous literature

---

10 Key used the eleven states of the Confederacy to define "the political South" due to its "consistency of attachment to the Democratic Party nationally. Eleven states and only eleven did not go Republican more than twice in the presidential elections from 1876 to 1944" (Key 1949, 10). You can also see evidence of Kentucky's two-party competition, and thus its political distinctiveness from the Old Confederacy, in its governor's elections. Republicans had won six of the state's fourteen most recent governor's contests when *Southern Politics in State and Nation* (Key 1949) was published. For a full account of how political scientists have defined "the South," including the importance of the eleven-state Old Confederacy definition, see Springer (2019).

11 In the Kentucky 2nd, 19.3% of residents identified their ethnic heritage as exclusively American in the 2017 American Community Survey. That is the eighth highest of any congressional district in the country. In Chapter 4, I will introduce a measure for unhyphenated concentrated at the congressional district level. Clearly, the Kentucky 2nd meets that definition.

on the subject. These center on the role of race in the wake of the successes of the Civil Rights Movement and the post-World War II suburbanized economic transformation of the South. Neither dynamic applies well to the Appalachias and upper South where Black populations have traditionally been smaller than in the Deep South, and where economic development has been slower than in the big city South.

I will thus argue that other factors—predominantly the increased importance of social issues and the nationalization of racial and geographic politics—are more relevant explanations for the shift taking place in unhyphenated America. Key to my argument is the different timelines applied to the shift in unhyphenated America and the Southern Republican realignment.

The 1994 election is a seminal moment here. It is not quite the apotheosis of the Southern Republican realignment, but it is quite close to the end of the process, most especially in congressional elections. Republicans continued to make gains in the South after 1994, but they were much more modest than their gains in previous years, and mostly at the state legislative and local levels.

But in unhyphenated America, 1994 represents the beginning. Republicans not only made gains in unhyphenated concentrated congressional districts such as Kentucky's 2nd that year, but they also held those districts and, over time, increased their vote share to landslide majorities. Similarly, Republican presidential candidates made gains in unhyphenated concentrated areas in the 1990s and continued to make similar gains into the twenty-first century. Therefore, the timing of the two Republican shifts are different, and, as a result, there are different explanations for these two electoral patterns.

This chapter has two principal objectives. The first is to use the literature that explains why the Southern Republican realignment happened to show why those explanations do not hold in the geographic area under study here—the regions of the Appalachian Mountains and the upper South, which feature concentrations of American ethnic identifiers. My second goal is to provide an explanation of why unhyphenated America has shifted toward the Republicans starting with the 1994 election, as detailed in the story of the Kentucky 2nd. To this, I argue non-economic issues—e.g. abortion, gay rights, gun policy, the environment, racial views—became more salient both as a consideration in voting and in polarizing the two parties. The conservative views of the Republicans on these issues were more attractive to residents of unhyphenated America, and the liberal views of national Democrats pushed these voters away.

1 The Southern Republican Realignment

In 1944, Franklin D. Roosevelt won all eleven states of the Old Confederacy for the fourth consecutive time. His smallest margin of victory in the South was in Tennessee, which he won by more than twenty percentage points. Democrats won 103 of the 105 US House seats contested that year in the South, almost all by landslide margins. Similarly, Democrats won elections that year to Senate seats in Alabama, Arkansas, Florida, Georgia, Louisiana, North Carolina, and South Carolina, all by at least forty points. They held all twenty-two Southern Senate seats (Clerk of the US House of Representatives 1945).

This was the Solid South, the South of yellow dog Democrats. The South that V. O. Key explored and explained in his classic treatise *Southern Politics in State and Nation* (1949). It was also a South that was about to change politically. In 1948, the states of Alabama, Louisiana, Mississippi, and South Carolina gave their electoral votes to Strom Thurmond, who ran as the nominee of the States Rights Party, more commonly known as the Dixiecrats. Since 1944, no Democratic presidential nominee has swept the South's electoral votes.

What began at the presidential level moved to the US Senate, starting with Republican John Tower winning a US Senate special election in Texas in 1961, and continued in the US House, where Republicans started making significant gains in the 1966 election. These gains continued over time. And while they are described by Angie Maxwell and Todd Shields (2019, 25) as fitting a "two steps forward and one step back" pattern, Republican gains continued over time. In 1994, Republicans won a majority of Southern seats in the US House and the US Senate and a GOP majority has been maintained in each election since then.

The Southern Republican realignment has had profound consequences not only for the politics of the South, but also for the United States. It is both a cause of and a result of the ideological polarization of modern politics (Hill and Tausanovitch 2018), helping to create the ideologically homogenous and nearly equally sized party coalitions that have marked twenty-first century politics (Lee 2016). Unsurprisingly, scholars have paid detailed attention to the GOP's Southern realignment and offered several categories of explanations for why the South shifted so strongly to the Republicans in the latter half of the twentieth century. Broadly, these explanations focus on two different categories—race and economics. I will detail both of these two explanations, explaining how they changed Southern politics in the wake of World War II, the success of the Civil Rights Movement, and the concurrent modernization of the Southern economy

1.1 Race and Realignment

What makes the South the most distinct region of the United States? At the center of this answer is the role of race. The South has—and has always had—the nation's largest share of African Americans, and relations between Black and white—which is to say the desire of whites to maintain economic and sociological supremacy over Blacks—dominated Southern life throughout slavery, Reconstruction, and Jim Crow segregation.

The importance of race to Southern economic and social life meant that race was also at the center of Southern political life (Kousser 1974). And at the center of Southern political life in the first half of the twentieth century was the Democratic Party. White supremacy and the Southern Democratic Party were melded together. "Southern one-party politics originated in the resolve of white southerners to hold Negroes to a well-defined economic, social, and political place" (Heard 1952, 145). Key (1949, 9) argued that Southern Democratic "unity on the national scene was essential in order that the largest possible bloc could be mobilized to resist any national move toward interference with southern authority to deal with the race question as was desired locally."

The effectiveness of Southern Democratic unity in maintaining segregation broke down as the national party moved to more broadly support civil rights. That broke the Solid South. The choice of Harry Truman to integrate the US military and the Democratic Party as a whole to adopt a pro-civil rights plank in its 1948 platform prompted the Dixiecrat revolt. John Kennedy's vocal support for a civil rights bill engendered an immediate reduction in support for him among Southern whites (Kuziemko and Washington 2018). Congressional passage of that bill in 1964, championed by Lyndon Johnson, caused five Deep South states to vote for Republican Barry Goldwater despite Johnson's national landslide (Cosman 1966).

The end of Jim Crow segregation did not extinguish the attitudes that created racial discrimination laws, but it did alter how racial issues were discussed in campaigns. For one, the Voting Rights Act, signed in 1965, enfranchised large numbers of African American voters (Grofman et al. 1992; Schuman et al. 1985; Hood et al. 2012).[12] Democratic support for the Civil Rights Act and the Voting Rights Act (and opposition from key Republicans like Goldwater) realigned newly

---

12 Though it should be noted that increases in African American voter registration began before the passage of the Voting Rights Act in 1965 (Rodgers and Bullock 1972; Stanley 1987; Timpone 1995).

enfranchised Southern African Americans into the national Democratic Party (Carmines and Stimson 1989) and in monolithic numbers (Campbell 1977).

Among white southerners, the reaction was different. Racial conservatism still prevailed among most of the population, and that made it difficult for national Democrats, with their liberal stands on civil rights, to win the votes of Southern whites. Steadily these voters began increasing their identification with the Republican Party (Aistrup 1996) and voting Republican for president (Black and Black 1992). Southern Democrats were able to maintain the loyalty of these same voters in the 1970s and 1980s, often by differentiating themselves from national Democrats by taking moderate and conservative positions on non-economic issues such as race (Black and Black 2002). Racial issues remained at the center of Southern campaigns of the 1970s and 1980s (cf. Bartley and Graham 1978; Bass and De Vries 1976; Havard 1972), but the ability of Southern Democrats to successfully appeal to both African Americans and whites (Glaser 1996) led to maintenance of a Democratic congressional majority in the South and to the conclusion that the South had engaged in either dealignment (Beck 1977) or split-level realignment (Aistrup 1996).

The South may have changed after the Civil Rights Movement, but the legacies of centuries of slavery and a century of *de jure* segregation still affected the attitudes of white southerners years later. Southern whites continued to hold more conservative attitudes on racial issues (Valentino and Sears 2005) and higher levels of racial resentment than northerners (Knuckey 2005b). Native-born white southerners hold more conservative attitudes on racialized issues than do migrants from the north (Glaser and Gilens 1997; Wilson 1986). Why do these attitudes persist? Valentino and Sears (2005, 686) attribute it to "the transmission of a broad culture of racial conservatism in the South across generations." How many generations? Acharya et al. (2016, 2018) believe the answer goes back to emancipation. They find that the share of slaves in a county's population in 1860 is an important predictor of racial and partisan attitudes 150 years later. They attribute this to the "historical persistence" of anti-Black attitudes that not only developed during slavery, but that were threatened by the potential for Blacks to gain political power during Reconstruction. These attitudes were reinforced across generations through not just the transmission of racist ideas from parent to child, but also through the socialization of expected behavior for both Black and white populations in the South.

At the center of the repression of former slaves and their descendants was the threat whites felt from the presence of African Americans. And the larger the share of Blacks in a local population, the greater threat that local whites felt from those African Americans. In 1949, V. O. Key formally developed this hypothesis, writing that the political focus of Southern politics is on "the maintenance of control by a white *minority*" (Key 1949, 5). The context of Southern politics has changed substantially since Key wrote that, but subsequent scholars found evidence of the connection between increasing shares of Blacks and support for conservative candidates (Black and Black 1973; Crespi 1971; Giles 1977; Giles and Buckner 1993; Giles and Evans 1986; Giles and Hertz 1994; Glaser 1994; Wright 1977). Support for the racial threat hypothesis is less identifiable when examining roll-call voting (cf. Bullock 1985; Coombs et al. 1984), which suggests the finding was limited to particular contexts, and academic disagreement over the effect of racial threat in explaining support for David Duke in Louisiana elections (Howell 1994; Voss 1996) raised the possibility that the hypothesis had faded over time.

Hood et al. (2012) have a more nuanced finding about racial threat, finding that it is not Black population size per se, but Black political mobilization that is a key variable in explaining the growth of Southern Republicans. As a higher share of Blacks mobilized into politics by registering to vote, Southern whites saw a relative advantage in joining the Republican Party, where they faced less competition in primary elections from liberal and African American voters and more opportunity to win elections and hence enact more conservative policies.

The school of thought presented in this section puts race at the center of the Southern Republican realignment. The national parties shifted their positions on race in the wake of the Civil Rights Movement. Over a long stretch of time, this broke down political loyalties in the South, especially as the racial liberalism of the national Democratic Party and the racial conservatism of Southern whites made it increasingly difficult for Southern Democrats to balance this conflict and win elections. Others disagreed, arguing that while race remained an important factor in Southern politics, its salience waned. Instead, politics in the South started to resemble the politics of the rest of the nation, which focused heavily on the division between the two parties over issues surrounding economics.

1.2 Economic Growth and Realignment

The second set of explanations for the Southern Republican realignment is rooted in the economic growth of the South after World War II. After generations as an economic backwater, centered in small towns and focused on agriculture, the Southern economy transformed into an industrial and trade-based economy focused on the region's biggest cities and their suburbs (Lassiter 2007). The economic growth brought large population growth, especially as northerners moved South in search of economic opportunities (Sosna 1987) and the more tolerable climates made possible by air conditioning (Arsenault 1984).

The shift in Southern economics created transformations in Southern politics as well. Northern politics after the New Deal had divided primarily on economic and class lines, with working-class voters tending to support the pro-labor and Keynesian policies of Democrats, with upper-class voters supporting the more moderate and budget-conscious politics of Republicans. These divides only increased from the 1960s to the 1980s as politics centered on opinions about the Great Society social welfare programs of the Johnson Administration and the tax cut policies pursued by the Reagan Administration.

In the South, the end of Jim Crow segregation and the growth in voting for Republican presidential candidates made these economic themes resonant on a partisan basis for the first time possibly ever. More and more upper-class voters drifted to the Republicans (Lamis 1988; Lublin 2004). The initial base of the Southern Republican Party was among the region's high-income voters, centered on suburban areas outside of the South's largest cities (Shafer and Johnston 2001). In this way, the politics of the South—or at least the suburban South—began to resemble the politics of the rest of the country, with upper-class voters tending to favor the Republicans and working-class voters tending to favor the Democrats (Shafer and Johnston 2006).

One factor pushing the region toward the Republicans was the region's population growth. Much of that population growth came from those who moved from the North to the South, especially into suburbs. Most of these migrants were white and middle-class and were thus more likely to identify and vote as Republicans. Migration thus pushed the South toward the Republicans (Scher 1997; Stanley and Castle 1988).

2 Why Race and Economic Growth Do Not Explain the Shift of Unhyphenated America

I have provided this detailed review of the Southern Republican realignment literature to show that what I am describing in this book is not the Southern Republican realignment. Obviously, the shift of unhyphenated concentrated regions toward the Republicans is a strong and durable political shift. As such, it has some obvious similarities to the Southern Republican realignment. There are other similarities. For example, unhyphenated America is centered in the states that make up the traditional definition of the "South." Looking beyond those surface similarities, one can identify several reasons why the shift of unhyphenated America toward the Republicans is different from the realignment of the rest of the South toward the Republicans.

The first reason is the timing of the shift. As I detail in Chapter 3, the biggest shift in unhyphenated concentrated counties towards the Republicans happened at the presidential level from the 2000 election to the 2008 election. By that time, the rest of the South had mostly stabilized into a clear preference for Republican candidates, and that lead stayed relatively constant. Most of the growth in Republican presidential vote share in the South had occurred by the 1980s and Republican vote share increased little after that (Maxwell and Shields 2019, 9–33). At the US House level, there is a similar pattern in the South. Republicans made small but clear gains in Southern House elections through the 1970s and 1980s, and then broke through to take a majority of Southern seats in the 1994 election, which they have held since then. But 1994 is toward the end of the Southern Republican realignment.

In contrast, the 1994 midterm elections were close to the beginning of the Republican shift in unhyphenated America. At the House level, Republicans won a majority of these seats for the first time that year. And the House gains in 1994 presaged gains at the presidential level that continued through the 2008 election. The different timing of these two changes suggests that the reasons for the shift in unhyphenated concentrated regions differ from those that brought about the Southern Republican realignment. That makes sense, because the reasons scholars found to explain the Southern Republican realignment do not apply as well to regions with large concentrations of American ethnic identifiers.

As noted, the changing politics around race is a key explanation for the Southern Republican realignment. The Democratic Party existed as the dominant party in the South as the political vehicle to achieve white social and economic supremacy in the region. With the success of the Civil Rights Movement, the Southern Democratic Party lost its post-Civil War *raison d'être* and prompted the region's white voters to slowly consider voting for Republicans. As Republicans embraced racially conservative positions, they attracted more Southern voters. The racial threat hypothesis holds that as the share of African Americans in the population increases, so too does the conservatism of the white voters in that region.

Part of what distinguishes regions with concentrations of unhyphenated Americans from the rest of the South is its rocky and hilly soil, which was never conducive to growing cotton on a mass-scale and the plantation-based slavery that came with it. As a result, the African American population of the region has always remained small (see Acharya et al. 2018, esp. Figures 3.1 and 3.5).

As Table 1.1 showed, the African American population of unhyphenated concentrated regions in the 2020 Census was 8.6%. That is lower than the national share of African Americans which is 12.1%. Of course, African American populations are even higher in the South. Every one of the eleven states of the Old Confederacy has a higher share of African Americans than the national share; the African American population of the five Deep South states are all over one quarter of their state's population.

The conclusion I draw from these data and from the history of Southern politics is that racial issues work differently in the Appalachias and the upper South than in rest of the South. That was true in V. O. Key's day, as he identified a strain of Mountain Republicanism in the Appalachian parts of the South, where no racial threat existed to organize politics around white supremacy. It worked differently in the post-civil rights era, as Southern Democratic candidates tried to differentiate themselves from their racially liberal national party (Glaser 1994) and conservative candidates tried to emphasize issues that implicitly cued racial stereotypes and resentments (Mendelberg 2001). As a result, unhyphenated America shifted less toward the racially conservative Republicans in this time period than did the rest of the South.

Another reason for the Southern Republican realignment was the twin effects of economic growth and migration on the region. Economic growth in the South helped create a Southern upper-middle class centered in the region's suburbs. These upper-middle-class southerners voted their economic, rather than their racial interests, and thus were attracted to the low-spending, low-tax policies of the Republicans. Economic growth also attracted population growth as northerners migrated South. Since northerners were on average more Republican than southerners, this increased the region's share of Republicans. And since many of these migrants moved to suburban areas, they also increased the concentration of Republicans in these localities (Lublin 2004; Shafer and Johnston 2001).

This economic growth and the migration that came with it tended to skip unhyphenated America. As noted in Chapter 1, the population of unhyphened concentrated counties is almost all in what Hood and McKee (2022) describe as "Small Town South." Even the parts of unhyphenated America that are not in the Old Confederacy are almost all in small towns and rural counties. As a result, this region has very few of the suburbs that provided a base for the Southern Republican Party of the 1970s and the 1980s. In general, population growth remains relatively small in unhyphenated America, indicating that few Northern migrants have moved into the region to help push it toward the Republicans in the twentieth century.

A fierce debate rages in the Southern politics literature on whether race or economics plays a more important role in the Southern Republican realignment (cf. Shafer and Johnston 2006; Kousser 2010). Certainly, this debate is important, but with regard to unhyphenated America, it is not relevant. The changes in racial politics that pushed the rest of the South toward the Republicans from the 1970s through the early 1990s meant little to a region with a disproportionately large share of whites such as unhyphenated America. Neither did the politics of suburbanized economic growth in a region with few suburbs and more modest levels of economic growth. These were important factors in the Southern Republican realignment, but they are not present in unhyphenated America. That is a large part of the reason why unhyphenated America did not move toward the Republicans at the same time as the rest of the South did. This conclusion, however, leaves open the question of why unhyphenated America moved to the Republicans when it did.

3 Changing Issue Salience in Twenty-First-Century Politics

Having shown that the Republican shift in unhyphenated America did not happen for the same reasons as the realignment in the rest of the South, I now turn to addressing why the shift did occur.

The difference in timing of the Republican shift in unhyphenated America and the Southern Republican realignment suggests that different sets of issues were at play in each case. I have identified four sets of issues which became more salient in political discourse starting in the 1990s and on which the two major party coalitions took different stands, allowing the issues to be politicized in the minds of voters. These issues include what are often called "social issues," but which I will specify as abortion and gay rights. In addition, I also identify gun policy and environmental issues centered on reducing the effects of climate change as issues that help explain unhyphenated America's shift to the right.

Issues around abortion and gay rights have increased in salience in American politics since the 1980s. The success of second-wave feminism in reshaping American social life in the 1970s and 1980s led to a Democratic Party that embraced feminism and which took a pro-choice (and thus pro-feminist) position on abortion (Adams 1997; Carmines and Woods 2002; Hout 1999). At the same time, Republicans have broadly opposed abortion rights and made common cause with Christian conservatives who have increased their political involvement since the early 1980s (Baylor 2017; Rozell and Wilcox 1996; Rozell et al. 1998), especially in the South (Green et al. 2010). Gay rights issues have increased in importance since the 1980s, as a result of increasing focus on issues such as AIDS relief and gay marriage (Haider-Markel and Meier 1996; Lax and Phillips 2009). The traditionalist views of the Republican Party would likely attract those who not only possess a traditional view of their ancestry, but are also concentrated in regions of the country such as the Appalachias which heavily feature religious observances and evangelical beliefs (White 2019).

Attitudes towards gun laws were similarly politicized along party lines through the 1980s and then gained newer salience in the 1990s (Lacombe 2021). Many attributed Republican gains in the 1994 election to Bill Clinton's signing of two gun control measures—the "Brady Bill" and the assault weapons ban. The National Rifle Association (NRA) had great success supporting Republican candidates who sought to repeal the ban and faced off against vulnerable Democratic incumbents (Kenny et al. 2004). Gun policy is an issue that divides urban interests from rural ones, and as the issue increased in salience, the small-town and rural voters in unhyphenated America moved toward the party that supported the pro-gun position of rural America.

Environmental issues have also shifted in the last political generation. Democrats, led by Vice President Al Gore, have proposed various methods to address global warming, mostly through increasing the cost of carbon-intensive energy sources. This push by Democrats to address climate change has been opposed by Republicans and has led to sharper partisan polarization on climate change among the mass public (Guber 2013; McCright and Dunlap 2011; McCright et al. 2014). Coal-producing regions, such as the Appalachias, have regarded these proposals as attacks on their livelihood (Bell and York 2010; Lewin 2019), which explains their attraction to the party that opposes attempts to reduce climate change.

Each of these four issues split the party coalitions. While there is variation within each party, broadly, the Democrats hold the liberal position and Republicans the conservative position on abortion, gay rights, gun rights, and climate change. More importantly, these are all issues that have increased in salience and partisan division since the 1980s. One would be hard pressed to find Dwight Eisenhower's or John Kennedy's position on abortion, and support for conservation and environmental protection seemed to have bipartisan support before the Reagan Administration. Political division on guns became more salient with the political activation and conservative positioning of the NRA in the late 1970s (Lacombe 2021), which is similar to how the gay rights movement increased the salience of their issues and compelled parties and elected officials to take a position on these issues (Garretson 2018; Karol 2023; Wuest 2023).

During the New Deal alignment, politics tended to revolve around issues of the economy, the budget, and redistribution. During that time period, candidates had little need to take positions on issues surrounding sexuality, guns, and the environment. Further, a local candidate's positions on these types of issues were not strongly identified with the position of his national party on the issue. But over the course of the 1980s, these issues increased in importance and became quite relevant in the 1990s. They have remained salient to politics in the twenty-first century.

Another issue of great relevance to explaining the Republican shift in unhyphenated America is one that was also relevant to the Southern Republican realignment—race. I argue that the context and meaning of race in American politics changed in the twenty-first century, and that change in context and meaning is important to understand why race pushed unhyphenated America toward the Republicans in the twenty-first century but did not after the Civil Rights Movement.

In the wake of the Civil Rights Movement, racial politics were dominated by the desire to maintain in some form the white supremacy of the Jim Crow South (Black and Black 2002) and to address the racial threat created by the emerging mobilization of Black voters into the electorate (Hood et al. 2012). As noted, the small Black population of the Appalachias and upper South meant that these concerns had less purchase in unhyphenated America. There are still reasons to think that racial attitudes in the region were conservative, but they were less activated than those attitudes in areas of the South with larger concentrations of African Americans.

The elevation of Barack Obama to the Democratic presidential nomination and then the presidency in 2008 changed the nature of race in American politics. The election of the nation's first Black president meant that race became not only a salient feature of American politics, but *the* salient feature of American politics.

In explaining how "Obama's legislative proposals have the potential to polarize issue opinions by racial attitudes and race," Michael Tesler (2012a, 691–692) wrote:

> Given the importance of elites' background characteristics . . . the salience of Obama's race in public perceptions of him should also spill over into public opinion about his visible policy positions. More specifically, source cues that connect racialized public figures to specific issues are expected to activate racial considerations in mass opinion much the way that code words and other subtle race cues have linked African Americans with public policies in prior research.

Tesler called this hypothesis the "spillover of racialization" and then found that opinions on the Affordable Care Act—the health care expansion more commonly referred to as "Obamacare"—polarized primarily based on voters' "race-based reactions" to Obama, over and above traditional partisan or ideological lines (see also Tesler 2015). Attitudes about race have "spilled over" to many issues unconnected with race, such as the economy (Chen and Mohanty 2017; Wilson and Davis 2018), climate change (Benegal 2018), and the federal response to superstorm Sandy (Sheagley et al. 2017). Unsurprisingly, racial spillover has been observed in voting results, particularly in congressional elections (Luttig and Motta 2017).

The implications of the racial spillover hypothesis for unhyphenated America are profound, as they presume that racial attitudes that had previously been more dormant due to the lack of local relevance became activated due to the national relevance of race. Tesler, in a later work, argued that the election of Obama "made racial attitudes a *chronically accessible* consideration in mass assessments" of Obama (Tesler 2016, 17). It did not matter how large or small the Black population was in a county or a state, that the president was an African American made race a meaningful consideration for all voters. Those who held racially liberal views polarized toward the Democrats. And those with racially conservative views—like whites who lived in the Appalachias and the upper South—polarized toward the Republicans.

The chronic accessibility of race in American politics did not end when Obama left office. One reason is that racial attitudes have long been relevant to partisanship (Enders and Scott 2019). A bigger reason is that Obama was succeeded by Donald Trump, whose openly racist rhetoric and policy making continued to provide opportunities for racial attitudes to spill over into other contexts, such as Trump's victory in the 2016 election (Hooghe and Dassonneville 2018; Mason et al. 2021; Schaffner et al. 2018; Reny et al. 2019). Rewarded for his racist rhetoric with victory in 2016, Trump continued to deploy it during his presidency with predictable effects—white voters with antagonism toward outgroups (Bartels 2020), high levels of white racial solidarity (Jardina and Mickey 2022) and high levels of racial resentment (Enders and Thornton 2022) increasingly supported Trump and his attacks on democratic principles, including his post-election attempts to steal the 2020 election and the January 6 attack on the US Capitol (Barreto et al. 2024; Davis and Wilson 2023; Filindra et al. 2024; Rhodes and Nteta 2024).

Putting this all together, my argument is that the Southern Republican realignment is a function of twentieth-century politics, which focused on issues of racial threat and civil rights in a localized racial sphere and economic redistribution in the national sphere. Southern politics tended to be defined by attitudes toward segregation and the Civil Rights Movement, with some level of economic voting developing in certain parts of the region by the last quarter of the twentieth century. Those changes did not affect unhyphenated America much. Only when politics changed in the 1990s—with non-economic issues such as abortion, gay rights, and gun rights emerging as highly salient issues and race becoming chronically accessible with the election of Obama and the resulting backlash that aided Trump's candidacy—that unhyphenated America moved toward the Republicans.

4 Ideological Polarization and Twenty-First-Century Politics

The politics of the twenty-first century focuses on ideology. In large part due to the Southern Republican realignment (Hill and Tausanovich 2018), the parties sorted into two ideologically homogenous and polarized coalitions. The decline of Democratic Party identification among white southerners and the development of a liberal base of African American voters in the Democratic Party pushed politicians of both parties—both inside and outside the South—to take more ideologically consistent positions in order to win primary elections. Voters responded by ideologically sorting themselves into the party closest to their issue positions, which only prompted politicians to further sort themselves ideologically (Hetherington 2009; Mason 2018).

The result is a Republican Party that has harmonized its conservatism on racial, economic, and social issues, facing off against a Democratic Party that has harmonized its liberalism on racial, economic, and social issues. One can find individual candidates in each party who moderate on some or on all of these issues. But with rare exceptions, a Republican candidate's positions will be more conservative than a Democrat's.

The second important characteristic of twenty-first-century politics is the increasing significance of non-economic issues in explaining the partisan choices of voters. In contemporary politics, voters divide based more on their attitudes to social, environmental, and racial issues than on economics.

These facets of twenty-first-century politics fit with my explanations of why unhyphenated America has moved toward the Republicans over the course of the century. The Republican Party is the conservative party—full stop—which attracts the conservative voters of unhyphenated America. A part of why voters in the Appalachias and the upper South are conservative is the increasing salience of social, environmental, and racial issues in national politics. Residents of unhyphenated concentrated counties tend to hold conservative attitudes on each of these types of issues and are thus attracted to the party that holds conservative positions on these issues and repelled by the one that holds liberal positions.

The ideological polarization of contemporary politics maps onto geographic polarization. As non-economic issues have increased in importance, areas with progressive attitudes on issues of feminism and gay rights, concern for climate change, and comfort with racial diversity have moved toward the Democrats. These voters tend to live in urban or near-urban areas. Voters with traditional views on social issues, skepticism about climate regulations, and racially conservative attitudes tend to live in rural areas and small towns (Brown and Enos 2021; Martin and Webster 2020). As discussed, unhyphenated concentrated areas are almost exclusively in small towns and rural counties.

Recent work on Southern politics has emphasized the importance of geography in explaining contemporary party coalitions. Hood and McKee (2022, 8) find that the Republican realignment occurred later in what they call the "Small Town South" than it did in the more suburban parts of the South, but that it has proven to be a more enduring realignment. The authors describe it as "America's longest and deepest realignment." The rural story that Hood and McKee tell is similar to the story I tell here. Small-town areas, especially in the Appalachias and the upper South—where white voters are dominant—have moved toward the Republicans.

Irwin Morris (2021) offers a potential explanation for this pattern. He identifies migration as a key variable affecting the politics of the modern-day South. Areas with high levels of population growth are moving toward the Democrats, as those who move tend to be younger, more optimistic, and more progressive on non-economic issues. Not only are they bringing more liberal attitudes to their communities, but they are also influencing those already there to adopt more liberal attitudes on issues of gay rights and racial diversity.

These findings are of course distinct from those who found migration into the South in the twentieth century pushed the region toward the Republicans because they were more likely to identify as Republicans than native southerners (Scher 1997; Stanley and Castle 1988). Studies of the twenty-first-century South find the opposite—migrants from the North are more likely to be Democrats and they push the new locales to the left (Hillygus et al. 2017; Hood and McKee 2010; McKee and Teigen 2016). What is happening in the twenty-first century though is bigger than northerners moving to the South. Morris (2021) finds that native southerners who move tend to be demographically (e.g. younger) and politically distinct from those who tend to stay in the counties where they were born. This is pushing the urban and suburban South to the left (Cooper et al. 2024). Influxes of migrants even seem to be having more effect on partisanship in the South than generations-long attitudes shaped by slavery and racial threat (Morris 2022).

Most important for the argument of this book, Morris also finds that migration has an effect not just on places where migrants go, but also in the places where non-migrants remain. Those who remain feel threatened by population stagnation economically, but also socially, and this threat tends to push residents toward the dominant party in their local area. In Black majority counties, Democratic allegiance is reinforced. But in white majority areas, a lack of population growth pushes residents toward the Republicans. Notably, Morris argues that residents of slow-growth areas blame stagnation not on local factors, but on national-level causes. I interpret this to mean that those who are moving toward the Republicans blame the national Democratic Party for their local decline.

Morris's findings fit well with the argument of this book. I am examining unhyphenated concentrated areas which are notably small-town areas, but also ones that lack the economic and social vitality provided by large levels of in-migration, and I am studying the "stayers," to use Morris's language. As shown in Table 1.1, population growth was half as large in unhyphenated concentrated counties between 2010 and 2020 than it was in the average American county. There are geographic differences in the scope of our two studies; Morris's study is of the eleven states of the South, whereas mine focuses on a subset of the South and then areas that are outside of the Old Confederacy. However, these differences are pretty minor, as the unhyphenated concentrated regions of the Ohio River Valley that I study are quite similar to the regions of "stayers" identified by Morris, especially when it comes to low population growth.

Further, I argue that the Republican shift in unhyphenated America was compelled by the Democratic Party's embrace of liberal positions on newly salient issues such as abortion, gay rights, and climate change. Similarly, racial issues started to take on national implications with the elevation of Barack Obama as leader of the Democratic Party. Thus, the Democrats became a party of the urban and urbane (like Barack Obama), and that seemed quite distant from small towns in the upper South and the Appalachias. I identify the shift as being driven by national-level forces as they are interpreted at the local level. Thus the shift in unhyphenated America happened in, and was the result of, twenty-first-century politics.

5 Testing These Claims

Much of this chapter has focused on showing what the rest of this book is not about. I argue that what I am describing is not the classic and well-studied Southern Republican realignment. I do this through a detailed examination of the findings of the literature on the Southern Republican realignment with a particular focus on the factors that scholars have argued prompted the Republican shift in the region. I then show that these factors are not that applicable to regions with concentrations of unhyphenated Americans. These regions have a smaller African American population than other parts of the South, reducing the potency of racial threat on a local level. Further, the lack of suburbanized economic growth in the area reduced the potency of Reagan-era Republican appeals for tax and spending cuts, which were a bigger draw in the South's emerging suburbs.

My task in this book is to describe and explain the shift in unhyphenated America toward the Republicans. In doing so, I also aim to explain when and why unhyphenated America made this shift. In the first two chapters I provide some general answers to this question. Yes, the shift happened, and it happened primarily over the course of the Clinton and younger Bush Administrations. And it continued in a less sharp form thereafter. I also argue that the shift occurred because of non-economic issues—such as abortion, gay rights, gun policy, and climate change—which not only increased in salience but also became more central to the images of each party. In addition, racial views also became more relevant with the emergence of Barack Obama as the leader of the Democratic Party. The appearance of these issues activated the conservative views of residents of unhyphenated concentrated regions, pushing them toward the GOP over the period from the mid-1990s to the mid-2000s, and sealing them as a landslide Republican region during the Obama Administration.

Over the next four chapters, I will use empirical evidence to try to prove the propositions raised in the last paragraph. In Chapter 3, I will examine the Republican shift in unhyphenated America in presidential elections and in Chapter 4 I investigate the shift in US House elections. The results show a strong and clear move to the Republicans in unhyphenated concentrated regions beginning in the early 1990s in both types of elections. In presidential elections, this shift is most stark between the 1996 and the 2008 elections. In House elections, it is most present in 1994 and in 2010—two wave elections for the Republicans that led to not only large Republican gains in unhyphenated America, but durable ones that held up for over a decade in both cases.

In Chapters 5 and 6, I analyze public opinion data to try to determine the issues on which unhyphenated America maintains more conservative views than not just the rest of the country, but also other Republican-leaning regions of the US. Chapter 5 examines opinions on non-economic issues such as abortion, gay rights, gun rights, and environmental issues. Using longitudinal public opinion data from the mid-2000s to the present, I find that residents of unhyphenated concentrated counties hold more conservative views on these issues than even voters in other Republican-leaning regions. In particular, views on abortion are not only more conservative, but seem to be caused by characteristics of the region itself and not just its more conservative character. In Chapter 6, I explore opinions on issues of race and immigration. Again, views in counties with concentrations of American ethnic identifiers are more conservative than not only other Americans, but also those who live in other Republican-leaning regions. This conservatism helped push the region away from the Barack Obama-led Democrats and helped seal it as a key component of the Donald Trump-led GOP.

The final empirical chapter focuses on that Trump-led Republican Party. As a region with more conservative views on race and immigration, unhyphenated America in particular proved to be a base for Donald Trump as he ran for president in the 2016 GOP nomination contest. Trump gained more support in unhyphenated concentrated counties in each state than he did in other counties. The value of this was limited though, as Trump's additional votes in the region did little to change the outcome of the 2016 contest. It also faded. Trump did not gain extra votes in the region in the 2020 or 2024 nomination contests. In many ways, this shows that Trump had bent the Republican Party as a whole to the views of unhyphenated America.

Thus, the concluding chapter focuses on the relevance of my findings. The first is that the views of unhyphenated America provide a key base within the contemporary Republican Party. The regional shift also helps to show the continued importance of partisanship and its overlap with geography as a determinant of vote choice. Even as our politics nationalizes due to the ideological homogeneity of the two parties and its overlap with geographic polarization, local influences can still matter. They matter in unhyphenated America in a unique way. I have argued here that it mattered when the region did not move when the rest of the South did from the 1960s to the 1980s. And it mattered when the region did move strongly toward the Republicans in the latter half of the 1990s and first decade of the 2000s.

In 1994, voters in Kentucky's 2nd District made a stark and surprising change, shifting from their long-established support of Democratic members of Congress to supporting a conservative Republican. These voters were swayed in 1994 by opposition to the liberal policies pursued by a Democratic administration and support for the socially conservative views of the Republican candidate, particularly on abortion. There is no evidence those voters regret their move. Voters in the Kentucky 2nd have continued to send conservative Republicans to Congress in every election since then. Democrats tried for a few years to run high-quality candidates against the new Republican incumbents, but after a few defeats, they essentially ceded the district. Republicans continue to win Kentucky's 2nd with near landslide margins in every election.

The story of the Kentucky 2nd is meaningful because it is the story of so much of unhyphenated America. These voters have moved strongly to the right, largely because of their support for the social, environmental, and racial conservatism of Republican candidates. The change is stark and clear, but most importantly, the change is durable, lasting for a full political generation at this point.

Chapter 3
Presidential Realignment in Unhyphenated America

The 2000 presidential election was the closest in American history, as George W. Bush officially won by four electoral votes. One might argue that it was even closer than that; the results were so close in Florida that the six-week saga of recounts and court challenges led to terms that will endure in political lore forever—hanging chads, the butterfly ballot, and the Brooks Brothers riot.

Officially, the Florida results showed Bush 537 votes ahead of Al Gore. Unofficially, one can legitimately claim any number of vote margins for the two major party candidates.

The closeness of the Florida results meant that it took up the lion's share of attention in the wake of Election Day 2020 and in historical memory. But the Electoral College was so close in 2000 that every state Bush won was pivotal to his victory. If any one of them—not just the exceedingly close Florida—had gone to Gore, then Bush would have returned to Texas to serve out his term as the state's governor rather than go to the White House.

One such key state was Tennessee. Bill Clinton had won Tennessee in both his presidential runs, Clinton won the Volunteer State by nearly five points in 1992, and then again in 1996, but this time by a smaller margin—2.4%. Of course, Clinton was likely helped in Tennessee by his running mate Al Gore, who had won three elections to Congress and two elections to the US Senate there. In the 2000 election, the expectation—noting that it was a less polarized electorate than today—was that presidential nominees would win their home states—none had lost their home state since George McGovern in 1972. But Gore lost Tennessee to Bush by four points, sending the state's eleven electoral votes into the Republican column.

Gore's loss of his home state attracted a great deal of commentary in the aftermath of the exceedingly close election, and a number of media outlets tried to explain Gore's loss. Republican Senator Bill Frist attributed the loss to Gore's support of Bill Clinton during the Monica Lewinsky scandal "From an integrity standpoint, Tennesseans have not been forgiving of Al Gore supporting Bill Clinton at a time that Clinton had lied to the American people" (Zuckerbrod 2000). One Bush voter interviewed by NPR focused on Gore's liberalism on social issues such as abortion, gay rights, and gun rights. "The abortion issue was a very heated issue here, emotionally sensitive to a lot of people," said John McCall of Carthage, TN. "He's had to align himself with some groups and some issues that

https://doi.org/10.1515/9783111615707-003

don't fly well in Tennessee" (All Things Considered 2000). The head of the Tennessee Farm Bureau Foundation thought Gore's environmental policies and the Clinton Administration's policies to reduce tobacco use cost votes in rural communities in the state (Zuckerbrod 2000). The *New York Times* summarized the problem in Tennessee: "While Tennessee has moved to the right . . . Gore has moved to the left since his days as a congressman" (Perez-Pena 2000).

Others attributed Gore's loss in Tennessee not to his and the national Democratic Party's issue positions, but to Gore's personality. Some thought Gore did not seem authentic enough to the state he called home. Gore was not actually born in Tennessee. Instead, he was born in Washington, DC while his father served in Congress. One young voter said, "Gore doesn't really live here. He only comes back when he wants votes" (Mansfield 2000). *Newsweek* thought Gore came across more as prep school student than a gold ol' boy: "Gore . . . shows a little too much of his St. Albans breeding to appeal to the Elvis vote" (Newsweek 2000). Republican congressman Bill Jenkins summed it up: "He left Tennessee. Tennessee didn't leave him" (Mansfield 2000).

It was a similar story in West Virginia. West Virginia was seen as a Democratic state coming into the 2000 election, The state was noted as a labor stronghold and had voted Democratic not just for Bill Clinton, but also for Michael Dukakis in 1988. But it swung to Bush in 2000.

Again, journalists tried to explain the results in West Virginia. Some attributed it to a more robust campaign effort from the Republicans. The Bush campaign targeted West Virginia in 2000 and put more effort into the state than did the Gore campaign. Bush himself visited the state three times, Dick Cheney came twice, as did other members of the Bush family as surrogates (Seiler 2000). The substantive reasons why West Virginia went for Bush were similar to those given in Tennessee. The Bush campaign "attacked Gore's position on environmental issues, especially his support for the Kyoto Protocol to limit emissions of pollutants that cause the greenhouse effect." Another key was the "gun issue" on which "the vice president was hammered by negative attacks by the Bush campaign" and from an effective issue advocacy campaign from the NRA (Nyden 2000).

Certainly, concerns about issue positions authenticity, and campaign effort are a part of the story of why Gore lost two states that Bill Clinton had won in his two runs for the presidency. But I will argue that the overriding factor that explains Gore's loss in these two states is that shift of unhyphenated America to the Republicans. Both states are a key component of the region. West Virginia has fifty-five counties and thirty of them have concentrations of American ethnic identifiers. In Tennessee, seventy-seven of the state's ninety-five counties are unhyphenated concentrated.

In West Virginia, the state's shift was quite strong. Bill Clinton won 58.4% of the two-party vote in the state in 1996, comfortably winning the Mountain State. In 2000, Gore won only 46.8% of the two-party vote, a decline of 11.6 points. In Tennessee, the decline was smaller, but pivotal. Clinton won 51.3% of the two-party vote in 1996, whereas Gore won only 48.0% of the two-party vote in 2000. Nationally, Gore ran 4.4% behind Clinton's 1996 two-party vote share. Nevertheless, he ran only 3.3% behind Clinton's 1996 vote share in Tennessee, suggesting that despite the attention paid to Gore's loss of his home state, his connection to the voters there may well have helped him.

The argument of this book is that the Gore campaign's inability to win Tennessee and West Virginia in 2000 was not primarily a function of the particular circumstances of the 2000 election. Instead, the changes observed in 2000 were part of a long-term Republican trend in this region that has lasted for a political generation. The 2000 election was the last time a Democratic presidential candidate came close in either state. No Democratic nominee has come within twelve points of a Republican nominee in either state since Al Gore.

Another reason why the 2000 election in the Appalachias and the upper South is important is it represents a key moment in the Republican shift in unhyphenated America. Prior to the 2000 election the shift in the region was gradual, but that year the area saw the beginning of an acceleration in support for the Republican Party. I drew this conclusion by examining presidential election results in unhyphenated America across nine elections, which helped identify when the Republican shift happened. My goal was to identify not only the shift in the vote in the Appalachias and the upper South, but also the causes of this shift. By identifying when the shift happened, it becomes possible to start understanding why the shift happened.

If the shift had happened in the 1990s, it would be evidence that unhyphenated America moved with the end of the classic Southern realignment or reacted in a conservative fashion to that decade's focus on budget politics. If the shift had happened in the Trump era (i.e. in 2016 or after), then it would be evidence that Trump's nationalistic politics (e.g. more restrictions on immigration) had attracted voters from a region with less experience with immigration than most other areas of the US or that the shift was part of the broader national shift of white working-class voters into the Republican Party.

Instead, I find that the shift happened in presential elections in the first decade of the 2000s, primarily between the 2000 and the 2008 elections. The issue environment in the 2000s focused heavily on the war on terror and on conservative attempts to ban gay marriage while the idea was still popular. These conservative positions seem to have appealed to a region with long martial and evangelical traditions. Of course, the nomination of Barack Obama in 2008 brought race to fore of American politics, and the region had a conservative reaction to this development.

1 The Republican Shift in Unhyphenated America

I argue that the results of the 2000 election in Tennessee and West Virginia do not represent an anomalous event tied to the nomination of a specific candidate. Instead, they are a part of a broader secular shift over the last political generation toward the Republicans in this region. To show these changes, I start by looking specifically at the region under study—counties with large concentrations of American ethnic identifiers.[13]

Figure 3.1 shows the aggregate Democratic two-party presidential vote share for these unhyphenated concentrated counties from 1988 to 2024. For comparison's sake, I included the national Democratic two-party share. The chart shows that this has never been a region of Democratic strength. In the last three elections of the twentieth century, Democrats ran behind their national vote share in unhyphenated America. But the differences were relatively small. In 1988, Michael Dukakis ran 6.2% behind his national vote share in counties with concentrations of unhyphenated Americans. Bill Clinton improved his vote share over Dukakis more in these counties than he did nationally—8.6% in unhyphenated America, as compared to 7.4% across the country as a whole.

In 1996, unhyphenated America began to diverge from the rest of the country. Bill Clinton increased his national vote share slightly, but it decreased in counties with concentrations of unhyphenated Americans. The shift became bigger in the twenty-first century. Nationally, Democrats gained a small but persistent plurality of presidential popular votes from 2008 through 2020. In unhyphenated America, the small shift against Clinton in 1996 became an avalanche starting in 2000. Al Gore won only 39.9% of the vote in unhyphenated concentrated counties. John Kerry did worse in 2004, winning 35.6% of the vote in unhyphenated America. Barack Obama increased his party's national vote share by 4.9% nationally, winning the largest Electoral College margin in the twenty-first century to date. But in unhyphenated concentrated counties, there was hardly any change at all. Obama ran 0.2% below Kerry in the region. The good news for Obama was that he increased his vote share in unhyphenated America when he ran for re-election in 2012. The bad news is that he increased it by less than a point to 36.1%.

---

13 As defined in Chapter 1, these are counties in which 19.4% of residents identify their ethnic heritage as "American," according to the US Census Bureau.

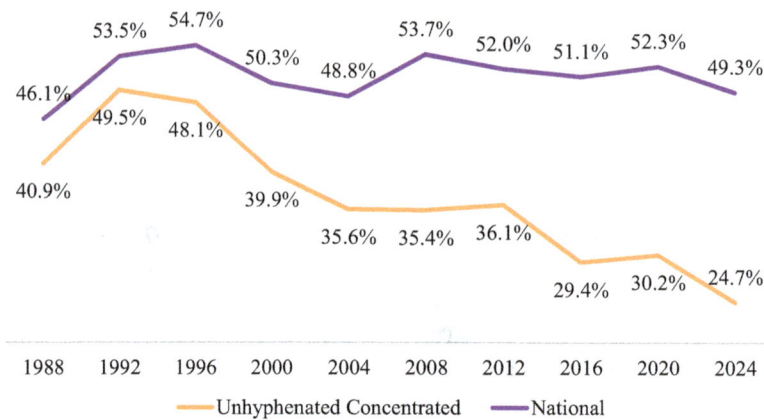

Figure 3.1: Two-Party Democratic Presidential Election Results, Unhyphenated Concentrated Counties, 1988–2020.
Source: Calculated by author, based on data from Dave Leip's Political Atlas (1988 to 2004) and the Associated Press (2008 through 2024).

It seemed that it could not get worse for Democrats in unhyphenated America, but in 2016, it did. Hillary Clinton won less than 30% of the vote in unhyphenated concentrated counties. Joe Biden improved the Democrats fortunes in 2020, but only slightly; he won 30.2% of the vote in the region. Democratic fortunes again dipped in 2024; Kamala Harris ran 3.0% below Biden nationally, but 5.5% worse in unhyphenated America.

Figure 3.2 shows the same data but in a different format. In this figure, the Democratic presidential two-party vote share in unhyphenated concentrated counties has been subtracted from the national vote share. In short, it measures the difference between the two lines in Figure 3.1. This figure reveals that most of the Republican shift in the region happened between the 2000 and 2008 elections. In the 2000 campaign, Gore was the first Democrat to run ten points behind his national vote share in unhyphenated America, and that underperformance hurt him in both West Virginia and Tennessee. But Democratic fortunes continued to decline in the region, as Kerry ran 13.2 behind his national vote share and then Obama ran 18.3 behind his national vote share in unhyphenated concentrated counties. Another big decline occurred between 2012 and 2016 as Hillary Clinton lost over five points off the margin in the region. The decline continued in the two elections in the 2020s.

Another depiction of the Republican trend in the region is presented in Figure 3.3. It shows the raw vote total for each party's presidential nominee from 1988 to 2024. One can see that almost all of the growth in vote totals in the region

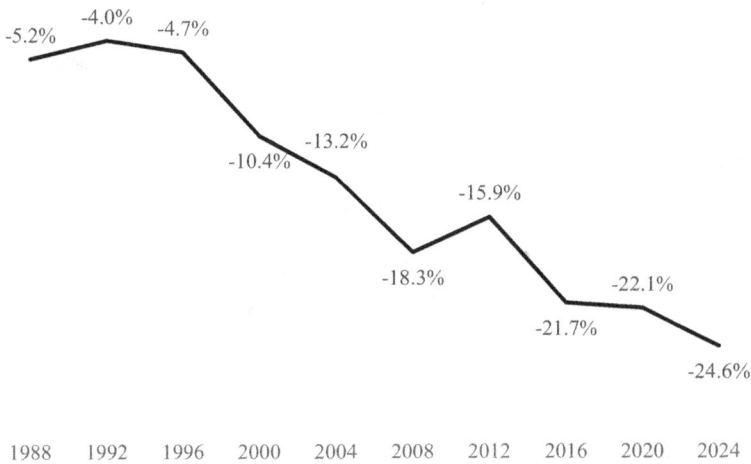

Figure 3.2: Difference from Democratic Presidential Vote Share in Unhyphenated Concentrated Counties, 1988–2020.
Source: Calculated by author, based on data from Dave Leip's Political Atlas (1988 to 2004) and the Associated Press (2008 through 2024).

are on the Republican side. In 1988, George H. W. Bush won 2.8 million votes in counties with concentrations of American ethnic identifiers. In 2024, Trump won over twice as many votes in the region—over 6.3 million.

Compare that to the Democrats. In 1988, Michael Dukakis won 2.0 million votes in unhyphenated America. Fast forward thirty-six years and the electorate in the region had expanded by nearly 3.3 million votes. But the Democratic nominee won barely any more votes in 2024 than in 1988. Bill Clinton won more votes in unhyphenated America in 1992 than his wife won in 2016; Kamala Harris fared even worse in 2024.

It is also instructive to look at the shift in how many counties each party has won in each election. Figure 3.4 shows this via a stacked bar chart for the 533 unhyphenated concentrated counties. Michael Dukakis, who lost nationally by about nine points, won 119 counties with high concentrations of American ethnic identifiers. Bill Clinton made gains on that in 1992 and won a majority of the counties in the region. Clinton fell back in 1996, losing thirty-eight counties that he had won in 1996. Republican nominee Bob Dole thus won the majority of counties in the region.

Still Clinton was competitive in the region in 1996. Democrats stopped being competitive in the region starting with the 2000 election. Al Gore won only eighty-one counties in unhyphenated America. John Kerry lost more, winning only forty-two counties. Barack Obama lost more, winning only eighteen counties in 2008 and only ten when he ran for re-election in 2012. Hillary Clinton fared

63,78,300

55,95,213

51,28,418

56,36,968

44,27,583

34,46,379

46,79,329

24,88,506

28,39,150

24,43,385

22,88,796

25,68,233

24,44,117

23,94,779

28,93,353

24,42,960

23,30,838

20,87,531

19,65,719

23,02,697

1988   1992   1996   2000   2004   2008   2012   2016   2020   2024

—— Democrat   —— Republican

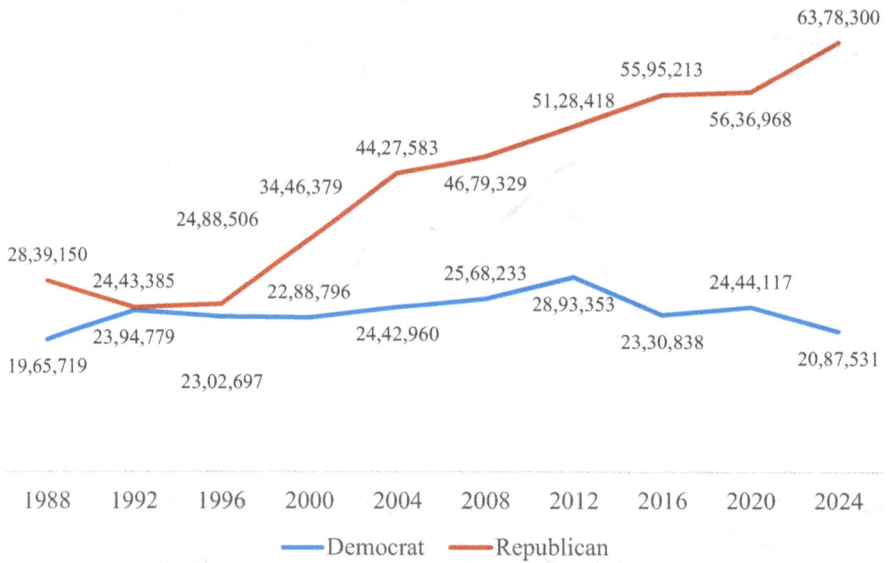

Figure 3.3: Raw Presidential Vote, Unhyphenated Concentrated Counties, 1988–2024.
Source: Calculated by author, based on data from Dave Leip's Political Atlas (1988 to 2004) and the
Associated Press (2008 through 2024).

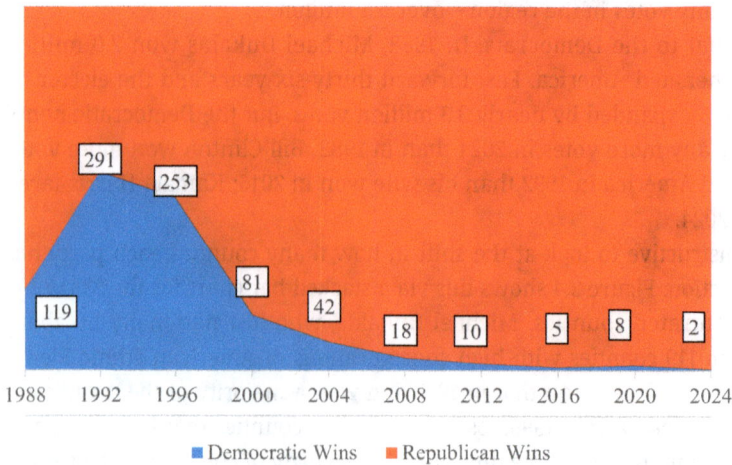

291

253

81

42

119

18   10   5   8   2

1988   1992   1996   2000   2004   2008   2012   2016   2020   2024

■ Democratic Wins   ■ Republican Wins

Figure 3.4: Unhyphenated Counties Won by Democrats, Presidential Elections, 1988–2020.
Source: Calculated by author, based on data from Dave Leip's Political Atlas (1988 to 2004) and the
Associated Press (2008 through 2024).
Note: N = 533.

even worse, winning only five counties with concentrations of unhyphenated Americans in the 2016 election. Republican nominee Donald Trump won 528 of them.

Joe Biden won more counties than Hillary Clinton but still only eight of them. Trump thus won 525 counties in unhyphenated America in 2020. Those gains were not only small, but they were illusory. In 2024, Kamala Harris won only two of the nation's 533 unhyphenated concentrated counties. The region has over the last generation gone from a competitive region that leans toward the Republicans in the twentieth century to a nearly monolithic Republican region in the twenty-first century. For each of these measures, the Republican trend is strong and the landslide margins that the GOP wins with in the region indicates that the trend will be long-lasting.

To give some context to the Democratic underperformance in unhyphenated America, it is useful to compare their results in the region to those in other regions of the country. Figure 3.5 presents the country divided into five geographic regions. One region includes all unhyphenated concentrated counties. The West region is defined by the Census, as is the Midwest except for its unhyphenated concentrated counties. The East comprises states in the Census's definition, as well as Maryland, Delaware, and the parts of West Virginia that are not unhyphenated concentrated. The South includes the Census South less Maryland, Delaware, and the region's unhyphenated concentrated counties. Each of the five lines in the figure represents the Democratic presidential candidate's two-party vote share for each of the five regions defined.

In 1988, there are relatively few differences between the regions. Dukakis wins a majority in none of them,[14] though he does worst in the South. But his numbers in unhyphenated concentrated counties are no different to his numbers in the rest of the South. Clinton makes across-the-board gains in 1992, including in unhyphenated America. In 1996, a divergence begins. Clinton improves his vote share in the East sharply, and slightly in the rest of the South. But in unhyphenated concentrated counties, his vote share declined. Democratic performance in these counties collapses in 2000, and then falls further in 2004 to 36%. What is particularly notable about these two elections is how Democratic performance in unhyphenated concentrated counties diverges from the other regions of the country. The gap is strong and big. In 2008, Obama makes gains across the country, except in unhyphenated concentrated areas, where he runs essentially even with John Kerry. This large gap continues through the rest of the timeline, growing particularly in the elections where Democrats lost—in 2016 and in 2024.

---

14 The Dukakis share for the East is 49.5%, which rounds up to the 50% shown in the figure.

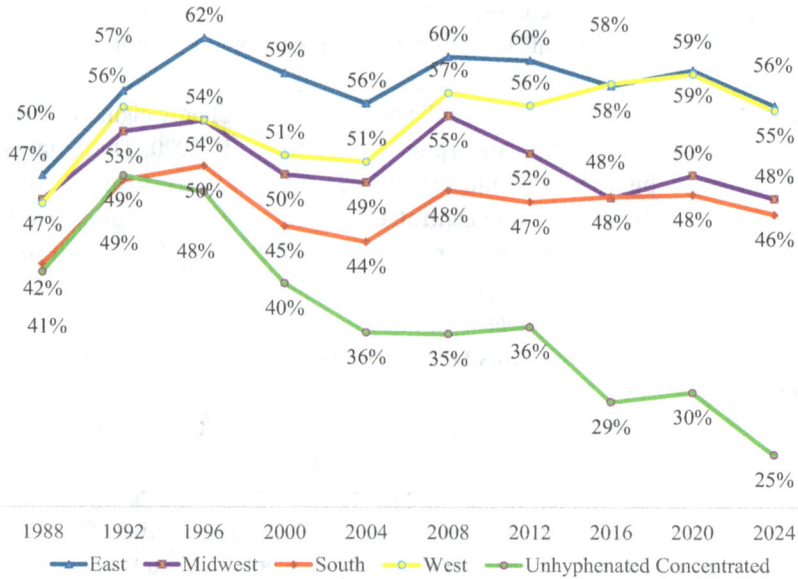

Figure 3.5: Democratic Presidential Two-Party Vote Share by Region, 1988–2020.
Source: Calculated by author, based on election data from Dave Leip's Political Atlas (1988 to 2004) and the Associated Press (2008 through 2024).
Note: The South comprises the eleven States of the Confederacy. The other three regions are their Census Regions, with West Virginia, Maryland, and Delaware included with the East, and Kentucky, Missouri, and Oklahoma included with the Midwest. Unhyphenated concentrated counties are excluded from all four of the regions.

Put together, these data reveal a clear and consistent pattern—unhyphenated America has moved strongly against Democratic presidential candidates and toward Republican presidential candidates over the last political generation. This move began in 1996 as unhyphenated concentrated counties began moving toward the Republicans—even as Bill Clinton improved his vote share in the rest of the country—and accelerated throughout the elections of the twenty-first century. The data show that Republicans have not only made significant gains in the region, but that these gains seem to be stable and long-lasting. The results of the 2020 election suggested that the Democrats may have reached the bottom of their fall in the region, but their decline in 2024 showed they could indeed fall further. But the bad news for Democrats (and the good news for Republicans) is that the bottom means a landslide loss. Republicans now win almost every single county in this region, and there is little reason to think that they will not continue to do so in the near future.

2 The Geography of the Republican Shift

Another way to obtain a sense of the Republican shift in unhyphenated America is via geography. Figure 3.6 is a map that shows the difference in Republican vote share by county between the 1988 and 2020 presidential elections. This allows one to broadly see geographic shifts in party voting that have emerged over the most recent political generation. One can see the blue of the Pacific coast, and New England, as those two regions shifted towards the Democrats, turning states like California, Vermont, and Connecticut—which voted for George H. W. Bush in 1988, into safely Democratic seats soon thereafter. One can also see some counties with deeper shades of red in places like west Texas and the northern Great Plains, where the Republican Party has made large gains over time.

Biden Minus Dukakis Vote Share

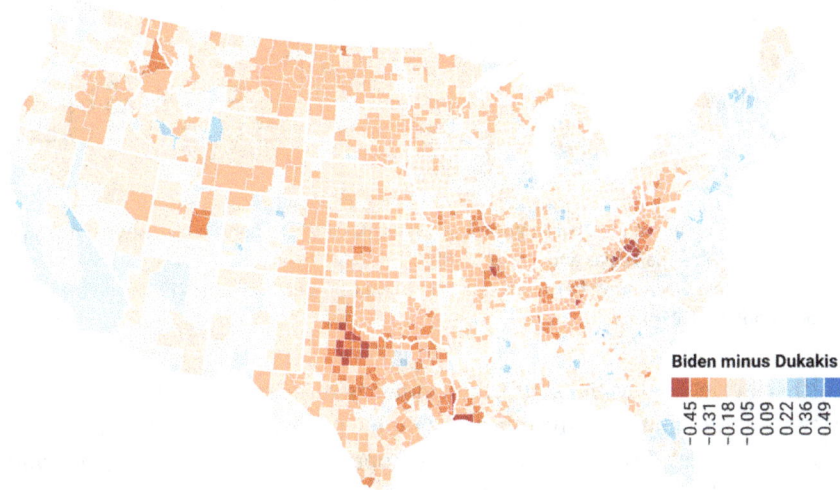

Figure 3.6: Difference in Republican Vote Share in Presidential Elections, by County, 1988–2020. National View.
Source: Calculated by author, based on data from Dave Leip's Political Atlas (1988) and the Associated Press (2020).

Another area of deep red is in the Appalachias and the upper South. This is shown more clearly in Figure 3.7, which takes Figure 3.6 and zooms in on the region. The concentration of Republican improvement is clearly centered in southern West Virginia and down the spine of the Appalachian Mountains into Kentucky, Tennessee, Georgia, and Alabama. It also moves west across the upper

South, with Republican improvement visible across the states of Tennessee and Kentucky and into rural Missouri, northern Arkansas, and the eastern parts of Oklahoma and Texas. In short, the deep red in this map follows the contours of unhyphenated concentrated counties shown in Figure 1.3.

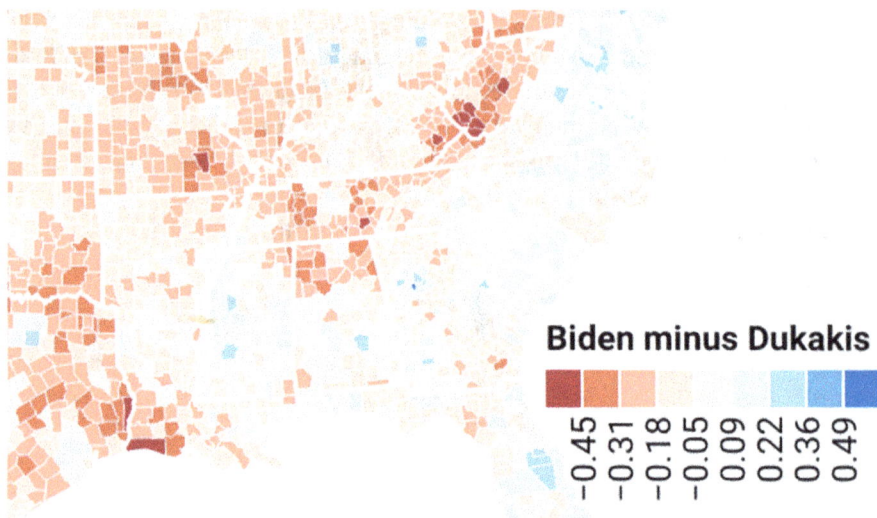

Figure 3.7: Difference in Republican Vote Share in Presidential Elections, by County, from 1988 to 2020. Focused on Appalachias and Upper South.
Source: Calculated by author, based on data from Dave Leip's Political Atlas (1988) and the Associated Press (2020).

Further evidence that the shift in unhyphenated America is distinct from the rest of the South is shown by the other geographic patterns on the map. An expanse of neutral counties stretches between the Appalachian Mountain counties and the more coastal or urban counties. These in-between counties—in-between in both an electoral and a geographic sense—run in a nearly continuous band from northern Virginia to central Mississippi.

On the other side of the in-between counties are the blue Southern counties, which is where Joe Biden ran better in 2020 than Michael Dukakis did in 1988. There are essentially two types of blue counties. First, the "black belt" counties, which are located in Low Country South Carolina, southeast Georgia, southern Alabama, and the Mississippi Delta. These counties have moved toward the Democrats as the Democrats have improved their performance with African American voters. Second, large metropolitan areas, as, for example, the concentration of blue around Washington, DC and its suburban counties. This extends to the urban counties of North Carolina. Another big concentration of blue is in Atlanta and its suburbs. Looking closely, only a small number of blue counties are visible in Tennessee, but these include Davidson (Nashville) and Shelby (Memphis) Counties. Similarly in Kentucky, the state has only two counties where Democrats made gains between 1988 and 2020, but those are the state's two most populous counties, Jefferson (Louisville) and Lafayette (Lexington).

Again, this map fits well with the map of unhyphenated concentrated counties in Figure 1.3. Unhyphenated concentrated counties are located in the Appalachian Mountains and then fan out west across Tennessee and Kentucky and across the northern parts of Alabama and Mississippi. They are heavily concentrated in rural and small-town locales and are not located in urban areas and in areas with large concentrations of African Americans. That pattern repeats itself in this map as well. Regions that moved strongly toward the Republicans are located in small-town Appalachia and the upper South. More lowland areas have larger African American populations and moved in the opposite direction politically. And urban areas have lower levels of unhyphenated American populations and have also moved toward the Democrats in recent elections.

3 Explaining the Republican Shift in Unhyphenated America

The map featured in Figures 3.6 and 3.7 is consistent with my argument that as the share of American ethnic identifiers in a county increases, the area has moved toward the Republicans over the last political generation. Those results fit with the results depicted in the previous figures which show the Republican shift in unhyphenated concentrated counties. These results are quite restrictive though, as they examine only those counties with the largest concentrations of unhyphenated Americans.

If I loosen this definition, the finding still holds, as seen in Figure 3.8. The figure is a county-level scatterplot with the x-axis being the share of American ethnic identifiers and the y-axis being the difference in two-party vote share for the Democratic nominee between 1988 and 2020. Positive values are counties where Joe Biden ran much better than did Michael Dukakis did in 1988;[15] negative values are counties where Dukakis outran Biden. To ease interpretation, I included a regression line in the figure.

---

15 Fun fact: Joe Biden ran for the Democratic nomination in 1988. It could have been him in the 1988 column if things had broken differently. Instead, he finally won the Democratic nomination on his third attempt, thirty-two years later.

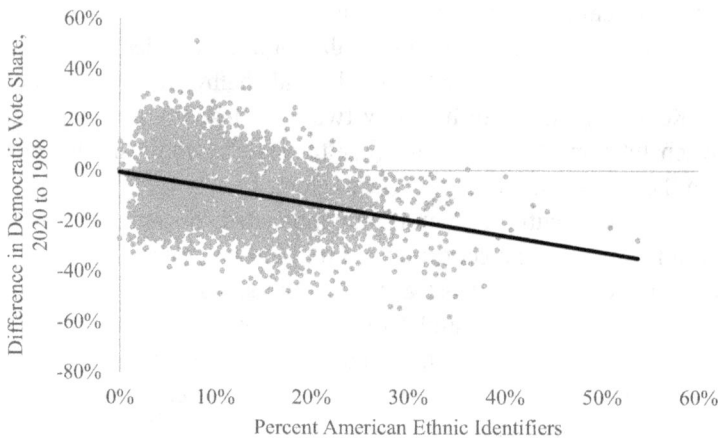

Figure 3.8: Difference in 1988 to 2020 Presidential Election Results by Percent Unhyphenated. Source: Calculated by author, based on election data from Dave Leip's Political Atlas (1988) and the Associated Press (2020), and American Ethnic Identifier Data from the US Census. Note: Data are at the county level.

The scatterplot of course shows great variance across the nation's 3,115 counties, but in general, one can see that the counties with large concentrations of unhyphenated Americans tend to have negative values—they moved away from the Democrats and toward the Republicans across the thirty-two years between the 1988 and 2020 elections. There is much greater variation in counties with low levels of American ethnic identifiers, as some have moved toward the Republicans over time and some have moved to the Democrats. But a larger concentration of these counties—including those that have moved the most toward the Democrats over time—comprises counties where Democratic presidential nominees have made gains between 1988 and 2020.

The regression line helps to confirm the negative slope of the scatterplot. The line's gradient is −0.63; that is, for every one percentage point greater a county's share of American ethnic identifiers, Joe Biden won 0.63% fewer of the vote than did Michael Dukakis. This is further evidence that regions with concentrations of unhyphenated Americans have moved toward the Republicans in the most recent political generation.

Further evidence for this shift is apparent when one looks at the counties that have shifted most toward the Republicans between 1988 and 2020. The five counties with pro-Republican shifts have two things in common—all five are in West Virginia and all five have large concentrations of unhyphenated Americans. Mingo County experienced the largest shift of any US county and 34.3% of its residents reported that they were American ethnic identifiers on the American Community

Survey (ACS). In 1988, voters there gave 71.8% of their votes to Dukakis. Democratic presidential nominees won Mingo County in the next four elections, but in 2008, Mingo went for John McCain (55% to 43%) and has kept moving toward the Republicans. In 2020, Mingo County voters gave 85.2% of their votes to Donald Trump.

A similar story has unfolded in Logan (29% unhyphenated American), McDowell (33% unhyphenated American), Webster (28% unhyphenated American), and Wyoming Counties. Dukakis won each of these four counties with vote shares above 64%. Each moved toward the Republicans, finally turning red somewhere between 2004 (Wyoming County) and 2012 (McDowell and Webster Counties). Further movement provided a landslide majorities for Republican nominees. In 2024, Donald Trump won all four of these counties with a vote share of over 78%.

These counties are specific (if unrepresentatively large) examples of the larger trend identified in this section of the chapter—areas with large concentrations of unhyphenated Americans have moved strongly away from the Democrats and toward Republicans in presidential elections. The evidence here shows the trend is strong and robust, and there is little evidence that it will change in the near future.

4 The Timing of the Republican Shift

So far this chapter tells us that a strong Republican shift has happened in counties with concentrations of unhyphenated Americans. The findings presented in Figure 3.8 indicate that this shift is broader than in just that specific subset of counties but connected specifically to the share of American ethnic identifiers in a county. None of these results do much to tell us when this shift took place, and answering that question is important to assessing why this shift has occurred.

I first examine the question of when the Republican shift in unhyphenated America occurred through the use of bivariate scatterplots. Figure 3.9 shows a scatterplot for each election between 1988 and 2020. Each scatterplot follows the method applied in Figure 3.8: the y-axis measures county-level vote share for the Democratic presidential nominee, and the x-axis shows the percentage of unhyphenated Americans in each county. A regression line has been included in each scatterplot to show the slope of the relationship between the two variables. When examining the scatterplots across time, a clear pattern emerges. In the first three elections under study, there is little relationship between the percentage of American ethnic identifiers in a county and Democratic vote share. In fact, the relationship in the 1992 election is positive (though insignificant).[16] But starting in 2000, the regression lines start following a downward trend and continue to get lower over time.

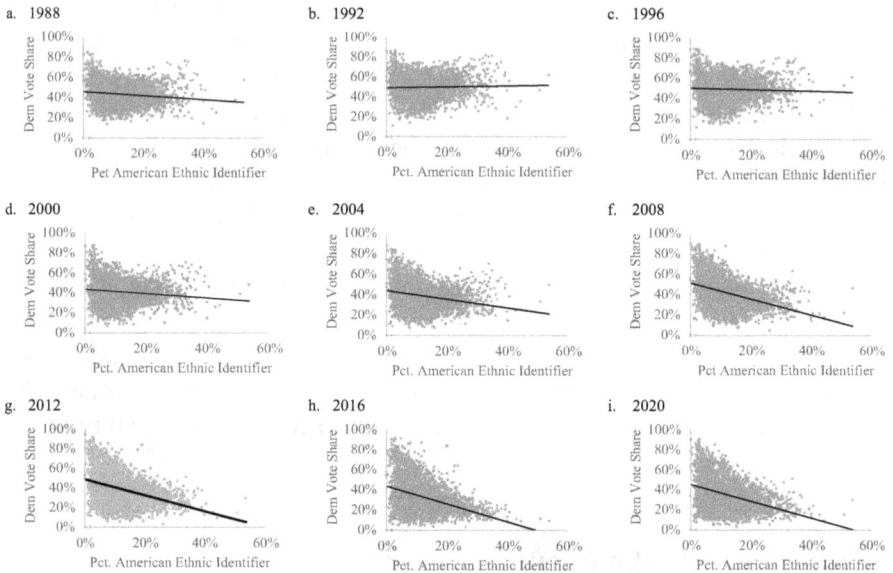

Figure 3.9: Bivariate Scatterplots, American Ethnic Identifiers and Democratic Presidential Vote Share, 1988–2020.

To provide a visual demonstration of the change in the relationship between percentage unhyphenated and Democratic vote share over the nine elections under study, Figure 3.10 shows the bivariate regression coefficient for the scatterplots in Figure 3.9. The line moves up between 1988 and 1992, but then begins a downward slide that is nearly continuous. It is notable that the movement is gradual in the 1996 and 2000 elections, followed by a slight acceleration in 2004. There is big movement in 2008; the coefficient moves from −.416 in 2004 to −.786 in 2008. That is the biggest drop in the time series and coincides with the nomination of Barack Obama as the Democratic nominee. The coefficient declines in both 2012 and 2016, then increases slightly in 2020. But for each of those four elections, the bivariate coefficient is around −0.8. That is, for every 1% greater the share of American ethnic identifiers in a county, the Democratic nominee loses 0.80% of their vote share.

---

16 Which, in a bivariate model with over 3,200 observations, is really hard to do. There really is no relationship here.

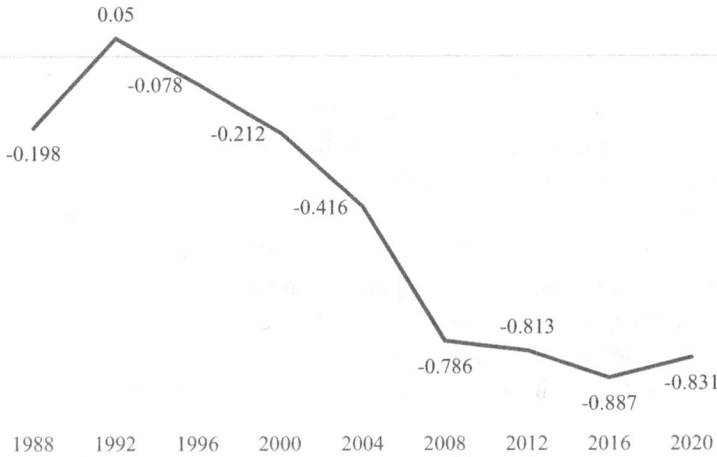

Figure 3.10: Bivariate Coefficients, Effect of Percentage of American Ethnic Identifiers on Democratic Presidential Vote Share.
Note: N=3115. Values are coefficients for bivariate regression; independent variable is percent American ethnic identifier in a county; dependent variable is Democratic two-party vote share.

I draw two conclusions from Figures 3.9 and 3.10. First, there is a long-term trend toward the Republicans which began in the 1990s. Unhyphenated America turned more against Bill Clinton in his run for re-election than it did against him in 1992, then turned further from Gore than it did Clinton and even further from Kerry than it did Gore. The trend gets sharper throughout these elections. Then it accelerates in the 2008 election, the election in which Democrats nominated an African American. After 2008, the trend reaches an equilibrium, but that level shows the region has moved strongly against the Obama-era Democratic Party. This conclusion is also bolstered by examining the stats presented in Figures 3.1 and 3.2.

These results suggest that the shift toward the Republicans in unhyphenated America began as reaction to the Clinton Administration and continued with support for the Bush Administration. This suggests that issues that emerged in the 1990s and early 2000s such as gay rights and environmentalism are key factors in pushing unhyphenated America toward the Republicans. But this trend accelerates significantly in the 2008 and 2012 elections, which is consistent with an Obama-based (and thus racial) explanation. In short, the bivariate data is consistent with multiple explanations for partisan change in the upper South.

5 Multivariate Results

The bivariate results in the previous sections are supportive of the idea that un-hyphenated America has moved toward the Republican Party in presidential elections in the most recent political generation, and that this shift is concentrated in the 2000s. But the results are not fully conclusive, as the shift could be the result of variables that are correlated with concentrations of unhyphenated Americans, such as lower levels of educational achievement or a higher share of evangelical Christians. A multivariate model makes it possible to control for variables that are correlated with the geography of unhyphenated concentrated areas. Thus, the question of whether the effect of concentrations of unhyphenated Americans on election results are just an artifact of one or more of these correlated factors can be tested.

I created a series of multivariate ordinary least squares (OLS) models, one for each election year between 1988 and 2020 and for each, the dependent variable is the percentage of the vote won by the Democratic presidential nominee.

The control variables include a series of socioeconomic factors measured at the county level: the percentage of residents with a professional degree or higher (e.g. an M.A. or a J.D.), the percentage of senior citizens, and the median county income in tens of thousands of dollars.[17] The model also includes other control variables. Counties' Black and Latino percentages are included in the model because of clear long-term evidence of distinct political views among members of these ethnic groups. Because of the historical correlation between religious affiliations and ethnic or ancestral origins, our model includes percentages for county-level religious church membership for Roman Catholics and evangelical Christians.[18] The percentage of veterans in a county is also incorporated to account for any residual political effects from the military tradition of the highland South. To ensure that the model controls for recent migration shifts, the model includes a "Born out of state" variable. It also includes a "Born out of the country" variable to control not only for migration patterns, but also for the level of consciousness in a community to immigrant roots.

Of course, the key independent variables are those that I am focused on as part of this research—the percentage of American ethnic identifiers in a county. Table 3.1 presents the results, with a column for each presidential election since 1988. Looking at the control variables, many behave in expected ways: *Percent*

---

[17] The socioeconomic and racial variables in the model come from US Census Bureau data.

[18] These two variables come from a study of the sizes of religious congregations by faith and county nationwide (Grammich et al. 2012). For the very small number of counties where these data are unavailable, the mean value of the contiguous counties' religious data was imposed.

White, Median Income, and *Evangelical* are always negative and significant. Republican fortunes improve as the share of white and evangelicals in a county are greater and when income is higher. *Population Density* is positive and significant in each model, which indicates that Democratic candidates do better in urban areas and Republicans do better in rural areas. Other variables work in unexpected ways. *Percent Foreign Born* is negative and significant in each model (a backlash effect?), while *Catholic* is positive and significant in eight of the nine elections under study. *Percent Black* is negative and significant in 1988 and only becomes a positive factor for Democrats in the 2004 and subsequent elections. *Percent Professional Degree* only becomes (positive and) significant in the final five elections of the study. The *Percent Born Out of State* is negative and significant in the first four elections under study, insignificant in the next four, and then positive and significant in 2020. The *Percent Veteran* variable is positive and significant in 1992 and then negative and significant in four of the last five election models.

Overall, the models show an increasingly demographically polarized electorate over time. The number of significant variables tends to increase across elections and every variable save one is significant in the 2020 election. The R^2 shows that the model tends to explain more and more of the variance in election results across time.

The variable of most interest though is the percentage of American identifiers in a county. The variable is negative and significant in 1988. For every 1% increase in the percentage of American identifiers in a county, Michael Dukakis loses 0.19% of the vote. Then in the next three elections, the variable is not significant. In fact, it is positive (if barely so) in 1992. But in 2004, the variable turns negative and significant. In 2008, the trend accelerates, as a 1% increase in the percentage of unhyphenated Americans in a county costs Barack Obama 0.44% of the vote *ceteris paribus*. The effect of the percentage of unhyphenated Americans in a county stabilizes in the remaining elections under study between −0.4 and −0.5. In fact, in both 2016 and 2020, the coefficient is the same to three significant digits—negative 0.404. That is, for every 1% higher the share of American ethnic identifiers in a county, Hillary Clinton and Joe Biden's vote share is reduced by 0.404% of the vote. Again, this result is controlled for the other independent variables in the model.

As with the bivariate regressions, Figure 3.11 shows the shift in the coefficients across the nine elections under study. The chart shows there are two eras of near equilibrium in the model. The results are essentially the same in the Clinton-Gore years. From 1992 to 2000, the coefficients hover around zero, and, as seen in Table 3.1, those coefficients are insignificant in each of those elections. The second era encompasses the Obama-Trump years, when the coefficients are

Table 3.1: OLS Regressions, Demographic Models, Presidential Elections, 1988–2020.

	1988	1992	1996	2000	2004	2008	2012	2016	2020
Percent American Ethnic Identifiers	-0.193*** (0.0336)	0.0691 (0.0363)	-0.0145 (0.0361)	-0.0415 (0.0336)	-0.178*** (0.0342)	-0.433*** (0.0350)	-0.467*** (0.0368)	-0.404*** (0.0329)	-0.404*** (0.0337)
Percent White	-0.192*** (0.0200)	-0.181*** (0.0216)	-0.195*** (0.0215)	-0.247*** (0.0200)	-0.196*** (0.0204)	-0.226*** (0.0208)	-0.257*** (0.0219)	-0.322*** (0.0196)	-0.314*** (0.0200)
Percent Black	-0.0796*** (0.0207)	0.00824 (0.0224)	0.0337 (0.0223)	0.0471** (0.0208)	0.0924*** (0.0211)	0.0769*** (0.0216)	0.143*** (0.0227)	0.204*** (0.0203)	0.197*** (0.0208)
Median Income	-3.573*** (0.290)	-4.120*** (0.313)	-4.054*** (0.312)	-3.194*** (0.290)	-3.868*** (0.296)	-2.968*** (0.302)	-2.935*** (0.318)	-1.659*** (0.284)	-1.654*** (0.291)
Percent Professional Degree	0.00344 (0.119)	0.127 (0.129)	-0.151 (0.128)	0.195 (0.119)	0.773*** (0.112)	0.785*** (0.124)	0.906*** (0.131)	1.944*** (0.117)	1.992*** (0.119)
Percent Senior	-0.178*** (0.0653)	-0.426*** (0.0706)	-0.409*** (0.0703)	-0.126 (0.0654)	-0.158** (0.0666)	-0.126 (0.0681)	-0.192*** (0.0716)	-0.267*** (0.0641)	-0.228*** (0.0655)
Percent Child	-0.724*** (0.0770)	-0.932*** (0.0832)	-0.944*** (0.0828)	-0.872*** (0.0771)	-0.824*** (0.0785)	-0.668*** (0.0802)	-0.601*** (0.0844)	-0.592*** (0.0755)	-0.550*** (0.0772)
Percent Foreign Born	-0.332*** (0.0533)	-0.241*** (0.0577)	-0.276*** (0.0574)	-0.381*** (0.0534)	-0.385*** (0.0544)	-0.415*** (0.0556)	-0.382*** (0.0584)	-0.149*** (0.0523)	-0.344*** (0.0535)
Percent Born Out of State	-0.0897*** (0.0159)	-0.0437** (0.0171)	-0.0647*** (0.0171)	-0.0335** (0.0159)	-0.00352 (0.0162)	-0.0192 (0.0165)	-0.0198 (0.0174)	0.0268 (0.0156)	0.0335** (0.0159)

Population Density (logged)	1.323*** (0.139)	1.935*** (0.150)	2.705*** (0.149)	3.831*** (0.139)	3.350*** (0.141)	3.385*** (0.144)	3.411*** (0.152)	2.805*** (0.136)	3.186*** (0.139)
Percent Evangelical	-0.0352*** (0.0130)	-0.0312** (0.0140)	-0.0649*** (0.0140)	-0.139*** (0.0130)	-0.202*** (0.0133)	-0.291*** (0.0135)	-0.267*** (0.0142)	-0.217*** (0.0127)	-0.242*** (0.0130)
Percent Catholic	0.0948*** (0.0152)	0.118*** (0.0164)	0.152*** (0.0163)	0.108*** (0.0152)	0.0989*** (0.0155)	0.0578*** (0.0158)	0.0570*** (0.0166)	0.0558*** (0.0149)	0.0110 (0.0152)
Percent Veteran	-0.185 (0.104)	0.262** (0.113)	0.0974 (0.112)	-0.191 (0.104)	-0.311*** (0.106)	-0.331*** (0.109)	-0.137 (0.114)	-0.312*** (0.102)	-0.394*** (0.105)
Constant	93.25*** (3.218)	95.23*** (3.479)	96.78*** (3.462)	82.00*** (3.222)	81.10*** (3.282)	85.38*** (3.353)	80.77*** (3.525)	72.79*** (3.156)	73.13*** (3.227)
Observations	3,112	3,112	3,112	3,112	3,112	3,112	3,112	3,112	3,112
R-squared	0.243	0.256	0.330	0.464	0.480	0.559	0.575	0.703	0.689

Note: Dependent variable is Democratic two-party presidential vote share. Standard errors in parentheses. *** p<0.01, ** p<0.05.

all in a range between −0.40 and −0.47. We obviously do not know what will happen in future elections, but as of now, there is an equilibrium for the effect of concentrations of unhyphenated Americans on election results.

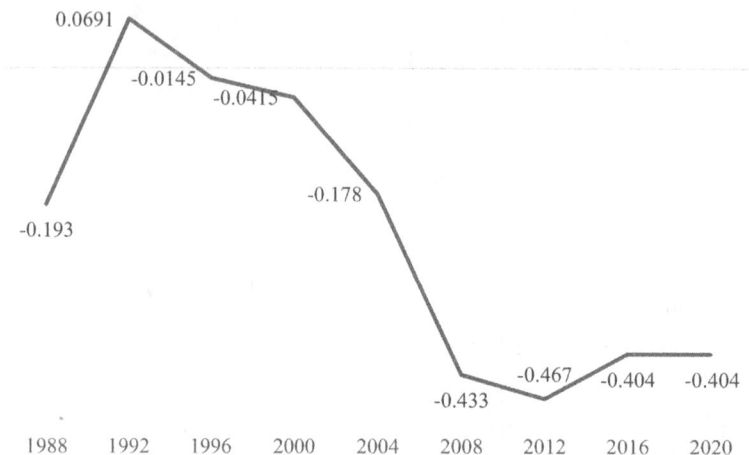

Figure 3.11: Coefficients, Effect of Percent American Ethnic Identifier on Democratic Presidential Vote Share, Multivariate Model.
Note: Calculated by author. Values are coefficients from the Percent American Ethnic Identifier variable in Table 3.1. Dependent variable is Democratic Two-Party Vote Share.

The data presented here provide support for the conclusions reached earlier in the chapter. First, concentrations of American ethnic identifiers are associated with reduced vote shares for Democratic presidential nominees—and increased shares for Republican nominees. The effect of concentrations of unhyphenated Americans is significant even when controlling for a large number of correlated variables, indicating the geographic effect is both unique and strong. Democrats run worse in this region because of characteristics of the region itself and not because unhyphenated America features many small towns, fewer residents with professional degrees, or a large share of evangelicals.

Second, the data here are consistent with the idea that the locus of this shift happens in the first decade of the twenty-first century. In the multivariate model, the percent American ethnic identifiers variable is not significant in the models in the 1990s but achieves significance in 2004 and increases in its importance in the 2008 model. This is evidence that the issues that rose in significance in the 2000s—the war on terror, gay rights, and global warming—are meaningful in unhyphenated America. This is also an acceleration of the trend in 2008, when Barack Obama was the Democratic Party's presidential nominee. Race was a key factor in the South's move toward the Republicans, but the lack of an African American population in the Appalachias and the highland South has blunted the presence of racialized appeals in these areas. The presence of an African American as the Democratic nominee in 2008 and 2012 brought race to the fore in this region, and accelerated its Republican trend.

6 A Distinctive and Long-Standing Shift

This chapter examined recent presidential elections in unhyphenated concentrated regions of the country and shows a clear and strong trend. Republican presidential nominees have gained vote share ever since 1992. In the twentieth century, Democrats could fight Republicans to a near draw in unhyphenated concentrated counties. But in the twenty-first century, the region has shifted toward the Republicans. The multivariate analysis allows me to conclude that this shift is not the result of some correlated variable found more readily in unhyphenated concentrated regions. Instead, it is a distinct geographic change in the region.

The results also show that the Republican shift in the region is apparent throughout the timeline after 1992. George H. W. Bush saw a slight decline in the region when he ran for re-election as opposed to his initial run for office. But after that election, Republican nominees posted gains in the region in nearly every election. The trend accelerated and intensified most in the three elections between 2000 and 2008. The Republican shift is present in elections before and after these three but is most intense in these years.

We can draw a few conclusions from the data presented in this chapter. First, unhyphenated America represents a distinct political region, and there has been clear movement in the region over the past generation toward Republican presidential candidates. Second, the trend in the region is notable because it stands in contrast to a national political trend that has moved modestly but clearly toward the Democrats. Third, the Republican trend is long-standing, having begun in 1996 and having lasted to the present day. I do not find any signs in the data that Democrats will make gains in the region any time soon. Fourth, while the trend is long-standing, it accelerated most in the period between 2000 and 2008. That the shift happened in this period suggests that the issues that rose to the fore at this time play a more important role in the shift than issues that were more important earlier or later in the time period. And of course, the move against Barack Obama in unhyphenated America may reflect part of the national increase in the salience of race in the Obama years.

These four conclusions help to answer the questions that I raised at the beginning of this chapter, but they also raise questions about the Republican shift in unhyphenated America. For example, is the Republican shift in the region simply a phenomenon of presidential candidates or is there a broader pattern that can be observed in down ballot races. Chapter 4 addresses this question. In addition, it is still unclear what is causing the Republican shift in the region. This chapter speculated on a couple of potential explanations (racial resentment and the presence of Barack Obama on the ballot; the rise of a set of new issues such as environmentalism and gay rights), but the data used so far is too crude to make any useful conclusions. Chapters 5 and 6 use survey data to examine what issues are driving unhyphenated America toward the Republicans.

What the results do show is that Al Gore's losses in Tennessee and West Virginia in 2000 were part of a long-term trend in the region. While one can praise the Bush campaign's decision to target the states or criticize Al Gore's inability to connect to voters in the region, it is clear the trend in the region is bigger than one campaign's targeting decisions or one candidate's personal characteristics. In Tennessee, George W. Bush earned 57% of the vote in 2004. John McCain matched that in 2008, despite losing 5% of Bush's national vote share. Republicans made more gains in 2012 (59%) and again in 2016 (61%) in the Volunteer State. The gains were bigger in West Virginia. After Republican nominees took 56% of the vote there in both 2004 and 2008, Mitt Romney topped that in 2012 with 62% of the vote. Donald Trump surpassed that in his three runs for the presidency, winning 68.5% of the vote. What happened statewide in Tennessee and in West Virginia mirror what happened in the rest of unhyphenated America. The region started turning strongly toward the Republicans in the 2000 election, denying Democrats votes and victories. After 2000, the region kept moving toward the Republicans and has not looked back.

Chapter 4
Congressional Realignment in Unhyphenated America

Some thought Republican Shelley Moore Capito's victory for a US House seat in West Virginia in 2000 was a fluke. She had drawn a Democratic opponent with huge vulnerabilities in state Senator Jim Humphreys and was aided by the greater attention that the George W. Bush campaign had given West Virginia compared to Al Gore's campaign. She squeaked out a two point victory (Cook Political Report 2000, 49–50). With a midterm environment likely working against a member of the president's party and West Virginia more likely to return to its Democratic roots, it was clear that Moore Capito was one of the most vulnerable incumbents in 2002, and her race was quickly labeled as a "Toss-Up" by the Cook Political Report (2001, 57).

Moore Capito caught some breaks leading up to the 2002 election. Despite murmurs that the district would be changed in redistricting, the Democratic state legislature did little to alter her district's lines. George W. Bush remained popular nationally in the wake of the September 11 terrorist attacks, which reduced (if not eliminated) the midterm penalty for House incumbents from his party. And the Democrats nominated Humphreys, with all his vulnerabilities, again, (Cook Political Report 2002, 130).

Humphreys won the Democratic nomination in large part because he was willing to spend his own personal fortune on the seat. But he also adjusted his strategy from 2000, using more positive and personal ads to increase his own favorable numbers in the district. He also found an important issue on which to attack Moore Capito—social security. Humphreys argued that Moore Capito supported the "privatization" of social security, thanks to a partisan but fair reading of her actual position and a tortured reading of one vote she took in the US House. The attacks compelled Moore Capito to defend her position, making semantic arguments about the definition of "privatization" in interviews (Clymer 2002) and more forcefully declaring "I want you to know that I oppose the privatization of Social Security" in stump speeches (Cohen 2002).

Fighting for her political life, Moore Capito turned to a place where West Virginia Republicans rarely turned—her national party. She received copious financial help from leadership PACs associated with Republican congressional leaders and from the National Republican Congressional Committee, allowing her campaign to keep Humphreys from dominating the airwaves with his personal fortune (Allen 2002). President George W. Bush made a campaign appearance for

https://doi.org/10.1515/9783111615707-004

Moore Capito at a rally in Charleston (Hernandez 2002). Bush's national popularity in the wake of the September 11 attacks and his personal popularity in a district he had won by ten points in 2000 helped boost Moore Capito. In the end, she won in a runaway, prevailing 60–40 over Humphreys.

What happened after 2002 in the West Virginia 2nd District is just as notable as what happened during 2022. Starting in 2004, Moore Capito won a series of comfortable victories for the rest of that decade, each by 14% or more. She ran up big numbers in 2010 and 2012, winning more than two thirds of the vote in each year (Barone et al. 2013). That made her the strongest Republican in the state, and in 2014, she was the consensus pick of her party to take on long-time incumbent Senator Jay Rockefeller, who announced his retirement rather than face off with—and almost certainly lose to—Moore Capito. In the 2nd District, Alex Mooney won a close election to hold the seat for the Republicans. He then established himself as a strong incumbent, winning re-election easily for the rest of the decade.

Why did Moore Capito win re-election in 2002? A big part of the story is the same partisan shift described in Chapter 3. The West Virginia 2nd is an unhyphenated concentrated district, where 17.4% of residents identify their ethnicity as American. Districts such as these moved towards the Republicans in presidential elections. Bill Clinton won the 2nd in both of his runs for the presidency, but George W. Bush won it in 2000, as part of his upset victory in West Virginia. That national Republicans—including Bush—were so prominent in Moore Capito's re-election campaign demonstrates that her campaign thought that voters would reward her for embracing her party.

Moore Capito's success in the West Virginia 2nd is also part of a trend apparent across unhyphenated America. Like many of these districts, it had a Democratic representative in the 1980s and 1990s. Moore Capito was able to win it as an open seat in 2000 as Bob Wise left the seat to successfully run for Governor of West Virginia. But once the district went to the Republicans, it stayed there. This pattern is repeated across unhyphenated America. Once one of these districts changes out a Democratic member of Congress for a Republican one, it tends to stay a Republican district.

In this chapter, I examine the results of US House elections. I do this from a longitudinal perspective, showing that the region has shifted from one where Democrats won a greater share of victories than they did in other regions of the country to one where Democrats win but a bare handful of seats. The region also moves from one where national trends are reflected in the results to one that seems impervious to national results—the Democratic wave of 2018 had basically no effect in unhyphenated America.

Using longitudinal data also helps to explore why the region moved toward the Republicans. The biggest changes came in 1994 and 2010 when the region reacted strongly and negatively toward first-term Democratic presidents. These changes proved durable, as they established new (and more Republican) equilibria on both occasions. These results indicate that the region reacted against Democratic governance in the Clinton and Obama administrations; Republican governance did not produce strong negative effects in the region.

1 The Distinctiveness of Congressional Elections

It is worth taking time to note how congressional elections work differently to presidential elections. At the center of most elections are the candidates. Presidential nominations are important prizes to win as they give a candidate a chance to be president and help set the policy direction and political frame for that party. As such, every out-party or open presidential nomination is fought over by candidates with high levels of political skills, and the nomination process weeds out those whose political skills top out at the state level. As a result, each presidential nominee is a high-quality candidate, even if differences in candidate quality still exist between party nominees.

This is not always the case in congressional elections. Some party nominations are quite valuable and thus produce either a large number of candidates (Herrnson and Gimpel 1995; Lazarus 2005) or compel parties to try to provide cues to primary voters on behalf of favored candidates (Hassell 2017). These types of primaries often attract high-quality candidates and can produce competitive elections (Jacobson and Kernell 1983). But in some seats, party nominations are not as valuable. The winner is nearly certain to lose in November and thus fewer candidates enter the primary and those that do are the political equivalent of "some dude." In some districts, a party will not be able to find anyone to run and the incumbent runs uncontested.

As a result, congressional elections are much more variable from election to election than presidential elections. The results in each district are premised on candidate quality and that shifts from election to election.

Another important difference between presidential and congressional elections is the geographic scope of the election. Presidential elections are of course national, and party nominees must make appeals to every region of the country. By definition, presidential nominees cannot run against their party; they, in essence, are their party. Presidential results tell us attitudes toward the national party and their nominees within a county or district. Congressional candidates of course come from that state or district and usually tailor their appeal to match that of the district, even if it puts them at odds with their party (Erikson and Wright 2000). Thus, congressional results can differ—and sometimes significantly so—from national results (Hunt 2022). Again, this leads to more variable results than in the presidential elections we examined in Chapter 3. Nonetheless, national forces are still quite present in congressional elections, and in recent years, that presence has only increased (Abramowitz and Webster 2016; Hopkins 2018; Jacobson 2015).

All of this is to say that there is greater variation from district to district in US House races. Local factors may matter more than national trends and good candidates can make their specific histories and personal characteristics matter more than perceptions of the president or the policy priorities of the national party. Party still matters, though, and as we saw in the West Virginia 2nd, is often the most important factor in US House elections. Over the course of time, that is what we see in unhyphenated America. As the region turned toward the Republicans, Republican candidates won more and more in House elections in the region.

2 Unhyphenated Concentrated Districts

To analyze congressional election results in unhyphenated America requires identifying the districts where there are strong concentrations of these unhyphenated Americans, and to do, as I did in Chapter 3, I draw on the percentage of American ethnic identifiers in a region. Here, I look at the numbers at the congressional district level, rather than at the county level.

Figure 4.1 shows a map of the seventy congressional districts in the 117th Congress where American identifiers are most concentrated. In these districts, at least 10.9% of the population identifies their ethnicity as American, which is one standard deviation above the national mean for congressional districts. (mean = 6.6%; standard deviation = 4.3%).

These districts are concentrated in the Appalachian Mountains, the Ohio River Valley, and the highland South. All six districts in Kentucky and seven of the nine districts in Tennessee have concentrations of unhyphenated Americans. In addition, there are districts here from the Deep South, though they tend to be from the northern or highland portions of these states (e.g. Upcountry South Carolina). The districts tend to skip over urban areas. For example, the two Tennessee districts that are not unhyphenated concentrated are the districts centered in Nashville and Memphis. A few districts come from the Rim South states of Florida, Texas, and Virginia, but these districts are in rural and more traditional areas of these states (Gulf Coast of Florida, East Texas, Southside Virginia). A handful of districts are found in the Midwestern states of Ohio, Indiana, and Illinois, but

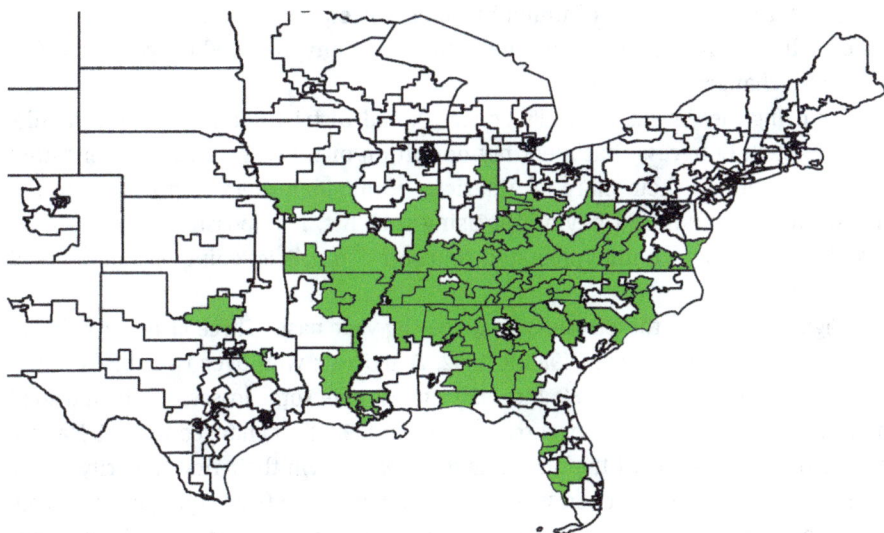

Figure 4.1: Map of Unhyphenated American US House Districts, 117th Congress.
Note: Unhyphenated concentrated districts are defined as those where 10.9% of residents or more identify their ethnic origin as "American"; 10.9% is the national mean for congressional districts plus one standard deviation.

these districts are concentrated near the Ohio River in the southern part of each state. We see something similar in Missouri, where the state's two southernmost districts are unhyphenated concentrated. Two of the three districts of West Virginia are unhyphenated concentrated.

This visual representation of unhyphenated concentrated districts is understandably very similar to the map of unhyphenated concentrated counties in Chapter 3. They are centered in the Appalachias and the upper South and concentrated heavily in rural and small-town areas of that region. These districts have one other characteristic in common—they are nearly monolithically represented by Republicans. The map comes from the 117th Congress, which was elected in November 2020. In that election, Republicans won sixty-five of these seats; Democrats won only five. These results were not flukes: Republicans won between sixty-five and sixty-seven of these seats between 2012 and 2024; Democrats won less than six of them in each election since 2012.

In the 2010s, Republicans dominated the US House election in unhyphenated America. But when did this domination begin? To answer that question, one needs to note that congressional districts are not static entities like counties but change with reapportionment and redistricting. Sometimes redistricting is conducted in the middle of a decade, but usually this process is done after a census is taken. As a result, the list of unhyphenated concentrated districts changes over time as district lines change. And the number of unhyphenated concentrated districts also changes over time.

By using the Census Bureau's Congressional District Summary Files, the districts in each Congress that meet my definition of unhyphenated concentrated can be identified—their share of American ethnic identifiers is greater than the mean plus one standard deviation. Using that list, it is possible to determine which party won each unhyphenated concentrated district going back a political generation.

Figure 4.2 shows these results on a year-by-year basis. Three clear periods are observable. The first is from 1988 to 1992. Democrats won over two thirds of the seats in the region in both 1988 and 1990, and despite some losses, still held a solid majority of unhyphenated concentrated seats in 1992. That changed in 1994. Nationally, Republicans gained fifty-four seats that year to win their first majority in the US House since 1954, and twenty-one of those seats came from unhyphenated concentrated districts. Or to put it another way, thirty-three of the seats Republicans gained came from the 361 seats in the rest of the United States; that is 9.6% of those seats. Republicans flipped 28.4% of the seats in unhyphenated America.

The results in districts with concentrations of American ethnic identifiers stayed remarkably stable over the next decade, as Democrats won between twenty-one and twenty-three seats in the period; Republicans won between forty-nine and fifty-four.[19] The 2006 and 2008 Democratic wave elections had a modest effect on unhyphenated America. Democrats gained four seats in 2006 and another five seats in 2008. Overall, the region was more favorable to Republicans.

The region entered its third period in the 2010 Republican wave election. Nationally, Republicans gained sixty-four seats in that year's election and twenty of them came from unhyphenated concentrated districts. Results have remained steady in the region ever since, with Republicans winning nearly monolithically each election year. The only time Democrats could count their victories on a second hand was in their wave election year of 2018, when they increased their victories to six. The Democrats may have taken over a majority in the US House that year, but unhyphenated America did not contribute to that effort; it stayed strongly Republican.

Figure 4.3 provides an alternative view of the Republican shift in unhyphenated America. It shows the list of these districts across time from 1988 to 2022—when a Democratic won them, they are shaded blue; when a Republican won

---

19 In 2000, Virgil Goode of Virginia switched his party affiliation from Democrat to independent. He won election that year easily over a Republican opponent. That victory is not included in Figure 4.2. In 2002, he switched again to the Republican Party.

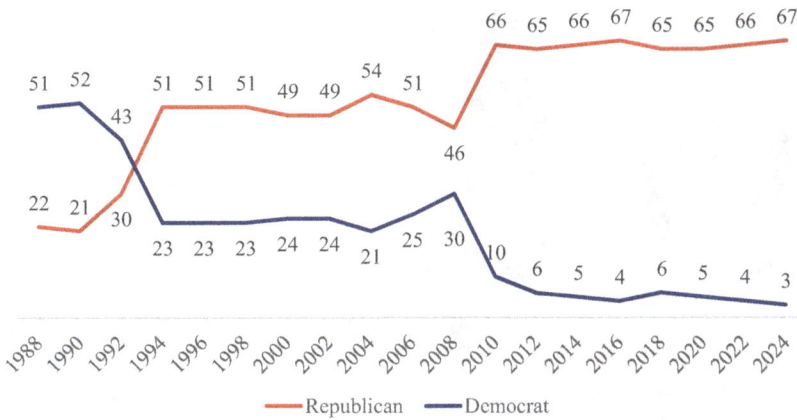

Figure 4.2: Election Results, Unhyphenated Concentrated US House Districts.
Source: Data are calculated by author based on the US Census Bureau Congressional District File for each Congress.
Note: Unhyphenated concentrated districts are defined as those where the share of residents who identify their ethnicity as "American" is greater than the mean plus one standard deviation for congressional districts that year.

them, they are shaded red. But because districts change over time, this is a slightly different list than I used in Figure 4.2. Here, I took the unhyphenated concentrated seats listed in the 117th Congress (see Figure 4.1), and matched up seats across redistricting based on where an incumbent ran for re-election. When the incumbent retired during a redistricting period, I matched the seat to the predecessor who had the highest share of the population of the current district.[20]

A visual examination of these districts shows that blue is the dominant color on the left-hand side of the figure, and red is nearly monolithic on the right-hand side. Over the three decades, these districts have moved into the Republican column. Of just as much importance is the chart's demonstration that Democrats can no longer win these seats back from Republicans. While Democrats were able to occasionally defeat a Republican incumbent or win a Republican-held open seat from 1982 through the 2008 election, ever since then, once they have lost a seat, they never get it back.

A clear example of this is the 6th Congressional District in Tennessee, which is located in the rural parts of middle Tennessee, to the east and north of Nashville. Democrat Bart Gordon first won election to the seat in 1984, succeeding Al

---

20 The vast majority of these districts are the same in both lists. I use this consistent list of districts because it makes it easier to see the change in partisanship over time via this method.

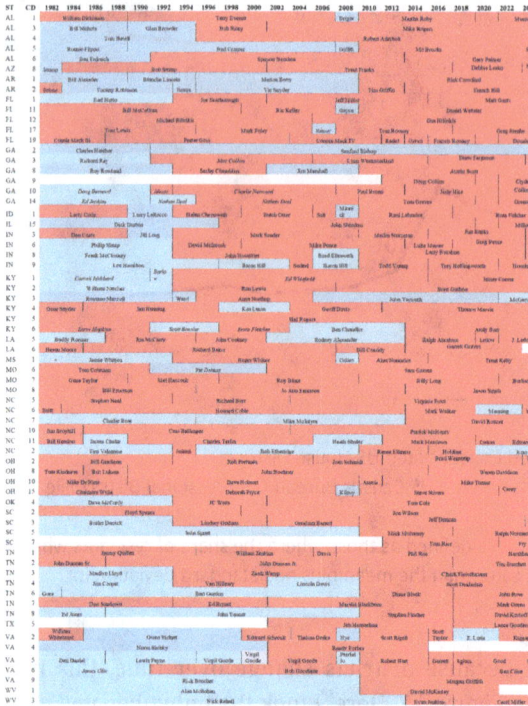

Figure 4.3: Unhyphenated Concentrated US House Seats, over Time.
Note: Unhyphenated concentrated districts are defined as those where the share of residents who identify their ethnicity as "American" is greater than the mean plus one standard deviation for congressional districts that year.

Gore, as both won election that year despite Ronald Reagan's landslide presidential win. Gordon won re-election to the seat twelve times. He fended off a difficult challenge in the 1994 wave and then defeated the same Republican more easily in 1996. He then returned to winning re-election by landslide margins and in 2008, Gordon ran unopposed. But in 2010, Gordon decided to retire, and between the seat's Republican lean (John McCain won 65% of the vote here in 2008) and the Republican wave year, it was a landslide. Republican state legislator Diane Black won in 2019 by thirty-eight points, and she won the 6th by landslide margins three other times. In 2018, Black ran for governor, but former Agriculture Commissioner John Rose won again by landslide margins to hold the seat for the Republicans. He has won easily in all three of his runs for re-election.

In short, the Tennessee 6th District quickly but permanently shifted from preferring a Democrat in the US House to a Republican. As a result, the district's Republicans have been able to win handily both in open seat contests and as incumbents. What is true in this district is true around unhyphenated America. The average Republican running in an unhyphenated concentrated seat in 2024 won 69% of the vote. Six Republican incumbents in unhyphenated concentrated districts ran unopposed by a Democrat. In short, these are districts that not only vote for Republicans but tend to do so overwhelmingly.

Figure 4.4 compares the Democratic winning percentage in these unhyphenated concentrated districts to the Democratic winning percentage in districts in two other regions—the Old Confederacy and the rest of the country, defined here as the North. For both the South and the North, I have removed unhyphenated concentrated districts from their region. Doing so makes it possible to see the distinct electoral pattern of unhyphenated America.

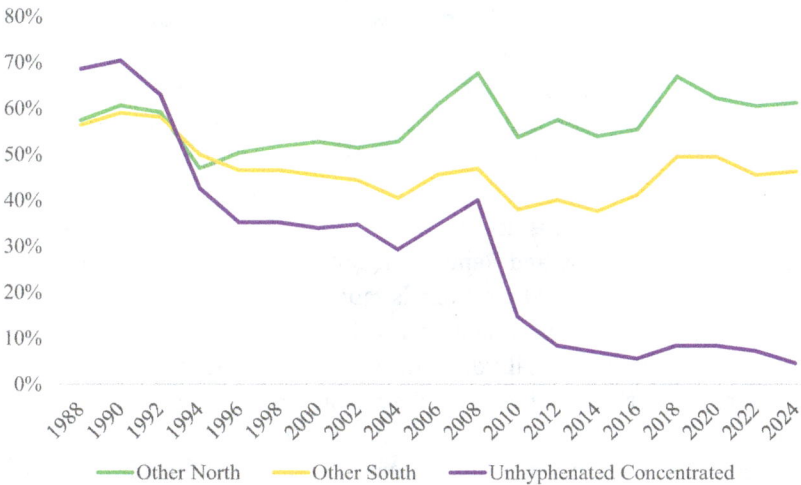

Figure 4.4: Democratic Winning Percentage by Region.
Source: Data are calculated by author based on the US Census Bureau Congressional District File for each Congress.
Note: Unhyphenated concentrated districts are defined as those where the share of residents who identify their ethnicity as "American" is greater than the mean plus one standard deviation for congressional districts that year. Other South is defined as the eleven states that joined the Confederacy minus unhyphenated concentrated seats. Other North is the thirty-nine states that did not secede minus unhyphenated concentrated seats.

In the 1980s, Democrats won a slightly higher share of elections in unhyphenated concentrated districts than they did in the other two regions of the country. Indeed, Democrats won a steady but clear majority in all three regions. This changed in 1994, as Democratic losses were heavily concentrated in unhyphenated America. Since then, the three regions of the country have moved in different directions. Democrats have performed best in northern congressional districts and the gap between their performance in the North and the South opened up in the 1990s and early 2000s. The winning percentage gap between the North and South reached double digits in 2004 and has stayed there ever since. In the "other South," Democrats were at an equilibrium from 1994 to 2014, winning between 40% and 50% of the seats. They increased their winning percentage in the region in 2018 to 49% and have won just under half of these seats in the three elections since then.

The results in the unhyphenated concentrated districts stand in stark contrast to those in the other two regions of the country. Starting in 1994, Democrats recorded their lowest winning percentage among the three regions in unhyphenated America. Democratic wins declined across the region until the Democratic waves of 2006 and 2008, though it remained the lowest of the three regions. And then the bottom fell out for Democrats in 2010, as they lost 87% of the seats in unhyphenated America in 2010 and 92% in 2012. The Democratic win share in the district stayed remarkably steady—and remarkably low—throughout the rest of the timeline.

The presidential election results shown in Chapter 3 demonstrate a steadier pattern of Democratic decline and Republican gain across unhyphenated America. The pattern in congressional elections is much less steady, owing mostly to the issues of incumbency and candidate quality discussed previously in this chapter. Instead, there are two critical points in the timeline. The first was in 1994, when Democratic majority equilibrium in the region was punctured, and the percentage of Democratic victories in the region declined precipitously from around 70% to 35%. But even with that decline, Democrats maintained some level of support in the region, winning 30–40% of elections there. In 2010, that support collapsed entirely, as Democrats became *party non-grata* in unhyphenated concentrated districts. They lost almost every seat in the region in every election from 2010 to 2024 and there is little reason to think they will regain many in the near future.

3 Unhyphenateds and Election Results, across Time

I want to go beyond just descriptive data to examine the long-term impact of unhyphenated Americans on election results. As in Chapter 3, it is not clear that concentrations of unhyphenated Americans are related to Republican victories in these districts. Other factors correlated with concentrations of unhyphenated Americans could be the more proximate cause of these election results.

The data presented in Figures 4.2–4.4 provide preliminary evidence of the importance of concentrations of American ethnic identifiers to the results of congressional elections, but they are only suggestive of this relationship. There are other demographic and political factors correlated with the percentage of unhyphenated in a district that may explain the negative trend for Democrats (and positive for Republicans) observed in Figure 4.2. Arbour (2011) found that heavily unhyphenated districts are whiter, more rural, older, and lower on the socioeconomic ladder than other districts. Changes in partisanship and the district opportunity structure (Black and Black 2002; McKee 2010) may attract better candidates and more funds into a district or may spur an incumbent to retire. This would be consistent with the fact that the large and long-standing changes in unhyphenated concentrated districts happen in wave election years.

To assess whether the negative relationship between the share of unhyphenated Americans in a district and Democratic vote share observed in the bivariate data is real or spurious, it is necessary to include variables to account for other factors, both political and demographic, that can influence election results. As I did in Chapter 3, I created OLS models for each general election from 1992 to 2020 with the Democratic share of the two-party vote in each congressional district as the dependent variable. Again, the key variable is the percentage of unhyphenated Americans in a congressional district. The model includes Previous Democratic Vote Share in US House elections as a key control variable, and includes racial (percentage white, percentage African American) socioeconomic (district median income, percentage of adults with a college degree), age (percentage of senior citizens, and percentage of children) and geographic (rural percentage) variables. In addition, the model contains political variables for the advantage (or deficit) in candidate quality held by the Democratic candidate,[21] an incumbency variable,[22] and variables for the amount of money spent by the Democratic and Republican candidates.

The results show that the coefficient for unhyphenated Americans is negative in fourteen of the fifteen elections under study, and significant in ten of the elections, including the last six under study. Figure 4.5 uses a line graph to show how the coefficient has changed over time. The coefficient for the percentage of unhyphenateds suggests that the relationship between concentrations of unhyphenated Americans

---

21 It is coded +1 if the Democratic challenger has held elective office, −1 if a Republican challenger has held elective office. In open seat races, it is coded +1 if the Democratic nominee has held office before but the Republican has not; and −1 if the Republican nominee has held elective office before and the Democrat has not. If both candidates have held elective office, or if neither candidate has held elective office, it is coded 0.
22 It is coded +1 if there is a Democratic incumbent, −1 if there is a Republican incumbent, and 0 for an open seat.

and Democratic Party vote share bounced around in the 1990s and the early 2000s. It was sharply negative in 2004, but then returned to more modest numbers in the Democratic wave years of 2006 and 2008. In the last six elections, the coefficient has become more and more negative until 2020, when it was exactly the same as it was in 2018 at −0.891. That is, for every 1% greater share of American ethnic identifiers a district has, the Democratic candidate receives 0.891% less of the vote, *ceteris paribus*. The declining coefficient indicates that the connection between concentrations of unhyphenated voters and Republican voting has strengthened over the last several elections. This suggests that that the negativity between unhyphenated Americans and Democratic candidates may be a more recent phenomenon.

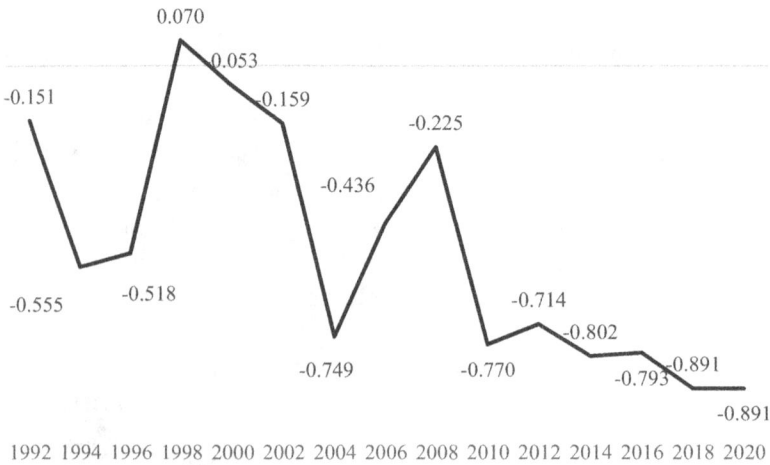

Figure 4.5: Coefficient for the Unhyphenated American Variable in Demographic Model.
Note: Figure shows the coefficient for the *American* variable. Models use two-party Democratic vote share as the dependent variable, and include measures for previous Democratic vote share, racial (percentage white, percentage African-American), socioeconomic (district median income, percentage of adults with a college degree), age (percentage of senior citizens and percentage of children), geographic (percentage rural), and political (challenger quality, incumbency, money spent, open seat) factors as variables.

In both the bivariate data in the previous section and in the multivariate regression data, 2010 is a pivotal year in the politics of unhyphenated America. As noted above, the bottom falls out of the Democratic winning percentage in the region that year and never recovers. We see similar results in the multivariate data, where the coefficient for the percentage of American ethnic identifiers goes strongly negative. These results are consistent with the idea that the region reacted negatively to the first two years of the Obama Administration. That this happened in 2010 instead of

2008 indicates that it was not necessarily Obama himself who caused the long-term shift in the region, but reaction to the policies he pursued in office.

The results here do not conclusively answer the question of whether the negative correlations between concentrations of unhyphenated Americans and reduced Democratic vote share is caused by a reaction to Barack Obama or are part of a longer-term pattern. This relationship does not follow a straight line of secular decline across time but bounces up and down. When Democrats gain House seats (1998, 2000, 2006, 2008), the effect of the percentage of unhyphenated Americans in a district declines from the previous election. When Republicans gain seats (1994, 2004, 2010), the effect increases. That the effect is more likely to matter in recent years suggests an intensification of this trend across time. And the results of the last four elections suggest that this intensification is most pronounced in districts with high concentrations of unhyphenated Americans, which are moving toward the Republican Party with great intensity.

4 National Trends and Unhyphenated Concentrated Districts

A large part of what is driving the shift toward the Republicans in US House elections in unhyphenated America is the increasing importance of national conditions in US House elections. In other words, US House results are increasingly mirroring presidential election results, even in midterm elections when a president is not on the ballot. In the 1980s and 1990s, it was common to see members of Congress use constituent service, pork barrel spending, and local connections to develop a personal vote and win election in seats that favored the opposing party in presidential elections (Cain et al. 1987; Fiorina 1977; Mayhew 1974). While candidates still try to use these techniques to win votes in difficult districts—and there are a handful of successful examples of such politicians (cf. Joe Manchin; Susan Collins)—the number of them, especially in House elections, have become fewer and fewer (Jacobson 2015; Hopkins 2018).

Nationally, voting between presidential and US House elections have harmonized as national forces have increased their impact on state results. Unhyphenated America is part of this trend. To examine this, I conducted a simple bivariate regression for each US House election in an unhyphenated concentrated district from 1992 to 2020. The dependent variable is the two-party Democratic performance in US House elections; the independent variable is two-party Democratic performance in the most recent presidential election in that congressional district. I conducted a separate regression for each election year.

Figure 4.6a presents the coefficient for each election via a line graph. Higher values indicate that presidential election results had a large impact on the results of House elections. These values are relatively steady from 1992 through 2006 in unhyphenated America. Presidential election results have a coefficient of around 0.9 throughout this period. This jumps greatly in 2010 to over 1.3, and the coefficient remains high throughout the rest of the timeline, even if it declined some in 2012 and 2014. In short, national factors have increased in importance in explaining the results of US House elections in unhyphenated America since the 2010 election. As the region has turned toward the Republicans at the presidential level, they have done so as well at the House level.

a. In Unhyphenated Concentrated Districts

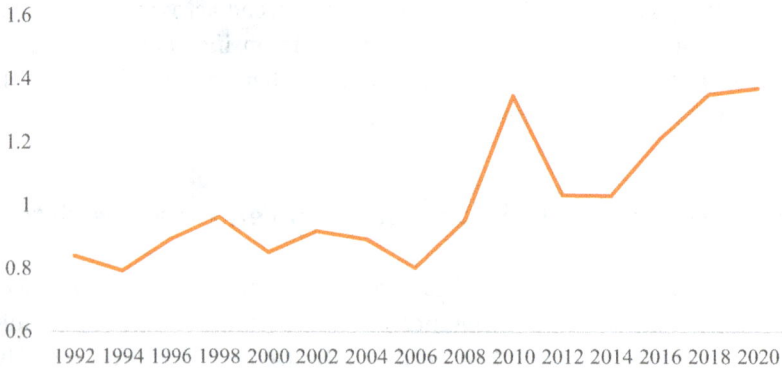

b. In Unhyphenated Concentrated and in All US House Districts

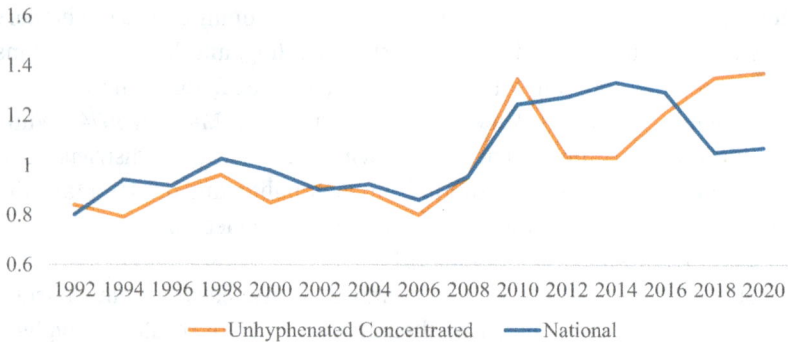

Figure 4.6: Impact of Presidential Vote on US House Vote, by Region, 1992–2020.
Note: Results are coefficients for a bivariate regression. The independent variable is the two-party Democratic vote share in the most recent presidential election and the dependent variable is two-party Democratic vote share in the US House election.

Unhyphenated Concentrated districts are defined as those where 12.8% of residents or more identify their ethnic origin as "American." Author matched districts across redistricting cycles based on where the incumbent ran. If an incumbent did not choose to run for re-election, the districts are matched to the predecessor which has the highest share of the population of the current district.

Of course, the impact of national factors in unhyphenated America is similar to the impact in the rest of the country. Figure 4.6b shows the coefficients for the same bivariate regression conducted across all 435 US House elections in the country. There are few differences observed between the results in unhyphenated concentrated districts and in districts across the country. Both stay steady before the Obama Administration and then increase sharply in 2010. But after that year, the results diverge. Presidential vote share is more important nationally in 2012 and 2014 than it is in unhyphenated America. But this reverses in 2018 and 2020. National forces increase in importance in unhyphenated America even as they decline (somewhat) in elections in the rest of the country.

Broadly, these results suggest that national forces have played a similar role in unhyphenated America as they have in the rest of the nation. Of course, as shown in Chapter 3, presidential results in unhyphenated America moved toward the Republicans in the 1990s and the 2000s, and that Republican trend shows up in congressional elections. The results over the last decade indicate a potential divergence between unhyphenated America and the rest of the country. Partisanship lessened, if slightly, in the rest of the country in response to the Trump Administration. It increased in unhyphenated America.

5 The Trend in Congressional Races in Unhyphenated America

This chapter examines congressional elections in unhyphenated America over the last political generation. And like the previous chapter on presidential elections, this one finds a sharp and durable shift toward the Republican Party in the region.

This shift is even sharper than in presidential elections. Before the 1994 election, voters in US House elections in unhyphenated America were more likely to send Democrats to Congress than Republicans. This changed after the realigning 1994 election when Republicans won a majority of seats in the region. And the Republican majority held remarkably steady in the region for another decade and a half. The equilibrium was only punctured by another Republican wave election—2010. In that election, Republicans won a near monolithic share of the seats in unhyphenated America, and that number has stayed remarkably steady ever since.

The results suggest that the key moment was 1994. In districts with high concentrations of unhyphenated voters, Democrats went from having a greater share of the seats than they did nationally to having a smaller share. Republicans continued to hold a similar share of these seats for the next seven elections. Seth McKee (2010, 2, 5) argues that the combination of "(1) increasing Republican identification among white southerners, (2) the partisan impact of redistricting . . . and (3) the emergence of viable Republican candidates who struck the right chords with an electorate primed for representational change" produced the "Republican ascendancy" in the South, and that the 1994 election represented the "critical moment" when one electoral equilibrium was punctured and a new one took its place. Thus, the change in these unhyphenated districts represents the end of a long trend of growing Republican identification among voters in these districts and the creation of new districts for the 1992 election.

While undoubtedly there are similar factors that explain the shifts observed in the 2010 election, the 2010 change was not created in part because of an exogenous event, like changing district lines. These districts had been in effect since redistricting after the 2000 Census. This shift may be more directly related to a response to events between the 2008 and 2010 election, which would make Barack Obama's policy agenda a likely explanation. That Democrats continued to lose seats in the region throughout the rest of the Obama Administration, despite holding so few seats to defend, provides further support for this conclusion.

The near monolithic Republican delegation from unhyphenated concentrated districts indicates that this region is closed off to Democrats for the extended future. Democratic defeats in the South from the 1980s to the middle of the 2000s would prompt handwringing about the dying off of the New Deal coalition. But Democrats have proven since then that they can win majorities in the US House and Senate primarily by being the party of urbanized America, stitching together urban districts with well-heeled suburban districts trending left and just enough working-class white districts (or states) to win a majority in the US House (or Senate). The Democrats have become a regional party, in part because they cannot compete in rural and small-town areas such as the Appalachias and the upper South.

Of course, both parties are now regional parties. In an increasingly polarized nation, both parties must write off particular regions as lost causes. The Democrats have had to do this with unhyphenated concentrated districts as the region has moved towards the Republicans, making even the highest quality Democratic candidates uncompetitive.

Republicans have done the same in an increasing share of well-heeled suburban districts, adding them to the majority-minority and big city districts where their candidates lose in landslide fashion. This has made their gains in Appalachia and the upper South more important. Republican gains here have made up for losses in other regions and allow the GOP to compete for and win House majorities despite their losses elsewhere.

The two major elections that shifted the region toward the Republicans were not only wave elections, but also elections that occurred in the first midterm after the election of a Democratic president. Both of those midterms came when Democrats held the *trifecta*—a majority in both the House and the Senate as well as the presidency—and the party pursued its policy agenda aggressively. The region holds steady through Republican presidencies but reacts negatively to Democratic ones. This suggests that it is the policies pursued by Democratic presidents and their co-partisan Congresses that repel voters in unhyphenated America.

But the data are only suggestive. The analyses in Chapters 3 and 4 are clear in showing that regions with concentrations of unhyphenated Americans are politically distinctive. In both presidential and congressional elections, concentrations of American ethnic identifiers have increasingly moved toward the Republicans and away from the Democrats over the last political generation. The data examined in Chapters 3 and 4 also show that this shift is not the result of correlated demographic factors such as median income or college graduation rates. Instead, the region's political distinctiveness is intimately tied to its ethnic distinctiveness. It matters that the region has concentrations of unhyphenated Americans.

What the county- and district-level results examined so far cannot do well is provide a full and detailed explanation for why: Why have regions with concentrations of American ethnic identifiers moved toward the Republicans in recent years? Why did these districts dislike the policies of Barack Obama? Why were voters in this region attracted to Republicans in general and Donald Trump in particular? To answer these questions requires individual-level data and focus on the actual issue positions of those who live in the region. The next two chapters move away from geographic and aggregate level data and use public opinion data to assess the individual-level priorities of those who live and vote in unhyphenated America.

Chapter 5
God, Guns, and Glacier Melting: Social and Environmental Issues in Unhyphenated America

In his southwestern Virginia congressional district, Democratic Rep. Rick Boucher looked like a fixture. The 9th District, deep in Virginia's Appalachian Mountains was the home of one base of "mountain Republicans," and featured more effective two-party competition than most Southern districts throughout the twentieth century.

In 1982, Boucher defeated eight-term Republican incumbent Willam Wampler to take the seat back for the Democrats. He easily held the seat for the next three decades. But the district started turning toward the right in national politics, voting for George W. Bush in 2000 after having voted for Bill Clinton in both elections in the 1990s. In 2004, national Republicans offered "significant support" to challenger Kevin Triplett, a former NASCAR executive, who criticized Boucher for voting against appropriations for the war in Iraq. These efforts were in vain, as Boucher turned aside Triplett's "spirited opposition" by a 59–39 margin. In 2006, Republicans tried again, running state legislator Bill Carrico. Boucher again won with ease, 68–32. In 2008, Republicans ceded the district to Boucher. They did not even nominate a candidate against him (Barone and McCutcheon 2011).

In 2010, it looked like Boucher would remain a fixture in the district. His race was initially rated as "Safe Democratic" by political prognosticators such as the Cook Political Report (Wasserman 2010). His assets were listed by a political foe—Republican Governor Bob McDonnell—who noted that Boucher was "a 28-year incumbent who got the NRA endorsement and did good constituent service." As a result, "people didn't think he was beatable" (Meola 2010a). Boucher focused his campaign rhetoric as he usually did on local concerns, "running on a record of bringing home federal funding for infrastructure projects and constituent services vital to the economically struggling region and its aging, Medicare-dependent population" (Whitley and Meola 2010). He used his perch on the Energy and Commerce Committee not just to steer federal money to his district, but to raise more money than his opponent (Meola 2010b).

Yet, despite these assets, political prognosticators started seeing signs in early 2010 that Boucher might be vulnerable to state Delegate Morgan Griffith. What made Boucher vulnerable? One important answer was his vote for a cap-and-trade bill. "All of a sudden, it's not much fun to be a Democrat from coal country

https://doi.org/10.1515/9783111615707-005

. . . where 'cap and trade' has become a political third rail," wrote Dave Wasserman in early 2010.

What was cap-and-trade? It was a plan to reduce greenhouse gas emissions by capping the amount of carbon emissions allowed by various businesses and then allowing businesses who emitted less than allowed to trade their extra permits to businesses that exceeded their limits. The goal of this system was to create a monetary incentive for businesses to emit less and monetary penalties when they emitted more than allowed.

At least that was the contention of proponents of "cap-and-trade," such as President Obama and the national Democratic Party. According to opponents of cap-and-trade, such as Griffith, the bill would "put electric rates through the roof" and "kill manufacturing jobs." He added: "Anybody who's been in coal country knows that" (Nolan 2010). Griffith's campaign ads and rhetoric "characterized Mr. Boucher's vote as a betrayal of the coal industry and the mining companies that provide much-needed jobs in the district" (Tracy 2010).

The focus on Boucher's cap-and-trade vote helped Griffith whittle down Boucher's early lead in polls (Pershing 2010) and compelled national Republican groups to spend money in the district to erode Boucher's spending advantage over Griffith (Luo and Palmer 2010).

The national money for Griffith fit with his campaign's attempts to nationalize the race in the 9th District. Boucher's vote for the cap-and-trade bill allowed Griffith to connect Boucher with the priorities and leaders of the national Democratic Party. One Griffith ad "features a repeated clip of President Barack Obama professing, 'I love Rick Boucher.' The narrator says: 'Love the Obama Washington agenda? Rick Boucher does. Obama's cap-and-trade plan kills our jobs and raises electricity costs. Boucher helped write it'" (Hester 2010). An ad funded by the National Republican Campaign Committee stated: "Big Numbers. 93. That's the percentage Rick Boucher voted for the Obama agenda . . . If Rick Boucher thinks Obama is right 93 percent of the time, is Rick Boucher still right for Virginia?" (The Hotline 2010).

The voters of Virginia's 9th District apparently decided the answer to that question was no. On election day, Griffith defeated Boucher by a five-point margin that "no one really saw coming" according to Governor McConnell. "The wave just caught him on Election Day," said McDonnell (Meola 2010a). There certainly was a wave in 2010, as Democrats lost sixty-three House seats and their majority in the body.

What caused the wave? One answer that pundits gave was the cap-and-trade bill. The bill was seen as "ideological and intensely out-of-touch" (Douthat 2010) and fed into voters "own perceptions of intrusive government" (Marcus 2010). In particular, the cap-and-trade bill was "reviled outside the bicoastal liberal enclaves" (Krauthammer 2010). But in districts throughout unhyphenated America, the bill "appears—like it or not—to be anti-coal" (Sabato, quoted in Tracy 2010).

Another interpretation of the results in the Boucher-Griffith race is that district's partisanship finally mattered in a House race. The Virginia 9th had started moving toward the Republicans in the 2000 election when George W. Bush won the district. At the presidential level, Bush made gains in the 9th in his re-election bid and John McCain made even more, winning 60% of the vote in the district (Barone and McCutcheon 2011). Democrats could not hold off the district's Republican trend forever.

1 An Urbanized Democratic Party

The defeat of a long-time and seemingly popular incumbent—and the general trend against Democrats in unhyphenated concentrated districts over time and specifically in 2010 (cf. Figure 4.2) begs the question of why districts like the Virginia 9th—where 25% of residents identify their ethnic heritage as American—moved so strongly toward the Republicans. One answer is Democratic attempts to address issues such as climate change through policies such as cap-and-trade. These policies were quite unpopular in unhyphenated concentrated areas which rely on extractive industries as keys to their economy. How unpopular? One state over, in West Virginia, Democratic Governor and Senate candidate Joe Manchin shot a copy of the cap-and-trade bill in a well-received campaign advertisement. Boucher apparently should have shot the cap-and-trade bill, rather than vote for it; Manchin won a close election to the Senate (Adler 2010; Jacobson 2010).

The Democrats moved toward environmentalist positions on issues such as climate change in large part because the party urbanized. That is to say, Democrats have adopted the views of their big city and suburban supporters whose perspective on the environment is that the emergence of climate change requires society to move away from using carbon-based fuel sources such as coal. In southwestern Virginia, coal means jobs and thus, efforts to limit the use of coal and fossil fuels are seen as a negative.

The urbanized perspective of the contemporary Democratic Party is not limited to issues around climate change. Guns are another set of issues where the Democratic perspective is urban. In urbanized America, guns are used by criminals and should only be used to prevent crime. In unhyphenated America, a more typical citizen will use guns for sporting activities like hunting and target practice—sometimes on bills supported by Democrats.

One can also see the urbanized perspective of the contemporary Democratic Party on issues of sex and sexuality. Urbanized America is generally supportive of concepts such as feminism, reproductive rights, and gay rights. Small towns, which are of course at the heart of unhyphenated America, have tended to be reticent about these changes and have opposed abortion and gay rights. Instead, these regions have retained their traditionalist views on these issues, often correlated with higher levels of church attendance and evangelicalism.

This urbanized Democratic Party has led to gains in urban and suburban regions across the country. But the tradeoff for Democrats has been losses in rural and small-town areas such as unhyphenated America. How much has its contemporary urbanized perspective hurt the Democrats in unhyphenated America? I explore that question in the rest of this chapter, examining how conservative unhyphenated concentrated regions stand on issues of sexuality, guns, and the environment.

2 God, Guns, and the Environment and the Politics of Unhyphenated America

The term "God, guns, and gays" refers to the political formula employed by modern-day Republicans to use what are described as social issues to win the votes of rural and blue-collar whites (cf. Baumgardner 2004; Gelman 2010; Norris and Inglehart 2006; Rozell and Wilcox 1995). The Appalachias and the highland South are regions known for their concentrations of blue-collar whites, their devotion to Protestant Christianity (Lieberson 1985; Lieberson and Waters 1989), and their reliance on manufacturing and extractive industries to provide a high share of the region's employment (Eller 2007).

In this chapter, I explore if that political formula has greater purchase in regions with large concentrations of unhyphenated American voters by studying public opinion on issues surrounding sexual morality and guns. The example of Morgan Griffith successfully attacking Rick Boucher for his support of the cap-and-trade bill shows that environmental issues may also be particularly salient in unhyphenated America.

In the previous two chapters, I examined the electoral shifts of regions with concentrations of those who identify their ethnicity as American. I found there is a long-term and durable shift in voting patterns in the Appalachias and the upper South to the Republican Party in both presidential and US House elections. But as noted in those chapters, the electoral analysis leaves open the question of what is motivating voters in unhyphenated America to move towards the Republican Party and away from the Democrats. Public opinion data provides the means to try to assess why such a move has happened in the region in recent generations.

The case study of the US House race in the 9th District of Virginia in 2010 helps shape a hypothesis that regions with concentrations of unhyphenated Americans possess conservative views on social and environmental issues. The high levels of devotion to Protestant churches, the rural character of the region, and the importance of extractive industries for the region's economic well-being should produce more conservative views on issues around abortion, gay rights (God), gun rights (guns), and the environment (glacier melting).

As noted in Chapter 2, the shift in the highland South to the Republicans stands in contrast to the classically defined Southern Republican realignment due to its time frame. The Southern Republican realignment happened between the 1960s and the 1990s (Black and Black 1989, 1992, 2002; McKee 2010). The shift in unhyphenated America happened from the 1990s to the 2010s and accelerated in the last half of this time period, in particular during the presidencies of Barack Obama and Donald Trump. The different timelines suggest that the issues that drove the Southern Republican realignment do not do a good job of explaining the shift in the highland South.

What issues became more prominent in American politics from the 1990s through the 2010s that were less prevalent in the 1960s to the 1990s? One answer is what can be defined as moral issues. Issues such as gay marriage and abortion have increased in salience since the 1980s, as a result of the successes of the gay rights and feminist movements, as well as shifts in sexual behavior and perceptions of gender roles. The traditionalistic views of the Republican Party would likely attract not only those who possess a traditional view of their ancestry, but also those concentrated in regions of the country with high levels of religious observance and evangelical belief.

In addition, the Appalachias are known for their high levels of gun ownership, a tradition of a sense of military obligation, and high levels of hunting (Singer 2018; Webb 2004). As such, there is good reason to think that residents of the Appalachias and the highland South would be more conservative on issues of abortion, gay rights, and gun ownership.

Environmental issues have shifted in the last political generation. Democrats, led by former Vice President Al Gore, have proposed various methods to address the problem of climate change, mostly through increasing the cost of carbon-intensive energy sources. Coal-producing regions, such as the Appalachias, have regarded these proposals as "an attack on their right to economic opportunity, their role in the national division of labor, their cultural identity as rural Americans, and their moral worth" (Lewin 2019, 51–52). From this conclusion, one can see why Democrats like Rich Boucher have lost popularity in the region, and why Joe Manchin felt compelled to shoot his party's proposal to regulate carbon emissions.

As noted, these three sets of issues tend to reflect the shift in the Democratic Party in recent generations to reflect the views of the urban and urbane. Changes in attitudes toward feminism, sex, and sexuality have brought issues such as abortion and gay rights to the fore in recent generations and the Democratic Party has embraced the liberal (and urban) positions on these issues. And that shift toward the views of the urban and urbane has given Republicans the opportunity to move toward the views of small-town and rural voters on these issues, in particular embracing the views of conservative Christians. Regions with concentrations of unhyphenated Americans, which are centered in small towns and rural areas and which have greater levels of religiosity that other regions of the country, can be expected to have opinions closer to Republicans than Democrats on these issues.

In this chapter, I examine the shape of public opinion in unhyphenated concentrated parts of the country on issues of God, guns, and gays. I also discuss issues of the environment (glacier melting). As noted, these regions vote strongly for Republican candidates, and it is thus likely that voters in this region share the conservative views of their favored candidates. As a result, it is worth comparing the views of unhyphenated Americans not to the rest of the country, but to other conservative areas. That moves the question from whether unhyphenated America is conservative (it undoubtedly is) to how conservative is unhyphenated America.

To do this, I compare the opinions of those who live in regions with concentrations of American ethnic identifiers to those of residents of other areas known for their support of Republican candidates. My expectation is that the views of residents of unhyphenated concentrated areas will be more conservative on social and environmental issues than those of residents of other Republican-leaning areas.

3 The Conservatism and Republicanism of Unhyphenated America

As shown in Chapters 3 and 4, unhyphenated America is noted for its contemporary loyalty to the Republican Party and its candidates. It is safe to assume, then, that voters in this region share some, and probably most, of the conservative views of contemporary Republican candidates.

To provide a more reasonable test of the distinctiveness of political opinion on issues of sexuality, guns, and the environment, I measure public opinion in regions known for their support of the contemporary Republican Party—the South (defined as the eleven states who joined the Confederacy) and Red States (defined as the states that voted for the Republican presidential nominee in every election from 2008 to 2020).[23] This enables a comparison of public opinion in unhyphenated America not with the rest of the country—which is less conservative—but with regions known for their conservatism and preference for Republican candidates.

The results presented in Chapters 3 and 4 showed that there are distinctly different voting patterns in presidential and congressional elections in regions with large concentrations of American ethnic identifiers. In particular, they revealed that voters in this region tend to favor Republican candidates and that the region's Republican vote share has grown in the twenty-first century. Here, I assess whether these pro-Republican views are also visible in public opinion data. The data used here is from the CES Cumulative File. The Cooperative Election Study (CES) is a biennial political science survey of the American electorate, conducted by YouGov. YouGov partners with individual political science departments or institutes to have each write their own module of the survey for private use. Collectively, they create a set of common questions that are available publicly. The survey is thus very large,[24] and since it has been conducted in the fall of every even-numbered year since 2006, it allows an examination of shifts in option across time.

Because the definition of unhyphenated Americans presumes that they are white, I limited my analysis to white respondents across all measures. I then calculated the difference between the views of those who live in each of the pro-Republican regions under study and that of the national sample.[25]

My analysis begins by focusing on broad and partisan aspects of public opinion. Figure 5.1 shows the results for party identification and ideology. The partisan data in panels A and B show that at the beginning of the timeline residents of unhyphenated concentrated counties were less likely to identify as Republicans and more likely to identify as Democrats than whites who live in the South or in

---

23 There is overlap between some of the South and Red States (Texas, Arkansas, Louisiana, Mississippi, Alabama, Tennessee, and South Carolina). There is no overlap with unhyphenated concentrated regions; I excluded unhyphenated concentrated counties from the South and Red States.

24 Size is a big reason for using the CES instead of other surveys such as the American National Election Study or the National Annenberg Election Survey. The CES has samples that range from 36,500 in 2006 to 64,600 in 2022, much larger than other studies. Unhyphenated concentrated regions make up just 5.2% of the US population, so the large sample size of the CES allows for a meaningful number of respondents from these regions, reducing the bands of confidence intervals in analysis of the subsample population.

25 For example, in 2022, 47.3% of residents of unhyphenated concentrated counties identified as Republicans. Nationally, 35.8% did. The difference is 11.5%, and that is what is reported in the results below (see Figure 5.1, panel a).

Red States.[26] That changes sharply through the 2010s as residents of unhyphenated concentrated counties become much more Republican (and less Democratic) than whites across the nation. This sharp move toward the Republicans (and away from the Democrats) is not mirrored in the other Republican-leaning regions under study. There is little shift in party identification there, and what movement exists is away from the Republicans (and toward the Democrats).

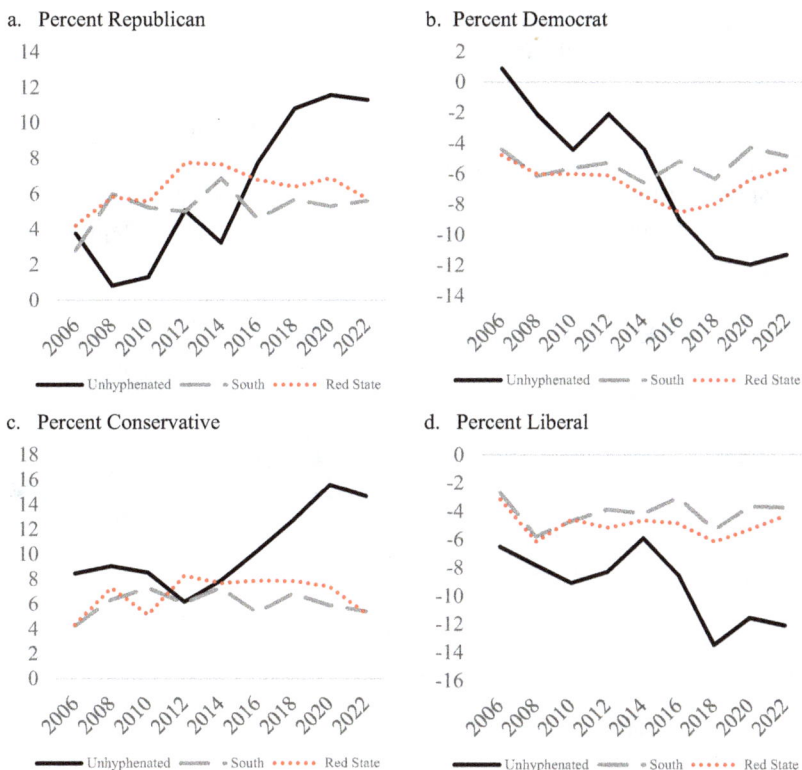

a. Percent Republican

b. Percent Democrat

c. Percent Conservative

d. Percent Liberal

Figure 5.1: Party Identification and Ideology, Difference from National Sample, 2006–2022.[27]

---

26 The CES asks independents to which party they are more likely to lean. I included these leaners with partisans, as the voting behavior of these independents mirrors partisans (Keith et al. 1992).

27 The following applies to Figures 5.1 through 5.3: values were calculated by the author and reflect the difference between opinions in the region mentioned and the national sample. Responses are limited to white respondents. Data come from the CES Cumulative File. The South is defined as the eleven states that joined the Confederacy. Red states are those won by the GOP presidential nominee in 2008, 2012, 2016, 2020, and 2024.

Panels C and D show that residents of unhyphenated concentrated areas have grown more conservative and less liberal in their ideology, particularly in comparison to residents of the South and of Red States.[28] Again, in the other Republican-leaning regions, ideology remains relatively steady over time. But in unhyphenated concentrated regions, respondents in 2012 were 6% more likely to identify as conservative than the national sample of whites. By 2020, that has grown to 15% more likely to identify as conservative. Similarly, residents of unhyphenated America went from being 6% less liberal than the national sample of whites in 2014 to 13% less liberal just four years later in 2018.

Figure 5.2 shows the results for vote intentions. Panel A looks at presidential elections and Panel B looks at House elections. Both have a similar pattern. Respondents who live in unhyphenated concentrated regions become more likely to vote for Republicans across the 2010s and by the end of the decade, this levels out but at a rate that is more strongly Republican than even the other Republican-leaning regions under study here.

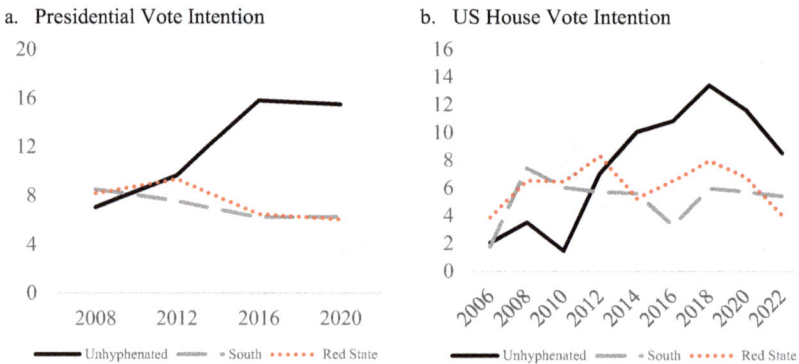

a. Presidential Vote Intention
b. US House Vote Intention

Figure 5.2: Vote Intention, Difference from National Sample, 2006–2022.

Figure 5.3 shows two general political variables—presidential approval and retrospective evaluation of the economy. Both variables are contingent on an individual's view of the president; these views are inherently partisan and thus shift when the president's party changes. To account for this, I transformed these results so

---

28 The CES questionnaire asks respondents if they are very liberal, liberal, moderate, conservative, or very conservative. For these results, I collapsed the very conservative and conservative answers into a single measure, and did the same for very liberal and liberal.

that positive values are always the pro-Republican position.[29] The presidential approval variable indicates very similar views between residents of unhyphenated America and those who live in other pro-Republican regions throughout the first half of the timeline. This shifts abruptly in 2016 as unhyphenated America moves against President Obama and then toward President Trump in 2018 and 2020. Again, the other two Republican-leaning regions stay mostly stable in their opinion with a slight shift in a Democratic direction.

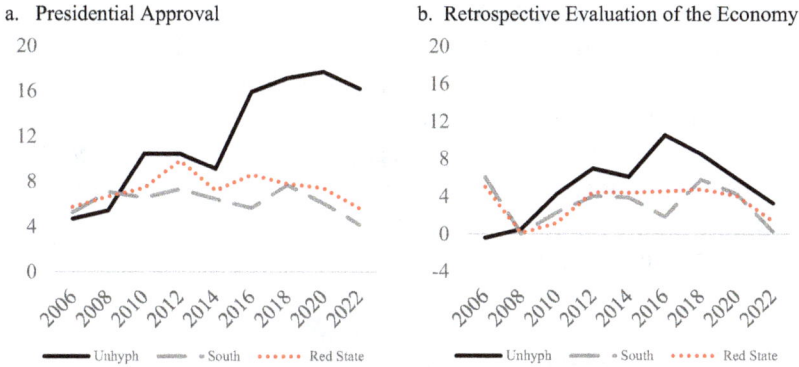

a. Presidential Approval   b. Retrospective Evaluation of the Economy

Figure 5.3: Political Variables, Difference from National Sample, 2006–2022 (Scaled so Pro-Republican Views are Positive).
Note: Values are transformed so that positive values reflect pro-Republican views. So, for the years when Obama and Biden were president (2010, 2012, 2014, 2016, 2022), I took the absolute value of the difference between opinions on these questions in these Republican-leaning regions and the national sample of whites.

The results for retrospective economic evaluation are different from the other results in this section. In 2006, unhyphenated America is less favorable to the economy during a Republican presidency than the other two regions under study. But over the next decade, economic opinions in counties with concentrations of American ethnic identifiers moves more rapidly in a Republican direction than the other regions. Then, after a peak in 2016, opinions in unhyphenated America shift back toward the other Republican regions. And this shift holds up as the party of the president changes between 2020 and 2022. The pattern is unique compared to the other survey responses.

---

29 In the years in which a Democrat was president, I took the absolute value of the difference between opinions on these questions in these Republican-leaning regions and the national sample of whites.

Overall, these data show that at the beginning of the timeline, opinions in unhyphenated America tended to favor Republicans, but at similar levels to the two other Republican-leaning regions under study. But over the 2010s, for nearly all of these questions, opinions in unhyphenated America moved swiftly in a Republican direction. Residents of counties with concentrations of American ethnic identifiers were more likely to identify and vote as Republicans and see themselves as conservatives. Notably, these shifts were happening at a time when residents of Red States and the South held steady in a set of views that are pro-Republican, but moderately so. The shift in unhyphenated America was distinct to that region, even compared with other regions that favor Republicans.

The one area where there is a different pattern is economic evaluations. There the pre-Republican shift of opinion in the region was arrested in the Trump Administration and continued through Joe Biden's term in office. This raises the possibility that economic issues work differently from other issues in unhyphenated America.

These results provide confirmation that the Republican shift in the region seen in the election data presented in Chapters 3 and 4 is also found in the individual-level public opinion data presented above. They also lead to the question of what is causing the pro-Republican attitudes and shift in the region. The rest of the chapter explores whether attitudes on moral and environmental issues are a large part of the cause.

4 Opinions on Issues of Morality, Guns, and the Environment

The results presented above show that in public opinion, just as in voting patterns, unhyphenated America not only supports Republican candidates and conservatism, but does so at much stronger rates than even other regions noted for their conservatism and support of Republican candidates. I have hypothesized that one important reason for this behavior is the opinion of residents of unhyphenated concentrated regions on social and environmental issues.

The CES survey not only asks respondents about their party identification, ideology, and vote choice preferences; it also asks a number of detailed issue questions. This is done in the yearly CES survey, each of which has an extensive questionnaire and a wide number of questions that solicit the policy views of respondents. As the issues and the policy proposals to address these issues change, so do the questions asked. I examined each individual year's CES from 2006 to 2022 and identified all of the questions that focused on issues of social morality, gun policy, and environmental issues.[30] As I did in the previous section, I limited the opinions listed to white respondents since unhyphenated Americans are, by definition, white.

I have focused on two major questions. Does unhyphenated America have a set of views on social and environmental issues that are distinct from those of the other conservative regions under study here? Second, has opinion on these issues shifted across the time period under study?

To answer the first question, I again compare opinion in unhyphenated America not with national opinion (it is almost universally more conservative) but with the South and Red States, as I did above. This enables an assessment of whether opinions in unhyphenated America are distinctly conservative on these issues, or at a similar level of conservativism to other Republican-leaning regions. To answer the second question, I look at results across time. The CES has been in operation since 2006, and while the questions differ, patterns are visible over time. Table 5.1 presents the results from the questions asked in the CES over the years about abortion. Again, the results are the difference between opinion in that region and national opinion on the same question. For each question, the region that is furthest away from national opinion is shaded. Bold indicates a response where the difference from national opinion is statistically significant.

The table reveals clear and unidirectional differences between the views of unhyphenated America and the other two regions of Republican-leaning voters on key questions about abortion. These are clearest on the questions asked most often. One asks if "by law, women should be able to obtain an abortion." On that issue, residents of unhyphenated concentrated counties are between 11.6% and 20.2% more opposed to this policy than the national sample. On the idea that "abortion should never be permitted," unhyphenated America is 6.5% to 11.5% more supportive of this idea than the national sample. Notably, these numbers are more conservative than those for the South and for Red States. Respondents from those two regions offer more conservative responses than the national sample across both questions and across the different years of the survey. But universally, the responses are not as far from the national opinion as those in unhyphenated America.

This pattern holds up on the various issues of abortion policy asked about by the CES over the years. Residents of unhyphenated concentrated counties are more likely to want to ban late-term abortions, to allow employers to deny abortion coverage in the health insurance they provide employees, and to prohibit the

---

30 The CES uses different issue questions each year, so I cannot compare results across time in the same manner I did in Figures 5.1–5.3.

Table 5.1: Differences in Regional Opinion from National Sample, Abortion.[31]

		2006	2008	2010	2012	2014	2016	2018	2020	2022
Abortion should never be permitted	Unhyphenated	5.7	9.1	7.0	6.5		8.7		11.5	7.3
	South	0.7	1.9	0.3	0.6		1.3		1.8	1.7
	Red States	2.4	3.4	3.3	2.3		2.7		2.8	1.6
Abortion allowed by choice	Unhyphenated	−16.7	−16.2	−11.6	−17.6	−16.9	−20.1	−20.2	−19.6	−14.4
	South	−2.5	−4.8	−2.9	−3.8	−4.6	−2.8	−4.5	−4.7	−6.1
	Red States	−6.8	−8.4	−5.1	−6.7	−8.1	−7.7	−7.6	−7.8	−6.6
Ban late term abortions	Unhyphenated	10.0								
	South	1.7								
	Red States	4.6								
Birth control exception	Unhyphenated				1.2	5.1				
	South				4.1	6.4				
	Red States				5.7	7.5				
Employers can decline abortion insurance	Unhyphenated					10.5	13.1	14.9	14.3	13.4
	South					6.4	4.7	6.1	5.1	5.1
	Red States					7.9	8.4	7.7	7.6	5.8
Prohibit government funds for abortion	Unhyphenated					10.9	13.3	16.2	14.7	12.2
	South					6.2	4.1	5.9	5.0	5.5
	Red States					7.4	7.6	6.9	6.9	5.1
Fund stem cell research	Unhyphenated	−11.9	−13.6	−11.6						
	South	−2.4	−3.6	−2.9						
	Red States	−4.7	−5.4	−5.1						

Note: Shaded values are those most distant from the national average among the three Republican-leaning regions. Bolded entries are statistically significant at the p < .05 level.

use of government for abortion. Those who live in counties with concentrations of American ethnic identifiers hold stronger anti-abortion views than not just the national sample, but also the samples of residents of the two other Republican-leaning regions under study. Those in unhyphenated concentrated counties are

---

31 The following applies to Tables 5.1 through 5.5: values are calculated by the author and reflect the difference between opinions in the region mentioned and the national sample. Data come from the CES Common Content for each individual year. The South is defined as the eleven states that joined the Confederacy. Red states are those won by the GOP presidential nominee in 2008, 2012, 2016, 2020, and 2024.

also less likely to support funding stem cell research than the national sample or those who live in the South or in Red States.

Table 5.2 shows opinions on issues around gay rights. Although the CES asked fewer questions about this issue than it did about abortion, the same patterns that we saw in Table 5.1 appear. Opinions among residents of unhyphenated American concentrated counties are much more conservative than those of the national sample. Residents there hold opinions that are 10.5% to 18.9% more conservative than the national sample on their support of a constitutional amendment to ban gay marriage, allowing gays to serve openly in the US military, ending the military's "don't ask, don't tell" policy, and allowing gays and lesbians to marry. Again, we see that opinions in the South and in Red States are more conservative than in the national sample, but opinions in unhyphenated concentrated regions are even more so.

Table 5.2: Differences in Regional Opinion from National Sample, Gay Rights.

		2006	2008	2010	2012	2014	2016	2018	2020	2022
Amendment to ban gay marriage	Unhyphenated		17.3	15.6						
	South		5.2	2.7						
	Red States		6.8	6.4						
Allow gays to serve openly in military	Unhyphenated				−10.5					
	South				−4.8					
	Red States				−5.5					
End "don't ask, don't tell"	Unhyphenated				−12.5					
	South				−5.4					
	Red States				−6.2					
Allow gays & lesbians to marry	Unhyphenated					−18.9	−18.5			
	South					−6.4	−4.4			
	Red States					−7.2	−7.0			

Note: Shaded values are those most distant from the national average among the three Republican-leaning regions. Bolded entries are statistically significant at the $p < .05$ level.

Table 5.3 examines issues around guns. The results show that the difference in opinion between unhyphenated America and the national sample is not as sharp as it is on abortion and gay rights. But the pattern still exists—opinions in counties with outsized numbers of American ethnic identifiers are more conservative than the national sample. For example, residents of unhyphenated concentrated counties are 9.6% less likely to say that gun laws should be more strict than the national sample in both 2010 and in 2012. That is a larger difference than observed in the South and in the Red States. That pattern is not as strong on guns as it is on gay rights or abortion—there are three examples in the table where Red States hold more conservative views than unhyphenated concentrated counties. But with that small handful of exceptions noted, the views of unhyphenated concentrated areas are much more conservative in nearly all of the issues and years under study.

Table 5.3: Differences in Regional Opinion from National Sample, Guns.

		2006	2008	2010	2012	2014	2016	2018	2020	2022
Gun laws should be more strict	Unhyphenated			**-9.6**	**-9.6**					
	South			-2.3	-3.0					
	Red States			**-6.3**	**-7.6**					
Prohibit publishing names of gun owners	Unhyphenated					6.1	4.4	9.5	5.4	8.5
	South					1.8	2.2	2.6	3.1	3.5
	Red States					3.9	5.1	6.0	5.1	4.1
Ban high capacity magazines	Unhyphenated					-7.2				
	South					-4.6				
	Red States					-7.6				
Ban assault rifles	Unhyphenated					-7.2	-9.1		-11.8	-11.8
	South					-4.7	-3.7		-4.0	-3.8
	Red States					-7.7	-9.0		-7.1	-6.0
Legalize concealed-carry permits	Unhyphenated					8.6	11.3	9.5	10.9	11.7
	South					2.8	2.8	2.6	3.0	2.8
	Red States					5.5	6.2	6.0	6.2	5.1
Background checks	Unhyphenated						-3.5	-2.4		-4.0
	South						-0.5	-0.7		-1.0
	Red States						-3.0	-2.7		-2.3
Funds to encourage states to take guns	Unhyphenated									-12.8
	South									-4.2
	Red States									-6.9
Allow teachers to carry guns	Unhyphenated									12.2
	South									4.7
	Red States									6.8

Note: Shaded values are those most distant from the national average among the three Republican-leaning regions. Bolded entries are statistically significant at the $p < .05$ level.

The final two tables in this section show opinions on general issues about the environment (Table 5.4) and about climate change specifically (Table 5.5). They again show a similar pattern to the previous three tables—views of those who live in unhyphenated concentrated counties are more conservative than those who live in the other two Republican-leaning regions under study. There are again a handful of exceptions, but the pattern is the same across environmental issues and climate change as we saw for abortion, gay rights, and guns. Unhyphenated America is more conservative than the country as a whole and more conservative than other regions that also vote Republican.

Table 5.4: Regional Public Opinion, the Environment.

		2006	2008	2010	2012	2014	2016	2018	2020	2022
More important to protect environment than jobs	Unhyphenated	−6.1	−9.1	−5.3	−6.4					
	South	1.4	−2.1	−2.1	−2.9					
	Red States	−1.8	−4.0	−3.5	−4.4					
Support Keystone Pipeline	Unhyphenated				3.7			14.1		
	South				2.4			6.0		
	Red States				3.5			6.2		
EPA should regulate CO2 emissions	Unhyphenated					−4.4	−8.7	−10.6	−8.8	−10.7
	South					−4.2	−2.0	−3.0	−3.4	−2.5
	Red States					−7.5	−6.5	−5.8	−5.9	−5.0
Raise fuel efficiency standards	Unhyphenated					0.7	−3.0	3.4	−3.7	−5.5
	South					−2.7	−1.7	2.0	−2.7	−2.1
	Red States					−4.0	−4.1	1.8	−3.8	−3.3
Minimum levels of renewable fuels	Unhyphenated					−9.0	−9.5	−9.8	−10.6	−11.4
	South					−3.6	−2.3	−3.8	−4.0	−3.8
	Red States					−5.3	−5.2	−6.6	−5.4	−4.3
Strengthen Clear Air Act enforcement	Unhyphenated					−10.9	−12.5	−14.6	−9.8	−10.9
	South					−3.4	−2.7	−4.0	−4.3	−3.4
	Red States					−6.6	−5.6	−7.1	−6.5	−5.1
Increase fossil fuel production & exports	Unhyphenated									7.7
	South									4.0
	Red States									3.5
Federal agencies to buy clean energy	Unhyphenated									−11.8
	South									−3.6
	Red States									−4.5

Table 5.4 (continued)

		2006	2008	2010	2012	2014	2016	2018	2020	2022
Repeal Clean Power Plan rules	Unhyphenated							14.4	10.6	
	South							5.8	3.1	
	Red States							6.0	3.8	

Note: Shaded values are those most distant from the national average among the three Republican-leaning regions. Bolded entries are statistically significant at the p < .05 level.

Table 5.5: Differences in Regional Opinion from National Sample, Climate Change.

		2006	2008	2010	2012	2014	2016	2018	2020	2022
Climate change has been established. Immediate action is necessary	Unhyphenated	−10.8		−3.9	−6.5					−13.3
	South	−3.4		−2.7	−2.4					−4.1
	Red States	−4.2		−5.9	−4.3					−5.2
Favor carbon tax	Unhyphenated		−8.1							
	South		−1.6							
	Red States		−3.0							
Withdraw/ rejoin Paris Climate Agreement	Unhyphenated							12.9	11.5	−13.2
	South							6.6	5.5	−4.5
	Red States							6.8	6.6	−5.0

Note: Shaded values are those most distant from the national average among the three Republican-leaning regions. Bolded entries are statistically significant at the p < .05 level.

There is one key difference between the results on environmental issues and those on abortion, gay rights, and guns. Opinions on the environment seem to be growing more distinct from national opinion over time. The clearest example of this is the question about supporting the Keystone Pipeline. In 2012, residents of unhyphenated concentrated counties were more supportive of this policy than the national sample but were only 3.7% more supportive than the national sample. In 2018, just six years later, unhyphenated America was 14.1% more supportive than the national sample.

One can see the increasing conservatism of residents of unhyphenated concentrated counties in opinions on policies such as whether the EPA should regulate carbon dioxide emissions and requiring car companies to raise fuel efficiency standards. On both of those issues, respondents in 2014 were relatively close to the national sample. They then diverged from national opinion more strongly in the subsequent years of the survey.

The evidence for this claim is limited though. The CES only asked one question about environmental issues in 2006 through 2010, and the modest divergence between unhyphenated American and the national sample may be a specific response to that particular question. On the question of whether climate change has been established and requires immediate action, there is a large divergence between unhyphenated America and the national sample in 2006 though that divergence declined sharply when the question was asked again in 2010.

Furthermore, the evidence of divergence across time seen in relation to some of the environmental issues is not observed on issues of abortion, gay rights, or gun policy. Results on each of these issues seem to be relatively stable across the 2006 to 2022 time period. Some occasional difference is observable across time, but for the most part, the year-to-year differences in the questions under study seem to be mostly noise.

Looking over the various measures of public opinion in Tables 5.1 through 5.5, one finds that residents of unhyphenated concentrated regions express more conservative views on a number of different issues than do comparatively similarly conservative and Republican regions. This applies to all issues under review but is strongest on issues of abortion and gay rights.

5 Multivariate Tests

The bivariate findings presented so far exhibit a broadly consistent pattern: residents of unhyphenated concentrated counties are more conservative in their opinions on issues of abortion, gay rights, guns, and the environment and climate change than not just the rest of the country as a whole, but also other Republican-leaning regions in particular.

But these findings do not prove that the reason behind them is the political geography or culture of unhyphenated America. As noted, unhyphenated Americans are not just a random collection of people who have a particular ethnic identification. They are concentrated in the upper South in the Appalachias, are more Protestant than the country as a whole, and less likely to have graduated from college. And as noted throughout this book and previously in this chapter, this region has moved sharply toward the Republicans in recent decades. It is therefore possible that any one of these factors, not just the presence of large numbers of unhyphenated Americans, may explain why these regions have more conservative opinions than other regions. Concentrations of unhyphenated Americans may thus be correlated with, but incidental to, the real reason for conservative opinions in the region.

The way to test such potential spurious correlations is through a multivariate test. To ascertain the relationship between ancestry, geography, and demography, I created a series of multivariate logistic regression models. If the presence of un-hyphenated Americans in a county is a factor that explains conservative opinions in the region, then it will be a significant factor controlling for other correlated variables. If the correlation is spurious, then one of the other variables will account for the shift, and the unhyphenated American variables will not be significant.

For my dependent variables, I focused on one of the public opinion questions that were used in each survey year from each of the three elements identified in the title of this chapter—God (social issues), guns, and glacier melting (then environment). For consistency, I tried to use a question that was asked in multiple years.

For social issues, I use the question on whether to "always allow a woman to obtain an abortion as a matter of choice." A variant of that question was asked in every single CES survey. For guns, no questions about the issue were asked in 2006 or in 2008. For 2010, I examined the question "In general, do you feel that the laws covering the sale of firearms should be more strict?" That question was also asked in 2012, but not asked after that. Instead, the CES started asking respondents if they supported a number of specific policies about guns, including whether to "Make it easier for people to obtain a concealed-carry gun permit." That question was asked in each version of the survey from 2014 to 2022 and I use it for each of these years. For the environment, I examine responses to the question of whether it is "much more important to protect environment even if costs some jobs or otherwise reduces our standard of living." This question was used in surveys from 2006 through 2012. From 2014 to 2022, I examine responses to the policy question of whether to "Give the Environmental Protection Agency power to regulate carbon dioxide emissions."

Each is a dichotomous variable, and I coded the response so that the more conservative option is coded as 1 and the more liberal option is coded as 0.[32] I conducted a separate logistic regression for each question in each survey year in which it was asked. As in the tables above, results were limited to white respondents.

---

[32] This eases interpretation and comparison across the four questions. On the "abortion allowed by choice" statement, agreement is the liberal position and is thus coded as a 0; disagreement is coded as 1. On "urge more concealed carry permits," support is conservative and coded as 1; opposition is 0. On one of the gun measures ("gun laws should be more strict") and the two environmental measures ("protect environment over jobs" and "EPA should regulate CO2 emissions") disagreement is conservative, so support is coded as 0; opposition is 1.

The independent variables are the same in all models and include a number of well-known correlates of public opinion based on each respondent's answers to survey questions. These start with *party identification*, which is on a seven-point scale with Republican responses being the higher numbers. The CES used a five-point scale to ask about *ideology*, with conservative answers higher. There are also demographic variables for *age*,[33] gender (*woman*), education (a dichotomous variable for *has a bachelor's degree*), and race (*white*), income (two dichotomous variables: *income under $30,000* and *income above $100,000*), and whether the respondent would describe themselves "as a 'born-again' or evangelical Christian."[34]

Of course, the key independent variables are those that are the focus of the present research—the geographic region in which the respondent lives. I created dichotomous variables for *Unhyphenated Concentrated*, the *South*, and *Red State*. Because of the overlap between the South and Red States, the three variables cannot be placed in the same equation; consequently separate equations for each of the three regions, and for all three survey years, were created.

Because my interest is in whether the conservatism of these Republican-leaning regions is attributable to some element of their political geography, or due to other correlated factors, such as socioeconomic status or partisanship, I again compare the differences between the three conservative regions under study. To do this, I calculated the marginal effects of each of the three regions and present those in Table 5.6.[35] These marginal effects are the increased change that a respondent in an unhyphenated concentrated county, the South, or a red state give the conservative response on that issue question, controlling for all other independent variables. As in the previous tables, the marginal effect appears in bold when the coefficient is significant.[36] Furthermore, regions that were most different from the alternative, which is the nation as a whole, have been shaded.

Table 5.6 begins with the results for the question of whether abortion should "be allowed by choice." On this issue, residents of unhyphenated America are decidedly more conservative than the rest of the county.[37] The marginal effects are

---

33 The CES asks respondents for their birth year, allowing the calculation of each respondent's age. Age is a continuous, rather than categorical, variable.

34 I chose dichotomous variables for these demographic measures for education, income, and religiosity because it preserves the assumption of linearity.

35 These figures were calculated using the "margins" command in Stata. The dichotomous variables were held at their most common response; party identification, ideology, and age are held at their mean.

36 Again, at the p < .05 level.

37 Notably, the coefficient for the South is negative for seven of the years under study and negative and significant for six of these years. The effect of region in the rest of the South pushes its

Table 5.6: Marginal Effects of Logit Regressions, Issue Opinions, 2006–2022.

		2006	2008	2010	2012	2014	2016	2018	2020	2022
God (Social Issues)										
Abortion allowed by choice	Unhyphenated	.086	.077	.088	.093	.094	.089	.096	.101	.047
	South	-.038	.004	-.063	-.034	-.024	-.034	-.036	-.013	.013
	Red States	.029	.055	.029	.003	.034	.014	.021	.022	.044
Guns										
Guns laws should be more strict	Unhyphenated			.002	-.007					
	South			-.024	-.008					
	Red States			-.007	.007					
Urge more concealed-carry permits	Unhyphenated					.070	.027	.016	.017	.032
	South					-.017	.022	-.019	-.003	-.011
	Red States					.011	.036	.021	.025	.020
Glacier Melting (The Environment)										
Protect environment over jobs	Unhyphenated	-005	.054	.021	.028					
	South	.006	-.009	-.014	.005					
	Red States	-.002	.007	-.001	.010					
EPA should regulate CO2 emissions	Unhyphenated					.029	.066	.029	.000	.006
	South					-.008	-.021	-.028	-.015	-.033
	Red States					035	.044	.011	.024	.016

Note: Values are marginal effects for the coefficient for each regional dichotomous variable. Shaded values are those most distant from the national average among the three Republican-leaning regions. Bolded entries are statistically significant at the p < .05 level.

The dependent variables for abortion and the environment were reversed so that the more conservative choice—opposition to these proposals—is coded as 1 and the liberal choice is coded as 0. This allows for easier comparison across all of the measures.

Independent variables in these models include party identification, ideology, age, gender, having earned a bachelor's degree, reporting an annual family income under $30,00, reporting an annual income of over $100,000, and identifying oneself as an "evangelical" Christian.

significant for every year in the unhyphenated row and they are the strongest effect among the three regions in every year under study. The multivariate test shows there is a regional effect here, and one that goes beyond the Republican,

white residents towards a more pro-choice position, *ceteris paribus*. Of course, on many of the other variables—party identification, ideology, evangelical status—Southern whites are more likely correlated with anti-abortion views, which pushes the region overall to more conservative views on the issue (see Table 5.1).

the conservative, or the evangelical nature of the unhyphenated concentrated region. The conservative responses on abortion in counties with concentrations of American ethnic identifiers seen in Table 5.1 reflects a distinct set of opinions in that region.

That is not the case on issues related to guns and the environment. On guns, I examined a question on the issue over seven different survey years. Only on one occasion was the coefficient for unhyphenated concentrated counties significant —on urging more concealed-carry permits in 2014. And only on two occasions was the largest marginal effect recorded in unhyphenated concentrated counties. On two occasions, the largest marginal effect was in the South. And on three occasions, it was in the Red States.

On the environment, the coefficient for unhyphenated America is significant in only two of the nine years under study. The effect is strongest in unhyphenated concentrated counties on five separate occasions, but statistically significant in only two of those years. Similar results are visible for the other two Republican-leaning regions under study. The South is significant only in 2022 (though negatively significant). Red States have the largest effect only twice (2014 and 2020) and are significant on three occasions.

The pattern for gun and environmental policy suggests that region has some effect on the views of individuals, but the effect is less strong and less consistent than for the abortion measures. The strongest regional effects on environmental views come from residing in unhyphenated concentrated counties, but the effect is muted. It appears that the conservatism of unhyphenated America on issues of guns and the environment seen in the bivariate data in Tables 5.4 and 5.5 is primarily driven by the region's support for Republicans and ideological conservatism. Figure 5.1 shows that Republican Party identification and conservatism grew in regions with concentrations of American ethnic identifiers from 2006 to 2022 with larger increases from 2014 to 2022.

Opinions in unhyphenated America on issues of guns and the environment are thus clearly conservative, but not distinctly so. Opinions there are conservative on these issues because respondents there are conservative and Republican leaning. This is distinct from abortion, an issue on which residents of unhyphenated concentrated counties hold distinctly conservative views.

6 Distinct Opinions on Abortion; Partisan Opinions on Guns and the Environment

This chapter turned the focus on the Republican shift in unhyphenated America from election results to public opinion. In Chapters 3 and 4, I found that there was a significant, durable, and seemingly permanent shift in the region toward the Republicans that was present in both presidential and in US House elections. This chapter explored the public opinion basis for this shift.

The initial finding was that unhyphenated concentrated regions began the timeline favoring Republicans, but at a similar rate to two other Republican-leaning regions—the South and Red States. But over the course of the 2010s, Republican Party identification and conservatism grew and became distinct in unhyphenated America. This pattern was also found in vote intentions for presidential and US House elections, as well as in presidential approval. In short, Republican and conservative views grew over time in the region.

The next step was to examine the basis for the conservatism and Republicanism of unhyphenated America, hypothesizing that the region has distinctly conservative opinions on issues surrounding sexual morality, gun policy, and the environment. These views are driven by the region's religiosity, rural character, and dependence on manufacturing and extractive industries as key job sources. Issues surrounding sexuality, gun policy, and the environment have risen in importance since the 1990s and help account for the distinctive time period when unhyphenated America shifted toward the Republicans.

The finding was that opinions in the region are indeed distinctive on these issues. Applying bivariate measures shows that residents of unhyphenated concentrated counties have conservative views on these three categories of issues, and more distinctly conservative views than in the other Republican-leaning regions under study. In multivariate tests, this finding holds up for opinions on abortion. Living in a region with large concentrations of unhyphenated Americans leads to more conservative views on abortion than in other regions, a result that is robust for controls not only for partisanship and ideology, but also for religiosity.

But multivariate tests show that opinions on gun policy and the environment are not as distinct in unhyphenated America. Opinions there on these issues are certainly more conservative than in the rest of the country and even other Republican-leaning regions. But these opinions are driven by the conservatism and Republicanism of the region, not from anything distinct in the region itself.

I focused on three different sets of issues in trying to examine why unhyphenated America had moved toward the Republicans since the mid-1990s. There is some reason to think that opinions on issues surrounding guns and the environment have a distinct role in pushing unhyphenated America toward the Republicans, but this effect is modest. The more important effect in pushing unhyphenated America to the right on the environment and gun policy comes from the effect of these issues as a component of its identification with contemporary conservatism and Republican policy positions.

There is a much clearer effect in relation to abortion, and presumably other social issues such as gay rights, in explaining the shift in unhyphenated America toward the Republicans. As these issues increased in salience in the 1990s and the 2000s, Democrats more unanimously embraced liberal positions on abortion and gay rights. This seems to have played an important role in the region's Republican shift.

This chapter opened with the story of Republican Morgan Griffith successfully attacking Democratic incumbent Rick Boucher for his vote in favor of the Democrat's cap-and-trade bill in the 2010 election. The results shown here indicate why these attacks were successful. Voters in unhyphenated America hold conservative views on issues around the environment and climate change, and Boucher's support for limiting carbon emissions was not an asset in a district that so strongly supports Republican candidates in presidential elections. Boucher seems to have lost in 2010 because he could no longer disentangle his personal reputation with his voters from the reputation of his national party. Unhyphenated America had a specific disregard for Democrats and liberalism in 2010, and Boucher's decision to support his party's policy—and his choice to help shape that policy—hurt him in 2010. Griffin's strategy to drive home Boucher's connection to the national party by emphasizing his opposition to the cap-and-trade bill proved effective in 2010 and helps show why unhyphenated America became unhospitable territory for Democrats after 2010.

Chapter 6
Race and Unhyphenated America

As part of its coverage of the 2008 election, the *New York Times* published a map showing counties where John McCain won a higher share of the vote than George W. Bush won four years earlier. In 2008, the overall electorate favored Barack Obama over McCain by over 7%, shifting 9.6 points from the two-and-a-half point margin that John Kerry trailed Bush in 2004. Despite that large Democratic shift, "22% of the nation's counties voted more Republican" in 2008 than they did in 2004 (Carter et al. 2011).

These counties were not randomly scattered across the country, Instead, blogger Matt Yglesias (2008) noted the distinct pattern of these red trending counties, and the band that runs from southwestern Pennsylvania and then south into West Virginia, eastern Kentucky, Tennessee, northern Alabama, Arkansas, eastern Oklahoma, and the rural parts of north and east Texas. In short, the region was centered in unhyphenated America. Or as Ben Smith of *Politico* noted in quoting an email from one of his readers: "you'll see that the interior south, where Obama could get no traction and almost the only part of the country where people voted more Republican in 2008 is the part of the country dominated by people who describe their ancestry as not German or English or Spanish or Irish but 'American'" (Smith 2008).

Some blogospheric analysis of the "McCain belt" focused on themes discussed already in this book. Clay Risen of *The New Republic* argued the division in the map between the deep and highland South described "a fissured and rapidly changing" South (Risen 2008). Chris Kroom of the Institute for Southern Studies argued that the McCain belt was "clearly not—as some pundits see it—'the South'" (Kroom 2008).

Others examined this map and saw another element at work—race. Yglesias (2008) offered tongue-in-cheek analysis: "[y]ou can see why John McCain's principled stand against higher taxes on the wealthy would have a special resonance in this region. Liberals who thought race had something to do with those appeals should be ashamed of themselves." *Atlantic* blogger Andrew Sullivan followed up quickly on Yglesias's post to write with similar levels of sarcasm, "Ah, yes, Appalachia and Arkansas. Obviously concerned about marginal tax rates for those earning over $250,000 a year, I suppose" (Sullivan 2008).

Underlying both Yglesias's and Sullivan's sarcasm is the implication that this region of the country moved toward the Republicans in 2008 not because of support for McCain's policy agenda—which both bloggers saw as overly solicitous to the demands of the well-off. Instead, they argue that it was something about the

https://doi.org/10.1515/9783111615707-006

2008 Democratic nominee Barack Obama that turned off voters in this region. Yglesias, in particular, is forthright in arguing that Obama lost votes in this region because of his race.

Other contemporary analysts put race at the fore of explanations for the region's move to the right. The most detailed look at the map came from political scientist Eric Oliver of the University of Chicago. Writing on the *Freakonomics* blog, Oliver (2008) found that "the counties where Republican margins grew the largest tended to be predominantly white places in otherwise racially mixed states . . . Historically, the greatest levels of racial violence occurred within white enclaves near larger black populations, particularly when these enclaves are poor and uneducated." In short, race explains the pattern. Or as John Sides wrote about Oliver's post at *The Monkey Cage*, "these results should dispel the idea that with the election of Obama, America has somehow 'transcended' race. Undoubtedly, racism is still pervasive in the United States, but where it appears depends a lot on social context" (Sides 2008).[38]

To this point in the book, the issue of race has sat mainly on the sidelines. In Chapter 2 it was discussed in great detail, noting its importance to the Southern Republican realignment. Both Chapters 1 and 2 noted the relatively small African American population in unhyphenated America, both historically and in the modern day.

The results of the 2008 election suggest that racial attitudes might play a role —possibly an important one—in explaining why regions with concentrations of American ethnic identifiers moved toward the Republicans. In 2008, Barack Obama earned 4.6% more of the national vote than did John Kerry, Obama's predecessor as the Democratic nominee. Outside of places where home state effects altered the results in 2004 and 2008 (e.g. Arizona, Alaska, and Massachusetts), Obama ran ahead of Kerry throughout the country—with the notable exception of unhyphenated America. The nation was rapidly diversifying, as demonstrated by the election of the nation's first African American president. Yet at the same time, here was a not insignificant chunk of the country that was resisting the broader national trend toward diversity and rejection of the nominee of the party of George W. Bush.

Unhyphenated America did not warm to Obama once elected and after he started implementing his policies. As discussed in Chapter 4, Democrats lost heavily in congressional districts with concentrations of American ethnic identi-

---

[38] For a contrary perspective, see Astor (2008), who argues that Obama's poor performance in the Appalachias is because Obama "never spent time in the region getting to know voters" and because coal production declined in the region, which meant Obama's poor performance had more to do "with the decline of coal mining unions than race."

fiers in the 2010 midterm election. In 2016, Donald Trump made bigger gains in unhyphenated America than in any other region of the country (see Figure 3.5).

The elections of Barack Obama in 2008 and Donald Trump in 2016 stand not only as two of the most surprising in American political history, but they also demonstrate the fractured and polarized character of American racial politics. The election of Obama represented a shining example of America's strive to make its ideals that "all men are created equal" a reality. Yet the election of Obama brought race to the fore in American politics in a way that it had never been before and created what political scientist Michael Tesler describes as a "spillover effect." The salience of racial issues became a strong predictor of attitudes on non-racial issues such as health care (Tesler 2012a), economic evaluations (Chen and Mohanty 2017; Wilson and Davis 2018), and the environment (Benegal 2018). In 2016 and again in 2024, Donald Trump was able to both ride the nation's extant racial divisions and exploit the resentments of a significant enough number of voters to win two presidential elections.

Election results and the pattern of racial spillover raise the question of whether attitudes on racial issues serve as a meaningful explanation for the Republican shift in unhyphenated America. Chapter 5 showed that this region has more conservative opinions on issues of abortion, gay rights, gun policy, and climate change than not just the rest of the country, but also other regions known for their support of Republican presidential candidates. This chapter examines if those conservative attitudes apply to issues surrounding race and immigration. It also assesses if opinions on these two categories of issues are diverging in unhyphenated America from the rest of the nation in response to the racialized politics of the Obama and Trump administrations.

1 Race, Racism, and Racial Resentment in Unhyphenated America

As discussed in Chapter 2, the Appalachias and upper South have a distinct history from the rest of the South on racial issues. The hills of the region were not conducive to plantation farming and thus have never had large populations of African Americans, reducing the sociological and political potency of racial threat. This is an important reason why the region was more Republican than the rest of the South before the Southern Republican realignment (Key 1949; Black and Black 2002).

While the low levels of African Americans in the region indicate the region did not react to localized racial threat during or after Jim Crow segregation, there is evidence that the region has long held racially conservative attitudes. For example, Arbour and Teigen (2011, Table 3) find that even before Barack Obama became a national political figure, unhyphenated Americans were less likely to say they would support an African American nominee of their favored political party. In addition, unhyphenated Americans are, by definition, white. Levels of racial resentment, racial stereotyping, and implicit bias against African Americans are higher among whites (Kam and Burge 2018, 2019; Tesler 2016). One would thus expect to find higher levels of racial conservatism in regions with such a large concentration of whites.

The nomination and election of Barack Obama increased the salience of racial issues across the country. The fact that the president—and the nation's most important Democrat—was an African American "made racial attitudes a chronically accessible consideration in mass assessments" of Obama, according to Michael Tesler (2016, 17).

Scholars have found that attitudes of race have spilled over to a large set of issues seemingly unconnected to race (Tesler 2016), on issues such as health care (Henderson and Hillygus 2011; Knowles et al. 2010; Lanford and Quadagno 2016; Grogan and Park 2017), views of the economy (Chen and Mohanty 2017; Wilson and Davis 2018), climate change (Benegal 2018), gay marriage (Tesler 2012b; Vavreck and Enos 2012), the federal response to superstorm Sandy (Sheagley et al. 2017), attitudes toward Michelle Obama (Knuckey and Kim 2016), and voting in congressional elections (Luttig and Motta 2017). Racial spillover has even affected opinions on attitudes about something with "no manifest political content whatsoever"—opinions on President Obama's dog Bo (Tesler 2012c).

The chronic accessibility of race and the "racialization of seemingly nonracial political issues . . . extends beyond [the Obama] presidency" (Enders and Scott 2019, 275). The racialized rhetoric of Trump, in addition to his focus on restricting immigration in both his rhetoric and policies, kept race at the fore for many Americans. Racial attitudes remained a significant predictor of vote choice in the 2018 (Knuckey and Kim 2020) and 2020 elections (Sides et al. 2022). Racial attitudes have also spilled over into reactions to the January 6 attempt by Trump supporters to keep Congress from certifying the legitimate results of the 2020 election (Rhodes and Nteta 2024; Davis and Wilson 2023).

The increased salience of racially based issues is part of the explanation for why unhyphenated Americans moved toward the Republicans in presidential and congressional elections throughout the Obama and Trump years. As such, an examination of these attitudes adds important context to this story of partisan shift.

I examine public opinion in unhyphenated America on race through the study of two specific issues. The first is race, and the most common measure of racial opinion in contemporary political science is the concept of racial resentment. Based on research by Don Kinder and his colleagues and codified as a set of questions in the American National Election Study (ANES), the racial resentment scale attempts to distinguish between those who attribute racial inequalities to structural factors and those who attribute it to individual actions (Kinder and Sanders 1996; Kam and Burge 2018). As such, this measure tries to distinguish what some scholars call modern (McConahay 1986), symbolic (Kinder and Sears 1981; Sears 1988), cultural (Kinder 2013), or laissez-faire racism (Bobo et al. 1997) from "old fashioned racism" (Bobo and Kluegel 1997; Kinder 2013). The measure was adapted as the amount of what is called "old fashioned racism" declined to microscopic levels of public opinion (Schuman et al. 1997), and politicians adopted new coded rhetoric to invoke racial themes without being openly racist (Knuckey and Kim 2015; Mendelberg 2001). Scholars have found that measures of racial resentment are highly correlated with many measures of political behavior—from attitudes on racial issues (Kinder and Sanders 1996; Sears et al. 1997) to attitudes on non-racial issues such as voter identification laws (Wilson and Brewer 2013) and health care (Henderson and Hillygus 2011; Maxwell and Shields 2014) to party identification (Valentino and Sears 2005; Knuckey 2017) and vote choice (Howell 1994; Knuckey 2011; Hooghe and Dassonneville 2018). Unsurprisingly, higher levels of racial resentment are correlated with reduced vote share for Barack Obama (Knuckey 2011) and increased vote share for Donald Trump (Abramowitz and McCoy 2019; Hooghe and Dassonneville 2018).

I also examine views on issues surrounding immigration. Immigration is a wide-ranging issue that touches on concerns about economic growth, class, inequality, and foreign policy. But one of the key elements of discussions of immigration in the United States is its focus on its racial implications. Scholars across different eras of immigration politics have found that racial attitudes have a strong influence on views on immigration (Ayers et al. 2009; Burns and Gimpel 2000; Casellas and Wallace 2020; Hood and Morris 1997; Reny et al. 2020). These views are also connected to racial resentment, as high levels of symbolic racism lead native-born Americans to be more likely to favor reducing legal immigration levels and federal aid to legal immigrants (Berg 2013). While southerners used "color-blind rhetoric to avoid sounding overly racist or nativist," they also "racialized the discussion" of immigration through the use of racial stereotypes and tropes (Lippard 2016, 25).

Attitudes on immigration are also highly connected to measures of partisanship and vote choice. Hajnal and Rivera (2014, 778) find negative attitudes toward immigrants and immigration are strongly correlated not only with Republican Party identification and vote for Republican politicians, but also with long-term shifts in party identification toward Republicans. And these findings are based on data collected *before* the emergence of Donald Trump and his 2016 calls for building a wall to keep Mexican and Central American immigrants out of the US and 2024 calls for mass deportations of all illegal immigrants in the United States. Not surprisingly, attitudes on immigration are highly related to votes in the 2016 presidential election, and those with more negative attitudes toward immigrants favoring Trump (Hooghe and Dassonneville 2018). In addition, support for Trump shapes individual's attitudes on issues as those who support Trump "shifted their survey responses on questions related to race and immigration to align with their support for Trump" (Enns and Jardina 2021, 539).

Unhyphenated America, which was described as "Trump Country" in a number of media reports from the 2016 primary (Arbour 2018), should mirror these patterns. The region is strongly Republican and supportive of Donald Trump. As a result, we should expect to find conservative views of immigration policy in the region.

2 The Distinctiveness of Public Opinion in Unhyphenated America

As in Chapter 5, public opinion in unhyphenated America is examined here through the Cooperative Election Study (CES). The CES is taken every two years, in the fall of even-numbered (i.e. election) years. The large size of the CES gives it an advantage over other surveys because it allows for a large enough sample from unhyphenated concentrated counties for meaningful analysis. The CES also has a long and detailed questionnaire that includes questions about race and immigration. There are questions about racial issues in every CES going back to the first survey in 2006 and a battery of questions about immigration policy in every CES since 2010. As in Chapter 5, analysis is conducted by comparing attitudes in unhyphenated America not to the nation as a whole (attitudes would undoubtedly be more conservative), but to other Republican-leaning regions—the South and Red States.[39] As in Chapter 5, analysis is limited to white respondents, because unhyphenated Americans are by definition white.

The first question that I address asks if opinions on issues of race and immigration in unhyphenated America are distinct from those of other Republican-leaning regions of the country. As noted, the CES asked questions on racial issues in every survey year and asked a battery of questions on racial resentment in every survey since 2010. Table 6.1 show the results of these racial questions. Again, the cells show the difference in opinions in the region under study from the opinion of the national sample. As in Chapter 5, bolded entries indicate where

---

39 The definitions of these are the same as in Chapter 5. The South includes only the eleven states that seceded to form the Confederacy. Red States are those that voted Republican for president in every election from 2008 to 2020. While there is overlap between the South and Red State measures, there is not between either of those measures and unhyphenated concentrated; I excluded unhyphenated concentrated counties from the South and Red States.

the difference with national opinion is statistically significant.[40] Shaded cells highlight the responses that are most distant from the national average among the three Republican-leaning regions under study.

Table 6.1: Differences in Regional Opinion from National Sample, Race.[41]

		2006	2008	2010	2012	2014	2016	2018	2020	2022
Support Affirmative Action	Unhyphenated	−11.2	−7.2	−10.6	−10.0	−9.1				
	South	0.4	2.6	1.7	**3.1**	1.2				
	Red States	−3.8	−4.4	−1.5	−1.5	−1.0				
Blacks Can Overcome Prejudice Like Other Groups	Unhyphenated			**7.9**	**10.8**	**6.6**		**13.9**	**15.0**	**10.7**
	South			1.6	1.7	1.8		1.4	1.3	**4.8**
	Red States			2.2	**3.6**	1.8		2.4	**3.2**	0.7
Generations of Discrimination Make It Hard for Blacks	Unhyphenated			**−9.2**	**−9.8**	**−7.8**		**−13.9**	**−18.0**	**−15.4**
	South			−2.1	−1.2	−2.2		−1.4	−1.1	**−4.0**
	Red States			−2.8	−3.1	−3.7		−2.8	−3.8	**−4.2**
White People Have Advantages	Unhyphenated						**−14.9**	**−18.0**	**−18.9**	**−15.5**
	South						−0.5	−0.2	−0.9	**−4.7**
	Red States						−3.7	−2.1	**−4.1**	**−4.2**
I'm Fearful of People from Other Races	Unhyphenated						2.3			
	South						0.5			
	Red States						−0.3			
Racial Problems Are Rare, Isolated Incidents	Unhyphenated						2.6	**3.3**	**8.2**	**5.9**
	South						1.8	1.4	2.5	**4.2**
	Red States						2.2	2.4	**3.8**	**3.8**

Note: Shaded values are those most distant from the national average among the three Republican-leaning regions. Bolded entries are statistically significant at the p < .05 level.

The results show a clear pattern. Residents of unhyphenated concentrated counties record sharply more conservative views than do respondents from the nation

---

40 As in Chapter 5, these are different at the p < .05 level.

41 The following applies to Tables 1.1 through 6.4 and Figures 2.2 and 2.3: values are calculated by the author and reflect the difference between opinions in the region mentioned and the national sample. Data come from the CES Common Content. The South is defined as the eleven states that joined the Confederacy. Red States are those won by the GOP presidential nominee in 2008, 2012, 2016, and 2020.

as a whole. This is true for every single question on race in every single survey year. For example, in 2006, residents of unhyphenated America were 11.2% less likely to support affirmative action than the national sample of voters. One can see a similar answer sixteen years later to the question of whether "generations of slavery and discrimination have created conditions that make it difficult for Blacks to work their way out of the lower class." On that issue, 15.5% of white residents of unhyphenated concentrated counties were less likely to agree with that statement than the national sample of voters. Both of the differences that I described here are significantly different from the national sample. Those answers are not surprising. Among the twenty-six questions on race asked over the nine survey years of the CES, the difference between unhyphenated America and the national sample is statistically significant in twenty-four of them. In short, it is very clear that unhyphenated America holds more conservative views on race than does the nation as a whole.

But even more notable is how distinct the views of unhyphenated America are on these issues from those of the other Republican-leaning regions under study. The differences between the views of southerners and Red State residents are only occasionally different from the rest of the country. Their views are usually more conservative—though notably Southern attitudes on affirmative action are not. It is in this context that the views of unhyphenated concentrated regions most stand out. On every single question on race in every survey year, opinions in unhyphenated America are the most distinct from the national average. And as noted, each of these views is more conservative.

It is notable that the pattern of more racial conservatism in unhyphenated America was already present in 2006, when Barack Obama was one of a hundred senators and Donald Trump was seen entirely as a businessman and a reality show star. Both became the dominant political figure of their era, but these results are from before that era. Yet, we can see that the voting behavior in the unhyphenated concentrated counties—moving away from the cosmopolitan and African American-led Democratic Party and toward the nationalist rhetoric of Trump—did not reflect changes in attitudes in the region in reaction to political events and rhetoric. Instead, unhyphenated concentrated regions already possessed more conservative attitudes on issues of race and immigration before they increased in salience over the Obama and Trump administrations.

I now turn to attitudes on immigration. The CES began asking a battery of questions on immigration policy in 2010 and has continued to ask such questions in every survey year since then. The survey instrument asks, "What do you think the government should do about immigration?" and then lists a number of different policy options. Respondents can click as many as they choose to support. The CES's format keeps the question the same over time but varies the policy options as different immigration policy options were debated over time. As a result, there are a large number of specific immigration policy ideas in the survey, which have here been separated into three tables.

Table 6.2 includes policy ideas addressed in the earlier set of CES surveys, and includes items asked across multiple survey years. Yet, they show the same pattern as observed in Table 6.1. Opinions in unhyphenated America are strongly conservative on issues of immigration just as they were for issues of race, and these opinions remain consistently conservative across time. For example, in 2010, white residents of unhyphenated concentrated counties were 15.5% more likely than the national sample to support allowing "police to question anyone they think may be in the country illegally." Fast forward twelve years, and the conservative views of unhyphenated America remain. On the proposal to "increase border patrols," opinion in the region is 13.3% more supportive than the national sample.

Table 6.2: Differences in Regional Opinion from National Sample, Immigration.

		2010	2012	2014	2016	2018	2020	2022
Grant Legal Status for Good Behavior	Unhyphenated	**-8.8**	**-7.7**	**-7.4**	**-12.4**		**-10.4**	**-10.4**
	South	0.6	1.9	-0.3	1.1		0.1	0.1
	Red States	-0.7	-0.7	-2.8	-0.6		-2.1	-2.1
Increase Border Patrols	Unhyphenated	**9.4**	**7.4**	**8.9**	**8.7**		**13.3**	**13.3**
	South	1.4	1.6	1.5	0.7		1.5	1.5
	Red States	**2.7**	**2.6**	**3.5**	1.8		**3.4**	**3.4**
Police Can Question Anyone They Think Is in Country Illegally	Unhyphenated	**15.5**	**11.9**	**7.7**				
	South	0.6	0.5	1.9				
	Red States	**3.4**	**3.4**	2.4				
Fine Businesses That Hire Illegal Immigrants	Unhyphenated		**5.9**	**5.6**	**4.4**			
	South		-2.2	0.0	0.8			
	Red States		1.6	2.3	2.0			
Identify and Deport All Illegal Immigrants	Unhyphenated			**9.1**	**15.0**			
	South			1.7	-0.3			
	Red States			**3.5**	1.4			

Note: Shaded values are those most distant from the national average among the three Republican-leaning regions. Bolded entries are statistically significant at the p < .05 level.

Table 6.3 continues to show results for other immigration policy ideas, and while these different to the policy ideas in Table 6.2, the results are essentially the same. Opinions in unhyphenated concentrated counties are more conservative on immigration policy than the country as a whole. In 2016, those who live in counties with concentrations of American ethnic identifiers were 12.8% less supportive than the national sample of the proposal to "grant legal status to all illegal immigrants who have held jobs and paid taxes for at least three years, and not been convicted of any felony crimes." In 2022, respondents in those same counties were 12.1% more likely to support the proposal to "reduce legal immigration by eliminating the visa lottery and ending family-based migration." Different proposals, but the same conservatism.

Table 6.3: Differences in Regional Opinion from National Sample, Immigration Policy Continued.

		2010	2012	2014	2016	2018	2020	2022
Grant Legal Status to Dreamers	Unhyphenated				-12.8	-15.8		
	South				1.1	-1.8		
	Red States				-0.3	-3.2		
Eliminate Visa Lottery Program	Unhyphenated					12.3	12.2	12.1
	South					1.6	1.9	2.7
	Red States					2.0	2.4	2.1
Police Must Report Legal Status of Detainees	Unhyphenated					15.2	11.8	
	South					1.9	2.5	
	Red States					3.3	4.1	
Increase Spending on Border Security	Unhyphenated						15.4	12.1
	South						1.6	4.8
	Red States						3.6	3.7

Note: Shaded values are the most distant from the national average among the three Republican-leaning regions. Bolded entries are statistically significant at the p < .05 level.

Table 6.4 contains opinions on policy issues that were asked about in only one survey year. Even though these are one-off issue questions, the underlying pattern of opinions is the same. Residents of unhyphenated America hold more conservative opinions than the national sample on each of these issues. In 2006, the CES asked questions about whether respondents would vote in favor of a proposal in Congress that year to allow illegal immigrants "more opportunities to become legal citizens"[42] and another on whether they preferred "opening a path to

---

[42] The full text of this question is: "Another issue is illegal immigration. One plan considered by the Senate would offer illegal immigrants who already live in the U.S. more opportunities to become legal citizens. Some politicians argue that people who have worked hard in jobs that the economy depends on should be offered the chance to live here legally. Other politicians argue that the plan is an amnesty that rewards people who have broken the law. What do you think? If

citizenship" to illegal immigrants or if they preferred "stricter enforcement of current restrictions."[43] On both proposals, residents of unhyphenated concentrated counties gave opinions that were more than 12% more conservative than the national sample. Similarly, in 2018, respondents who live in counties with concentrations of American ethnic identifiers were 15.8% more supportive than the national sample of a proposal to "increase spending on border security by $25 billion, including building a wall between the U.S. and Mexico."

Table 6.4: Differences in Regional Opinion from National Sample, Immigration Policy: Questions Asked Only in One Survey, 2006–2020.

Prefer Strict Enforcement to Path to Citizenship. 2006	Unhyphenated	**13.0**	Vote for Path to Citizenship. 2006.	Unhyphenated	**−12.6**
	South	2.6		South	1.0
	Red States	3.6		Red States	−1.2
Prevent Illegal Immigrants from Using Government Services. 2012	Unhyphenated	6.4	Increase Guest Workers. 2010	Unhyphenated	**−6.2**
	South	−1.3		South	−2.2
	Red States	2.5		Red States	0.2
Deny Citizenship to Children of Illegal Immigrants. 2012	Unhyphenated	6.0	Increase Visas for Overseas Workers. 2012	Unhyphenated	**−8.8**
	South	−1.3		South	−1.8
	Red States	2.5		Red States	0.3
Muslim Ban. 2016	Unhyphenated	**10.0**	Admit No Refugees from Syria. 2016	Unhyphenated	**12.5**
	South	1.4		South	2.2
	Red States	**3.5**		Red States	**4.3**
Build the Wall. 2018	Unhyphenated	**15.8**	Imprison Deported Individuals Who Return. 2018	Unhyphenated	**11.6**
	South	1.8		South	1.2
	Red States	**3.2**		Red States	0.5
Permanent Status for Children of Illegal Immigrants. 2020.	Unhyphenated	**−9.3**			
	South	0.2			
	Red States	1.4			

Note: Shaded values are those most distant from the national average among the three Republican-leaning regions. Bolded entries are statistically significant at the p < .05 level.

---

you were faced with this decision, would you vote for or against this proposal?" The response options were "for" and "against."

43 The full text of the question is: "Congress has been debating different policies concerning immigration reform. The Senate proposal has a path to citizenship for illegal immigrants. The House proposal, on the other hand, contains stricter enforcement and deportations of undocumented aliens. Which of these two items of reform do you think is more important?" The response options were: (1) "Stricter enforcement of current restrictions" and (2) "Opening a path to citizenship for current illegal immigrants."

More importantly than the conservatism of unhyphenated America is the *distinct* conservatism of unhyphenated America. On each of the forty different opinion measures in the three tables above, opinions in unhyphenated concentrated areas are more conservative than the opinions in the South and in Red States. Again, that is on every single measure.

Across a broad number of survey questions and in the fourteen different years under study, there is a clear pattern—residents of unhyphenated concentrated counties hold distinctly more conservative views on questions of immigration and race than even those who live in other Republican-leaning regions. The pattern begins before the emergence of the increased salience of racial matters in the Obama and Trump administrations, indicating that the pattern was not caused by the rhetoric and policy proposals of either president or their adversaries. And yet, these presidents had a significant impact on the racialization of politics across the nation (Tesler 2016; Abramowitz and McCoy 2019). I next address the question of whether opinions on race and immigration polarized in unhyphenated America.

3 The Divergence in Opinion in Unhyphenated America is Growing

The second question that I explore is whether attitudes about issues of immigration and race have polarized in unhyphenated America over the last few years. National politics became more racialized through the Obama years, as the fact that the president was an African American made race more present, even on issues where race was irrelevant (Benegal 2018; Chen and Mohanty 2017; Wilson and Davis 2018; Tesler 2012a). The backlash created by the Obama presidency led to the election of the openly racist Donald Trump (Mutz 2018; Gimpel 2017), who continued to regularly use openly racist language as President of the United States (Lopez 2020). Areas with concentrations of unhyphenated Americans were more receptive to Trump politically (cf. Irwin and Katz 2016; Arbour and Teigen 2016; Arbour 2018) and their conservative attitudes on issues of race and immigration may have grown more starkly conservative over this period.

To examine whether such divergence is happening in unhyphenated America, it is necessary to identify questions about race and immigration that were asked over multiple years. Unfortunately, the CES did not ask its battery of racial resentment or immigration policy questions in 2006 or 2008. As a result, no question was asked in every single year of the survey. But enough questions were asked across a number of their survey years to allow this type of analysis.

On race, the CES has asked a small battery of racial resentment questions starting in 2010. For most surveys, that battery comprised two questions. The first asked respondents if they agreed or disagreed with the statement "Irish, Italians, Jewish and many other minorities overcame prejudice and worked their way up. Blacks should do the same without any special favors." The second question determined agreement with the statement "Generations of slavery and discrimination have created conditions that make it difficult for blacks to work their way out of the lower class." The survey has added questions over time, and in 2016 replaced those statements with a different set of racial resentment questions but returned to these two statements in subsequent surveys.

The authors of the CES survey began asking their immigration policy battery in 2010 but have changed the policy questions over the years to reflect new policy ideas about immigration. As a result, no single policy idea was asked in each of the seven surveys with an immigration battery. But two questions were asked in six of the last seven surveys, and I use these questions to assess changes in immigration attitudes over time—the questions related to policies on granting legal status and increasing border patrol measures. The CES has asked about these policies in every survey year since 2010, except for 2016. This gives me four questions that were asked in six surveys over seven different election years to examine for opinion change over time.

Figure 6.1 includes line graphs for each of these four questions. As in the previous section, the percentage of respondents from each region who agreed with the statement in the survey instrument is subtracted from the percentage of respondents nationally who agreed with the statement. Each of the four panels shows the same pattern as that of the previous section—residents of unhyphenated concentrated counties have more conservative views on all four issues under study. This pattern continues across all seven survey years under study.

On the two questions about race (panels a and b), the attitudes of residents of unhyphenated concentrated areas tend to move further from the national average over the course of time. This movement is strongest in 2018 and 2020, as racial attitudes in unhyphenated concentrated regions became more than ten points more conservative than the national sample. There is something of a return in 2022 as views in unhyphenated concentrated areas on racial resentment move slightly closer to the national average than they did in 2020.

On immigration, there is some movement in unhyphenated counties away from the national average, though it is more modest on the measures on race. On the Grant Legal Status measure, almost all of the movement in a conservative direction happened between 2014 to 2016; the measure basically levels off after that. The Increase Border Patrols measure is steady through 2016 and then increases to a new, more conservative level in 2020 and 2022.

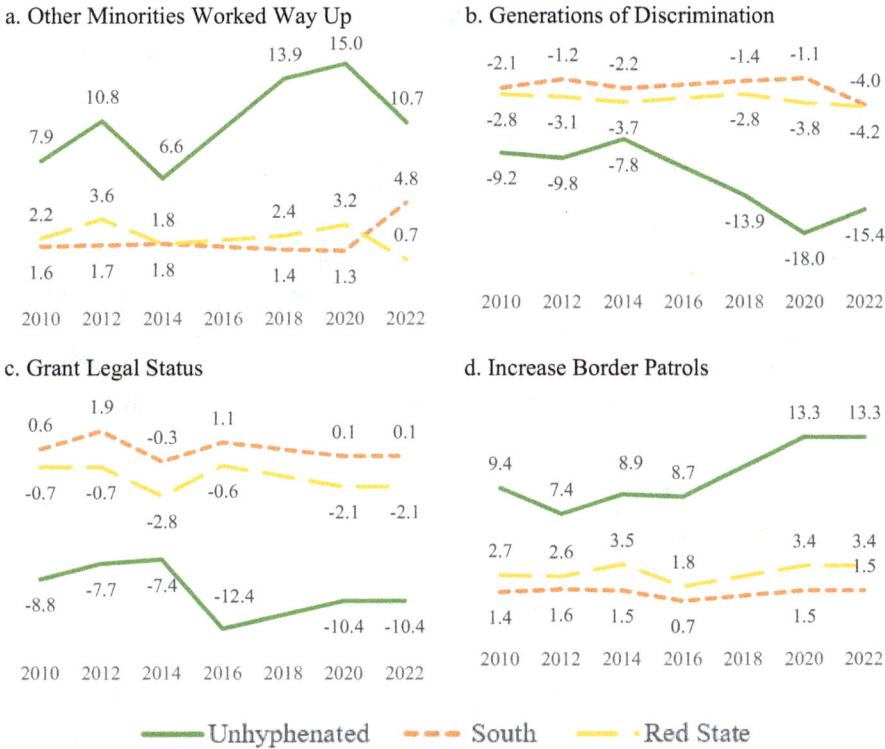

Figure 6.1: Divergence in Regional Opinion from National Sample across Time, 2010–2022.

Notable in these results is the lack of movement among the other two Republican-leaning regions under study—the South and Red States. In both, attitudes on racial resentment and immigration policy stay relative stable over the twelve years of the survey. There are certainly bumps and wiggles, but the results tend to stay within a few points of each other and snap back to normal after changes. For example, attitudes on Granting Legal Status to undocumented immigrants moved in a more liberal direction in the South between 2010 and 2012. But these attitudes started moving in a more conservative direction in 2014 and look similar to the 2010 numbers in the last two surveys recorded here. Panel a also shows that attitudes in Red States on the Other Minorities Worked Their Way Up statement moved sharply toward the national average in Red States in 2022. This shift was actually greater than the shift observed that year in unhyphenated concentrated counties. It remains to be seen if the shift in Red States is permanent or just a one-year blip.

There was one other question about race asked in five different survey years; from 2006 to 2014, the CES asked respondents whether or not they supported affirmative action.[44] This question was asked from 2006 to 2014. While that is not as long a time frame as the survey responses given in Figure 6.1, and pertains to only a single question, it is from a different time period than the 2010 to 2022 questions. Figure 6.2 shows that views on affirmative action in unhyphenated concentrated areas remained mostly steady across the five survey years. Overall, views converged closer to the national average over time. They converged more sharply in 2008 but then returned to their previous level in 2010. The results in Figure 6.2 suggest that the divergence of attitudes on race and immigration are a phenomenon of the latter half of the 2010s and were likely unleashed as part of the forces that drove Donald Trump to become the nation's most prominent political figure.

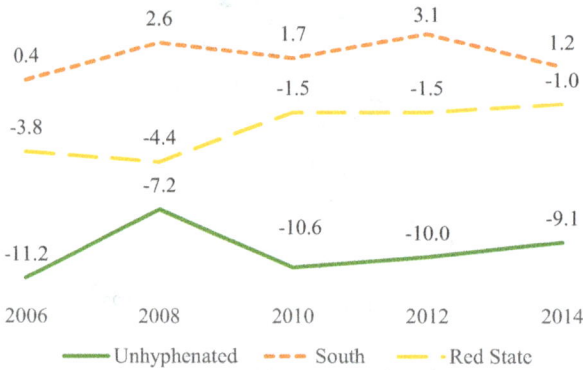

Figure 6.2: Divergence in Opinion on Affirmative Action from National Sample across Time, 2006–2014.

The results here provide supportive if not overwhelming evidence that the views of unhyphenated concentrated areas have indeed polarized over time. Views among residents of unhyphenated concentrated counties have grown more conservative than the views of a national sample on issues of race and immigration, especially during the Trump Administration.

---

44 The full text of the question is "Affirmative action programs give preference to racial minorities in employment and college admissions in order to correct for past discrimination. Do you support or oppose affirmative action?"

4 Multivariate Tests

The bivariate findings presented so far show a broadly consistent pattern: residents of unhyphenated concentrated counties are more conservative in their opinions on issues of race and immigration than the rest of the country as a whole and other Republican-leaning regions in particular. That pattern appears to be growing even more stark over time.

As noted in Chapter 5, these findings do not in and of themselves prove that the reason for these findings is the political geography or culture of unhyphenated America. As noted, unhyphenated Americans are not just a random collection of people who have shifted their ethnic identification. They are concentrated in the upper South in the Appalachias, are more Protestant than the country as a whole, and less likely to have graduated from college. It is therefore possible that one of these factors, not just the presence of large numbers of unhyphenated Americans, may explain why these regions have more conservative opinions than other regions. Concentrations of unhyphenated Americans may thus be correlated with, but incidental to, the real reason for conservative opinions in the region.

The way to assess such potential spurious correlations is through a multivariate test. To ascertain the relationship between ancestry, geography, and demography, I created a series of multivariate logistic regression models. If the presence of unhyphenated Americans in a county is a factor that explains conservative opinions of the region, then it will be a significant factor controlling for other correlated variables. If the correlation is spurious, then one of the other variables will account for the shift, and the unhyphenated American variables will not be significant.

For my dependent variables, I used the five survey questions discussed in Figures 6.1 and 6.2. These questions not only discuss important components of opinion on race and immigration, but the fact that they span multiple years makes it possible to examine potential changes in the relationship between geography and opinion over multiple years. Each survey response has been coded as a dichotomous variable, with the more conservative option coded as 1 and the more liberal option coded as 0.[45] A separate logistic regression was conducted for each question in each survey year in which it was asked.

---

45 The conservative responses coded as 1 oppose affirmative action, agree with the idea that since other minority groups worked their way up, African Americans can as well, oppose the idea that generations of discrimination make it hard for blacks, oppose granting legal status to illegal immigrants who have been in the country for years, held jobs, paid taxes, and avoided criminal conviction, and support increasing border patrols. This coding is done to ease interpretation and comparison across the five measures.

The independent variables are the same as those used in Chapter 5. They include *party identification* on a seven-point scale, *ideology* on a five-point scale, *age*, gender (*woman*), education (having a *bachelor's degree*), *race* (*white*), family income (*over $100,000* and *under $30,000*), and religiosity (*evangelical* identification).[46]

Again, the key independent variable is geographic region, with dichotomous variables for Unhyphenated Concentrated, the South, and Red State. Because of the overlap between the South and Red States, there is a separate regression for each region for each question in each survey year.

As in Chapter 5, I present the marginal effects for the geography variables in each model. That allows for a focus on the most important factor of interest in the models. Table 6.5 shows marginal effect for each geographic variable for each question in each survey year. As per earlier tables, shaded values indicate those that are most distant from the national average among the three Republican-leaning regions. Bolded entries indicate those that are statistically significant.

The results suggest that living in an unhyphenated concentrated area tends to have an effect on making opinions on race and immigration more conservative, but it is not a monolithically strong influence as observed in the bivariate data in Tables 6.1 through 6.4. The influence is nonetheless still present. For example, the marginal effect for unhyphenated concentrated areas is significant in three of the Affirmative Action models, three of the Work Way Up models, and five of the Generations of Discrimination models. The other Republican-leaning regions are significant in fewer of the models under study here. Living in a county with concentrations of American ethnic identifiers has the largest marginal effect in three of the Affirmative Action models, three of the Work Way Up models, and four of the Generations of Discrimination models. That is more than the other two regions put together.

Looking at the two immigration questions, one can again observe that the effect of living in an unhyphenated concentrated area is the strongest overall on these attitudes, but it is not consistently the most important opinion. On the Increase Border Patrols question, the unhyphenated measure is the furthest from zero among the three regions in four models and is significant on three occasions. Again, these are larger than for the other regions. The results for the Grant Legal Status measure are even stronger. The marginal effect is the largest of any of the three regions in five of the six survey years and is significant in three models.

---

46 I chose dichotomous variables for these demographic measures for education, income, and religiosity in order to preserve the assumption of linearity.

Table 6.5: Marginal Effects of Logit Regressions, Race and Immigration, 2006–2022.

		2006	2008	2010	2012	2014	2016	2018	2020	2022
Race										
Oppose Affirmative Action	Unhyphenated	.027	**.053**	**.039**	**.037**	.010				
	South	**.034**	−.015	−.000	−.002	**.016**				
	Red States	**.024**	.000	−.009	.010	−.011				
Work Way Up	Unhyphenated			**.056**	**.044**	.021		−.000	**.035**	.004
	South			.010	.027	**.031**		**.023**	**.023**	**.015**
	Red States			−.012	**.018**	−.010		−.021	−.007	.005
Generations of Discrimination Make It Hard for Blacks	Unhyphenated			**.061**	**.064**	**.048**		.030	**.063**	**.059**
	South			.016	.034	**.051**		**.034**	.033	.004
	Red States			.008	.029	.012		**.021**	.018	.008
Immigration										
Grant Legal Status	Unhyphenated			**.049**	**.032**	.024	**.067**		.014	.007
	South			**−.020**	**−.017**	−.007	−.007		.003	**−.016**
	Red States			−.014	−.011	**−.020**	−.005		−.007	.001
Increase Border Patrols	Unhyphenated			**.040**	.049	**.034**	.022		−.014	.015
	South			**.018**	**.071**	.003	**.037**		−.003	.004
	Red States			.014	**.046**	.002	.014		.007	−.012

Note: Values are marginal effects for the coefficient for each regional dichotomous variable. Shaded values are those most distant from the national average among the three Republican-leaning regions. Bolded entries are statistically significant at the p < .05 level.
The dependent variables for the Generations of Discrimination and Grant Legal Status measures were reversed so that the more conservative choice—opposition to these proposals—is coded as 1 and the liberal choice is coded as 0. This allows for easier comparison across the measures.
Independent variables in these models include party identification, ideology, age, gender, having earned a bachelor's degree, reporting an annual family income under $30,00, reporting an annual income of over $100,000, and identifying oneself as an "evangelical" Christian.

One can conclude that living in an unhyphenated concentrated county can have a strong and significant effect on opinions on issues of race and immigration. I also conclude that these opinions are tempered by other factors that are correlated with living in unhyphenated America. Opinions in the region on these issues are indeed more conservative than the opinions held in other Republican-leaning regions, as demonstrated by the data in Tables 6.1 through 6.4. But the fact that this conservatism holds up often, but not always, in a multivariate test indicates the geographic effect of living in unhyphenated America is muted by other factors, most importantly the region's conservatism and its support for Republicans.

5 The Racial Conservatism of Unhyphenated America

Race plays a central role in American politics generally and Southern politics specifically (cf. Key 1949; Black and Black 2002). In particular, race played a central role in the Southern Republican realignment, as the successes of the Civil Rights Movement ended legal segregation in the South and ended the *raison d'être* for the Solid Democratic South. That was the key part of the long and sure transition of the South toward the Republicans. As I have argued, because this shift was prompted by localized racial conditions, it mattered less in the Appalachias and the upper South. The region was more Republican to start with, due to its smaller African American population, and moved less to the Republicans from the 1960s to the 1980s than did the rest of the South.

The results presented in this chapter show that racial attitudes in unhyphenated America are starkly conservative on issues of race and immigration. The bivariate data in Tables 6.1 through 6.4 show that not only does the region hold conservative views on these issues, but that these views are more conservative than in other regions that also cast their votes in recent elections for Republicans. The multivariate models show that being in the region itself has an effect on attitudes on race and immigration, though this effect is not consistent nor is it consistently larger than the effect of being in the South. Much of the region's racial conservatism comes from its ideological conservatism and its fealty to the Republican Party, both of which strengthened in the twenty-first century.

In the twenty-first century, racial attitudes became more relevant to voters in large part because racial attitudes became more "chronically accessible" through the presence of Barack Obama's racial makeup (Tesler 2016) and the racist and anti-immigrant rhetoric favored by his successor in the White House (Hooghe and Dassonneville 2018; Abramowitz and McCoy 2019). The results in this chapter show that residents of unhyphenated concentrated areas hold conservative attitudes on these issues and the increased salience of these issues in nationalized contemporary politics help explain why racial attitudes are more influential today in unhyphenated America than they were in the days of segregation or in the aftermath of the Civil Rights Movement.

Racial politics are nationalized and thus, the local racial composition of unhyphenated America matters little. Instead, its long-standing conservatism on issues of race and immigration plays a more important role in pushing the region to the right. We saw that in Chapter 5 on issues such as abortion, gay rights, gun policy, and the environment. The increased salience of these issues in twenty-first-century politics helped activate the region's conservatism on these issues and pushed it to the right. Here, in Chapter 6, we find that the region's conservatism on race and immigration are also a factor in the Republican gains in the region.

At the beginning of the chapter, I highlighted a map of election results that showed a swath of unhyphenated America giving a higher share of votes to John McCain in 2008 than it did George W. Bush in 2004, despite McCain running five points behind Bush nationally. A number of commentators went beyond the data of the map to speculate that race played an important role in explaining McCain's gains in the region. I have probed this in much more detail than these bloggers—examining not only attitudes on race in the region in 2008 but across a much larger timeframe—but my results fit with the conclusions made by journalists such as Matthew Yglesias and Andrew Sullivan and political scientists such as Eric Oliver and John Sides; race matters in unhyphenated America. The region's racial conservatism helped push it toward the Republicans, both in 2008 when Barack Obama was on the ballot and in subsequent elections.

Chapter 7
Unhyphenated America in the Republican Primary: Is This Trump's Base?

In early May 2016, the presidential nomination contest came to West Virginia. The West Virginia primary was not very substantively important. Donald Trump had clinched the Republican nomination the week, before when he won in Indiana, prompting his last opponents—Ted Cruz and John Kasich—to drop out of the race. On the Democratic side, Hillary Clinton had not mathematically clinched the race, but journalists reported that she held "a nearly insurmountable lead" entering the contest (Meckler and Nelson 2016).

While the substantive stakes of the West Virginia presidential primaries were small, the symbolic stakes were large. These symbolic stakes were most stark on the relationship of the two presumptive nominees to the coal industry—the state's most important industry from this symbolic standpoint.

At a March town hall, Clinton, when asked by a voter to "make the case to poor whites why they should vote for you based on economic policies," discussed her plan "to bring economic opportunity using clean renewable energy . . . into coal country." Shen then focused on coal miners: "And we're going to make it clear that we don't want to forget those people. Those people labored in those mines for generations, losing their health, often losing their lives to turn on our lights and power our factories."

But in between the discussion of her policy proposal and her expression of sympathy for workers, Clinton described what was happening in the coal industry, "We're going to put a lot of coal miners and coal companies out of business."[47]

This is a first-class political gaffe. Clinton mangled her intent. As a result, the subtlety of what she said was lost, and the only thing that voters remembered was "miners out of business." When Clinton got to West Virginia in May, "angry protesters were on hand, booing and chanting 'go home!'" (Kercheval 2016). An unemployed coal worker named Bo Copley met Clinton as a roundtable event in Willamson, WV and asked her "I just want to know how you can say you're going to put a lot of coal miners out of jobs and then come in here and tell us how you're going to be our friend. Because those people out there [i.e. the protesters] don't see you as a friend" (Stewart 2016).

---

47 Quotes are from the full transcript of the town hall. It is available online here: https://cnnpressroom.blogs.cnn.com/2016/03/13/full-rush-transcript-hillary-clinton-partcnn-tv-one-democratic-presidential-town-hall/.

https://doi.org/10.1515/9783111615707-007

Protests were not limited to Clinton herself. Bill Clinton, Senator Joe Manchin, and Governor Earl Ray Tomblin were the targets of protests while campaigning for Hillary Clinton in Logan County. Manchin was greeted with "shouts of 'traitor Joe'" (Gutman 2016a).

The icy reception for Clinton continued on election day. She received only 36% of the vote, losing by fifteen points to Vermont Senator Bernie Sanders. West Virginia Democrats were not expressing support for a more progressive alternative to the Democratic frontrunner. Over half of the West Virginia Democratic voters told exit pollsters they "wanted the next president to be 'less liberal than President Obama'" (Weigel 2016). These voters were voting against the Democratic establishment that Clinton represented, which was consistent with the shift of unhyphenated America away from the Democratic Party and its center.

The reception for Donald Trump could not have been more different than the one for Clinton. Lines for a Trump rally at the Charleston Civic Center "stretched across the street . . . as people from all over the region waited in a cold rain . . . for a chance to see Donald Trump." The crowd was filled with people not only wearing the signature red "Make American Great Again" hats, but also the hard hats worn by coal miners (Kersey and Brown 2016).

At the rally, Trump donned one of those hard hats given to him by the Vice President of the West Virgnia Coal Association, a trade group, and feigned shoveling coal. Behind Trump as he spoke were miners wearing their own hard hats and waving signs that read "Trump Digs Coal." In his remarks, Trump praised the "courage of the miners" and called them "amazing people." Trump criticized "ridiculous [environmental] rules and regulations that make it impossible for you to compete" and made it so his hairspray is only "good for 12 minutes." Trump then promised, as he had before, that "If I win, we're going to bring those miners' [jobs] back" (all quotes from Gutman 2016b).

While an editorial in the *Charleston Gazette-Mail* described Trump's "political pitch" on coal as a "fantasy," it was a fantasy that West Virginia voters wanted to believe. Trump won 77% of the vote in the West Virginia Republican primary, a tally bested in only one state. In November, West Virginians continued to show they believed in Trump's promises to bring back jobs in the region—he won 68.5% of the vote in the Mountain State, his highest of any state.

1 Is West Virginia Trump's Base? The Pundits Debate

The focus of the national press on West Virginia in the week leading up to its primary, right after Trump had clinched the nomination, led national pundits to wonder if West Virginia—a central part of unhyphenated America—was Trump's base. Russell Berman of *The Atlantic* previewed the West Virginia primary by writing "The voters there are predominantly white, culturally conservative, and hard-hit economically by the loss of jobs in the coal and steel industries and as a result of outsourcing. In other words, they are Donald Trump's base of support" (Berman 2016).

Derek Thompson, Berman's colleague at *The Atlantic*, also identified blue-collar whites—the kinds that are abundant in West Virginia—as Trump's base. Thompson wrote "Trump's core constituency is clear: Republican whites, particularly men, and especially those who didn't go to college, who feel their American whiteness like a second skin" (Thompson 2016). An ABC News (2016) analysis of the West Virginia primary argued that Trump's "message of bringing back factory jobs, revitalizing the coal industry and pushing for protectionist trade policies has excited white, economically depressed and underemployed blue-collar voters in a geographic stretch from southern Pennsylvania to Kentucky." The article's sub-head said Appalachia was "a growing base for Trump."

According to these articles, West Virginia—the epitome of unhyphenated America—was Trump's base in 2016. This fits with the conclusions reached in the previous six chapters of this book. Regions with concentrations of American ethnic identifiers have moved strongly to the Republican Party over the last political generation. This move was based on the Democrat's increasing association with the urban and the urbane, highlighted by the nomination and election of Barack Obama. The last two chapters also found that voters in regions with concentrations of unhyphenated Americans hold distinctly conservative views on issues such as abortion, race, and immigration that have pushed them away from the Democratic Party over time.

Yet, there is evidence that Trump's wins in West Virginia were not a result of his unique connection to working-class voters, but instead were the results of him gaining momentum across the course of the Republican nomination campaign.

The week of the West Virginia primary, Nate Silver published an article at Five-ThirtyEight.com headlined "The Mythology of Trump's 'Working Class' Support." Based on exit poll data, Silver found that the "median household income of a Trump voter so far in the primaries is about $72,000 . . . It's well above the national median household income of about $56,000. It's also higher than the median income for Hillary Clinton and Bernie Sanders supporters, which is around $61,000" (Silver 2016). Using Silver's findings, Matthew Yglesias of Vox.com concluded that "Trump, in particular, built his big primary wins on the backs of people who are economically comfortable. There is no country on Earth where the median household income is higher than the median household income of a Donald Trump primary vote" (Yglesias 2016). In particular, Yglesias noted Trump's wins in affluent states such as Massachusetts and Connecticut and his polling lead in well-heeled California.

The analyses by Silver and Yglesias prompt the question of whether Trump's true base in the primary election was in small-town communities with low levels of median income and college graduates—i.e. the characteristics of unhyphenated America. From a geographic standpoint, Trump ran up big numbers in primaries in the Northeast, many of which were held in April of 2016. Trump's landslide wins in states like New York, Connecticut, Rhode Island, and Maryland—dense, urban states—challenged the established wisdom at that point that Trump's appeal was most concentrated in rural areas.

Further, the conclusion that unhyphenated America's shift toward the Republicans in general elections means the region is Trump's base in a primary election is questionable at best. Primary elections are quite distinct from general elections. In general elections, the choice is between two parties, and the choice of the Democrats to focus on issues that appeal to the urban and urbane (abortion, the environment, civil rights) has pushed away voters in unhyphenated America. In primary elections, the choice is between different members of the same party, so the same dynamics do not apply. Demographic groups or geographic areas may prefer one candidate in a primary and then switch back to the nominee in the general election. But sometimes, a candidate's weakness with a particular set of voters—such as Hillary Clinton's weakness with working-class whites in the 2016 primary—presage the same weakness in the general election.

In short there are many reasons to dig deeply into the question of whether Trump has a primary base in unhyphenated America. It will help to parse the question of whether that base exists just in the general election, and to answer the question about whether Trump's base is limited to small-town communities in unhyphenated America or if his base within the Republican Party is broader.

2 Voting in Primary Elections

In this chapter, I assess the geographic location of Donald Trump's base in the Republican Party, using data primarily from the 2016 Republican nomination contest, but also from the 2024 contest. To make this assessment requires an understanding of the specific dynamics of voting in primary elections in general and presidential primaries and caucuses more specifically.

Primary elections are contests within a party to determine its nominee for the general election. This means that many of the factors that influence voting in a general election do not apply in races between candidates of the same party. For example, party identification is crucial to understanding how voters receive and process information during a campaign, in addition to how they make their vote choice decisions. But party identification does not apply in a primary; all of the candidates are Republicans in this circumstance.

In previous chapters, the assumption behind most of the analyses was that partisan voting patterns are, for the most part, stable. And thus, shifts in these patterns are meaningful. In primary elections, voting patterns are ephemeral. That is, they reflect the specific set of candidates running in that primary election and the relative standing of those candidates in the minds of voters at one point in time. One way this works is through the process of "discovery, scrutiny, and decline." John Sides and Lynn Vavreck (2013, 36) describe a process whereby a candidate's share of news coverage increases due to them doing "something reporters and commentators judge to be novel, important, and therefore newsworthy." This surge in coverage leads to "increased scrutiny from both opponents and the news media." Voters follow along, often increasing the support for a candidate as he or she receives more media coverage and shift preferences if the scrutiny period leads to learning more unfavorable information about a candidate. As a result, many candidates drop in the polls after the scrutiny period.

Another important factor in presidential elections is their sequential nature. Primaries and caucuses are held on different dates and the results of one primary or caucus "can have a powerful impact on a candidate's odds of victory in the next primary or caucus" (Kamarck 2018, 27). The number of candidates is different in different primaries across the calendar. Candidates drop out of the race based primarily on their competitive standing in polls and fund raising, and secondarily the results from the earlier contests (Norrander 2006; Haynes et al. 2004; Steger et al. 2002; Feigenbaum and Shelton 2013). Through this process of winnowing, different sets of voters choose between different candidates.

The sequential process of presidential primaries also leads to the phenomenon of momentum. The concept of momentum holds that a candidate who does well in the early phases of a sequential primary contest will improve their standing in future contests. Candidates who do well in early contests, especially in Iowa and New Hampshire, receive increases in both media attention and donations as a result of beating expectations in initial contests. As a result, they do better in subsequent contests (Bartels 1988). It is unclear exactly how this process works in the minds of voters. It could be that voters take cues from their colleagues who vote in early states. It could be that increased press coverage leads to voters learning more about and approving the policy stances and personality of the candidate with momentum (Mutz 1997). Momentum may stem from voters wanting to be on a winning team or because they like "winners" over "losers" (Kenney and Rice 1994; Scala 2020). It could just be that information from candidates with momentum is more accessible for voters and they thus move to the top of the list for consideration (Shapiro et al. 1991). Perceptions of electability often influence primary voter decision making and increased poll standing and coverage leads to increased perceptions of a candidate's electability (Abramowitz 1989).

Winnowing and momentum certainly mattered in the 2016 Republican primary contest. Candidates dropped out before any votes were cast (e.g. Scott Walker, Lindsey Graham), after the Iowa caucuses (e.g. Rand Paul, Mike Huckabee), and after the New Hampshire primary (e.g. Carly Fiorina, Chris Christie). Marco Rubio lasted through the Junior Tuesday primaries of March 15, but then departed the race. Ted Cruz and John Kasich remained until they lost the Indiana primary on May 3, and then Donald Trump had the field to himself for the final month of the campaign. Different sets of voters had different sets of candidates to consider throughout the Republican contest.

Momentum was predominantly on the side of Donald Trump. Trump dominated press coverage of the campaign before votes were cast and his share of media coverage only grew as voting began (Confessore and Yourish 2016; Patterson 2016; Sides and Leetaru 2016). Trump shot to an early lead in the polls when he entered the race in the summer of 2015 and held onto it throughout the year. He did lose the first contest in Iowa but recovered quickly to win New Hampshire a week later. And while Trump did not win every race, he kept winning. As Trump proved his viability among Republican primary voters, his vote share began a steady climb starting on Super Tuesday. Voters in subsequent states seemed to take the choices of those who voted before them as a signal that they could also support Trump, and in time his numbers grew.

Voting in primary elections is quite different from voting in general elections. In previous chapters, I have shown that a broad shift toward the Republicans in unhyphenated America has grown over the last political generation. This shift does not appear to be the result of the actions of any one Republican candidate or president, but a broad reaction to the two parties. Trump's success in small towns and rural areas and other communities down the socioeconomic spectrum raises the question of whether he individually has a connection to the voters of unhyphenated America, and if we can observe this in primary election results.

3 Primary Vote in 2016

How did Trump do in unhyphenated America in the 2016 Republican primary contest? The simplest answer is that he did the same there as he did in the rest of the country. Table 7.1 shows the popular vote results for Republican presidential primaries and caucuses in 2016.[48] In unhyphenated concentrated counties, Trump won 1,223,630 of the 2,669,318 votes cast. That is 45.8%. In the rest of the country, Trump won 12,696,261 of the 28,000,261 votes cast; that is 45.3%. In general elections, Trump, and other Republicans, run stronger in counties with concentrations of American ethnic identifiers. But in the 2016 primary, Trump won essentially the same vote share inside and outside of unhyphenated America.

Table 7.1: Republican Presidential Primary/Caucus Vote Share by Region, 2016.

	Trump	**Cruz**	**Kasich**	**Rubio**
Unhyphenated Concentrated	45.8%	26.8%	5.7%	14.6%
	1,223,630	716,093	151,353	389,806
Rest of Country	45.3%	25.0%	14.6%	10.8%
	12,696,261	6,996,885	4,091,343	3,032,677

Note: Unhyphenated concentrated are defined as counties where 19.3% or more of the residents identify their heritage as "American." That value is the national mean at the county level plus one standard deviation. The data include both primary and caucus results, including for the District of Columbia. Election results are not available from Alaska, Colorado, Kansas, Minnesota, North Dakota, and Wyoming. The Republican Party in these states did not report caucus results at the county level. Election results come from a dataset available at the Bucknell Digital Commons (Pirrman et al. 2016).

Table 7.1 also includes the vote share for the three other leading Republican presidential candidates in 2016. The results show the largest differences for John Kasich, who won only 5.7% of the vote in unhyphenated concentrated counties, much less than the 14.6% of the vote he won in the rest of the country. Marco Rubio ran 3.8% better in counties with concentrations of American ethnic identifiers than in other counties, a modest improvement. Ted Cruz's numbers are similar in both regions. Much like Trump, he ran the same both inside and outside of unhyphenated America.

Further evidence of the lack of difference in Trump's vote share between unhyphenated America and the rest of the country is provided in the scatterplot in Figure 7.1. The x-axis represents the percentage of American ethnic identifiers in each county and the y-axis Trump's vote share. The results show basically no relationship. There are essentially no unhyphenated concentrated counties where Trump does poorly; it looks like he has a high floor in the region. But there are plenty of counties with low shares of unhyphenated Americans who returned

---

48 Several states did not report caucus or convention results by county, and thus, they are excluded here. Those states are Alaska, Colorado, Kansas, Minnesota, North Dakota, and Wyoming.

strong majorities for Trump. Consequently, we can conclude that there is basically no effect, either positive or negative, of American ethnic identifiers on Trump's primary vote share.

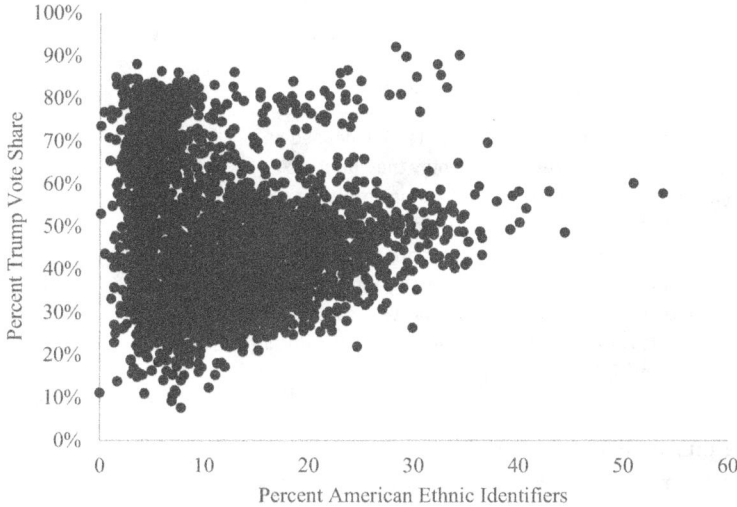

Figure 7.1: Scatterplot, Trump Vote Share by American Ethnicity, 2016 Republican Primary. Note: County level data. "Percent American Ethnic Identifier" is the share of residents in each county who write "American" as their answer to the Census question "What is your ancestry or ethnic origin?" The "Percent Trump Vote Share" is the county-level vote for Trump in the 2016 Republican primaries and caucuses, including the District of Columbia. Election results are not available from Alaska, Colorado, Kansas, Minnesota, North Dakota, and Wyoming. The Republican Party in these states did not report caucus results at the county level. Election results come from a dataset available at the Bucknell Digital Commons (Pirrman et al. 2016).

However, Table 7.2 presents something very different. This table examines the number of counties that each candidate won. Unsurprisingly, Trump won the most counties in both unhyphenated concentrated counties and in the rest of the country. But Trump won a much higher share of counties in unhyphenated America (88.5%) than he did in the rest of the country (69.9%).

Ted Cruz was the only other candidate to win any unhyphenated concentrated counties. Neither Kasich nor Rubio won any. They did win a handful of counties across the rest of the country—sixty in total for Kasich and thirty-eight for Rubio. Again, Ted Cruz won the lion's share of counties that did not go for Trump. He won 578 counties outside of unhyphenated America—just over one quarter of the total.

Table 7.2: Counties Won by Region, 2016.

	Trump	Cruz	Kasich	Rubio
Unhyphenated	470	61	0	0
Concentrated	88.5%	11.5%		
Rest of Country	1,573	578	60	38
	69.9%	25.7%	2.7%	1.7%

Note: Calculated by author. Unhyphenated concentrated are defined as counties where 19.3% or more of the residents identify their heritage as "American." That value is the national mean at the county level plus one standard deviation. The data include both primary and caucus results, including for the District of Columbia. Election results are not available from Alaska, Colorado, Kansas, Minnesota, North Dakota, and Wyoming. The Republican Party in these states did not report caucus results at the county level. Election results come from a dataset available at the Bucknell Digital Commons (Pirrman et al. 2016).

This presents a puzzle. If Trump got the same vote share in unhyphenated America as he did in the rest of the country, then how did he win such a higher share of counties in unhyphenated America? The answer has to do with the unique nature of presidential nomination contests and their differences from other types of elections. Presidential nomination contests are unique because they are sequential. General elections all happen on the same day, but presidential primaries happen on different days and the results of one contest can affect the results of the next one. Further, the effects of winnowing and momentum can help candidates who survive to the end of the primary season to increase their vote share across time. Candidates who do well early tend to do better as the contest goes along. This is what happened with Donald Trump in the 2016 nomination contest.

Figure 7.2 shows the vote share for Donald Trump for each week of the 2016 Republican nomination contest. Results on weeks with multiple contests across all states that had a primary that week have been pooled. Broadly, the figure shows Trump increasing his vote share over the course of the campaign. The increase is not linear, but is clear across time, and relatively steady when one accounts for some of the demographic and cultural differences between the different states in each week and their unique set of Republican voters.

The chart also shows two vertical lines. The one in Week 6 marks when Marco Rubio dropped out of the presidential race after losing the Florida primary to Trump. Trump's vote share increases slightly in the weeks after that, and much more sharply in Weeks 12 and 13 when the contest moved to the Northeast, where Trump ran quite strongly. The other line is in Week 14, which was the Indiana

Trump Vote Share by Week

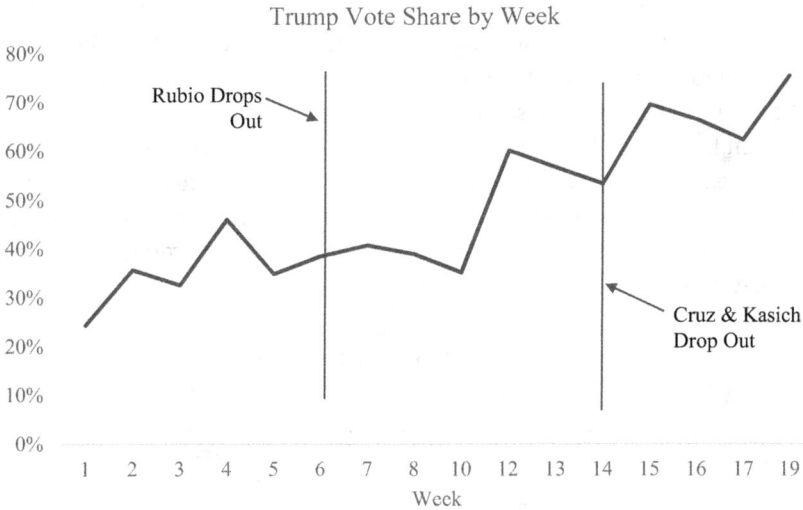

Figure 7.2: Trump Vote Share by Week, 2016 Republican Primary and Caucuses.
Note: Calculated by author. In weeks with multiple primaries or caucuses, results are aggregated across all contests that week. Election results come from a dataset available at the Bucknell Digital Commons (Pirrman et al. 2016). Data on the date of primaries and caucuses in 2016 come from www.thegreenpapers.org.

primary. After that primary, Ted Cruz and John Kasich both dropped out of the race making Trump the only candidate left standing. Trump won increasing shares of the vote in the subsequent primaries, starting with the West Virginia contest in Week 15.

Trump built momentum throughout the campaign, and while some conventional wisdom among the pundit class—especially among conservatives who have remained loyal to the Republicans but would prefer a different leader—suggests that Trump only won because his opposition was split between different candidates (Azari 2016; Maskin and Sen 2016; Stokols 2016), the data presented here provides evidence that Trump increased his vote share across time and seemed to take a proportionate share of the vote from candidates who dropped out of the race (cf. Woon et al. 2020 for further support of this contention).

The fact that Trump built momentum throughout the campaign demonstrates that it matters when different regions hold their primary contests. For example, Super Tuesday is an early primary contest, and it is dominated by Southern states (e.g. Texas, Tennessee, Georgia, Virginia). Six Northeastern states, where there are no unhyphenated concentrated counties, held their primary contests in late April, after Trump had gained significant momentum from his victories in primaries throughout the month of March.

Table 7.3 divides the Republican nomination contest into five different time periods—Early, Super Tuesday, March, Northeast, and Post-Clinch.[49] The table shows that Trump increased his vote share across each period. The increase was only slight from the Early contests, where Trump won 32.5% of the vote, to Super Tuesday, when he won 34.8% of the vote. But the increase for Trump grew as the campaign proceeded. He won 39.6% of the vote in the March primaries, and then a majority in the Northeast section of the contest in late April and early May. Finally, he won nearly 70% of the vote after the other candidates dropped out after his May 3 victory in Indiana.

Table 7.3: Trump Vote and Unhyphenated Concentrated Counties by Campaign Period, 2016 Primary.

Campaign Period	Trump Vote Share (%)	Share of Unhyphenated Concentrated Counties
Early (February)	32.8	6 out of 172 3.5%
Super Tuesday (March 1, 2016)	34.8	273 out of 888 30.7%
March (March 5-April 5)	39.6	200 out of 1,002 20.0%
Northeast (April 19-May 3)	56.5	20 out of 194 10.3%
Post Clinch (May 10-June 7)	69.7	32 out of 524 6.1%

Note: Calculated by author. Trump Vote Share numbers are aggregated across all contests during that period. Unhyphenated concentrated are defined as counties where 19.3% or more of the residents identify their heritage as "American." That value is the national mean at the county level plus one standard deviation. Election results come from a dataset available at the Bucknell Digital Commons (Pirrman et al. 2016).

---

49 The "Early" contests are the four held in the month of February (Iowa, New Hampshire, Nevada, and South Carolina). The Super Tuesday are the primaries and caucuses held in 12 states on March 1, 2016. The "March" period begins on March 5 and continues through the Wisconsin Primary on April 5. The "Northeast" period covers events on April 19 (New York Primary), April 26 (Five Northeastern states) and May 3 (Indiana). Cruz and Kasich dropped out after losing the Indiana primary, so all contests from May 10 to June 7 are "Post-Clinch," i.e. after Trump clinched the nomination.

The table also includes the number of unhyphenated concentrated counties that voted in each period, along with the total number of counties that voted in each period. There are 533 unhyphenated concentrated counties in the United States. Table 7.3 shows that 473 of them (88.9%) voted in the Republican presidential primary either on Super Tuesday or in the rest of March. Trump increased his vote share in the final two periods of the nomination contest.

Trump's increasing vote share across time and the concentration of unhyphenated concentrated counties in primaries in March raises the question of whether the lack of difference between Trump's results in unhyphenated America and the rest of the country reflects broad support for Trump across different regions or is primarily a function of when those primaries occurred.

Evidence to support the idea that Trump ran better in unhyphenated America is provided in Table 7.4, which examines nine states that held primaries on Super Tuesday 2016. The middle column displays Trump's vote share in unhyphenated concentrated counties in each state and the right-hand column displays the vote share of the rest of the state. For each of the seven Super Tuesday states with unhyphenated concentrated counties, Trump ran better in those counties than he did in the rest of those states. Across all the Super Tuesday states, Trump won 32.8% of the vote. In unhyphenated concentrated counties, he ran over ten points better, at 43.5%.

Table 7.4: Trump Vote Share by State, Super Tuesday (March 1, 2016).

	Unhyphenated Concentrated (%)	Rest of State (%)
Alabama	46.6	41.2
Arkansas	36.4	31.9
Georgia	45.6	36.2
Massachusetts	N/A	49.0
Oklahoma	36.6	28.3
Tennessee	44.3	33.5
Texas	27.1	27.0
Virginia	45.4	32.8
Vermont	N/A	32.4
Total	**43.5**	**32.8**

Note: Calculated by author. Unhyphenated concentrated are defined as counties where 19.3% or more of the residents identify their heritage as "American." That value is the national mean at the county level plus one standard deviation. Election results come from a dataset available at the Bucknell Digital Commons (Pirrman et al. 2016).

Despite those higher vote shares, Trump does not seem dependent on unhyphenated concentrated regions to overcome deficits in other regions. In fact, he does not usually lose in other regions. Looking at Super Tuesday states, Trump won both the unhyphenated concentrated counties *and* the rest of the state in six of the seven states that voted on Super Tuesday that have unhyphenated concentrated counties.[50] The one state where Trump did not win the rest of the state was in Virginia, where Rubio edged him out 33.9% to 33.0%. Trump's victory in the state came from his big margin in Virginia's unhyphenated concentrated counties; Trump won 45.3% of the vote there, compared to 21.0% for Rubio. It was a similar story in Arkansas, but here Trump won the rest of the state 31.9 to 30.5% over Rubio. In unhyphenated Arkansas, Trump won by a bigger margin—36.3% to 30.5%. But in places like Tennessee and Georgia, Trump won handily in both unhyphenated concentrated areas and in the other parts of the state. In Texas, Cruz won both regions with a similar vote share (44%). In Oklahoma, Trump won the unhyphenated concentrated counties while Cruz won the rest of the state.

The conclusion I draw here is that Trump was broadly popular in 2016 among Republican voters. He had advantages in unhyphenated concentrated regions, but those voters were not at odds with their fellow Republican voters in other parts of their states. Instead, Trump won across the board in Republican primaries. He was the most popular candidate and continued to gain vote share throughout the course of the campaign.

4 The Effects of Trump's Momentum

These results present a puzzle. They indicate that overall, Donald Trump did no better in 2016 in unhyphenated America than he did in the rest of the country. Yet, they also indicate that Trump ran better in unhyphenated concentrated counties on Super Tuesday. These descriptive data do not provide a good answer to the key question of this chapter.

Confounding the conclusions reached so far is the sequential nature of presidential primary elections. As shown, Trump continued to gain votes over the course of the campaign as the field winnowed and he gained momentum. Being able to account for Trump's growing vote share across time might in turn make it possible to find a clearer answer to the question of whether unhyphenated America is Trump's base within the Republican primary electorate.

---

50 Massachusetts and Vermont voted on Super Tuesday but do not have any unhyphenated concentrated counties. Trump won both states.

Table 7.5 provides evidence of the importance of accounting for Trump's increased vote share across time in analyzing voting patterns in the 2016 Republican presidential nomination contest. It presents three models. The dependent variable in each is Donald Trump's vote share by county in the 2016 primary contest.

Model 1 is an OLS regression model with the one independent variable—the share of American ethnic identifiers in a county. The result is a coefficient that is negative and significant. For every 1% greater a county's share of unhyphenated Americans, Trump's vote share goes down by 0.17%. That is vastly different to the results of the bivariate models presented in Chapter 3, which showed big jumps in Trump's general election vote share in these counties.

Table 7.5: OLS Regression, 2016 Republican Presidential Nomination Contest.

	Model 1	Model 2	Model 3
Percent American	−0.17***		0.48***
Ethnic Identifier	(0.040)		(0.024)
Week		2.55***	2.81***
		(0.036)	(0.036)
Constant	49.20***	25.70***	17.49***
	(0.58)	(0.35)	(0.52)
R-Squared	.0069	0.645	.692
Observations	2,780	2,780	2,780

Note: *** = $p < .001$; ** = $p < .01$; * = $p < .05$. Standard errors in parentheses. Dependent variable is Trump vote share at the county level. "Percent American Ethnic Identifier" is the share of residents in each county who write "American" as their answer to the Census question "What is your ancestry or ethnic origin?" Election results are not available from Alaska, Colorado, Kansas, Minnesota, North Dakota, and Wyoming. The Republican Party in these states did not report caucus results at the county level. Election results come from a dataset available at the Bucknell Digital Commons (Pirrman et al. 2016). Data on the date of primaries and caucuses in 2016 come from www.thegreenpapers.org.

In Model 2, the independent variable is the week of the campaign. The Iowa caucuses were held on February 1, 2016; that is Week 1. The New Hampshire Primary was February 8, which is Week 2. Super Tuesday—March 1, 2016—was Week 5, and so on until Week 17, the final set of Republican primaries in California, Montana, New Jersey, New Mexico, and South Dakota. The result here is positive and significant. Strongly so. The results show that Trump picked up—on average—2.55 percentage points per week of the campaign. As the campaign went along, Trump, like most primary frontrunners, gained vote share at an almost steady clip.

Model 3 includes both independent variables from the first two models. The *Week* variable is again positive and significant. But more importantly, the *Percent American Ethnic Identifier* variable is positive and significant. As noted above, a larger share of unhyphenated concentrated counties held their primaries in the month of March, in the first half of the nomination contest. Those who voted in April and May were more likely to vote for Trump in general, which the *Week* variable accounts for. Once the effect of momentum and time is controlled for in a model, the effect of having concentrations of unhyphenated Americans in a county produces a higher vote share for Donald Trump. Having 1% more American ethnic identifiers in a county is associated with a 0.48% higher vote share for Trump. This fits with the results of Table 7.4. Trump ran better in unhyphenated concentrated regions than in other places that voted on the same day.

The results of Tables 7.4 and 7.5 indicate that the period in which each state's primary or caucus is held is an important variable in explaining the results of the 2016 Republican presidential nomination contest. When one accounts for that, the effect of unhyphenated concentrations on Trump's vote share becomes not only positive but also meaningful. Adding the *Week* variable is thus a big improvement upon the bivariate data discussed in Tables 7.1 and 7.2 and Figure 7.1.

5 A Multivariate Test

Of course, two variables are not sufficient to answer the key question of this chapter —whether unhyphenated America is a base for Donald Trump within the Republican Party. One needs to assess that question with a broader series of potential variables.

Much as in Chapters 3 and 4, a fuller test is needed, one that examines American ethnic identity in a model that controls for variables that are correlated with the geography of unhyphenated concentrated areas (e.g. lower levels of educational achievement and higher levels of evangelical Christians). This makes it possible to test whether the effect of concentrations of unhyphenated Americans on Trump's results in the 2016 Republican nomination contest are unique to the region or an artifact of other correlated factors.

The same set of socioeconomic control variables are applied here as were used in Chapters 3 and 4. Each is measured at the county level: the percentage of residents with a professional degree or higher (e.g. an M.A. or a J.D.), the percentage of senior citizens, and the median county income in tens of thousands of dollars.[51] The model also includes other control variables. Counties' Black and Latino percen-

---

51 The socioeconomic and racial variables in the model come from US Census Bureau data.

tages are included. Because of the historical correlation between religious affiliations and ethnic or ancestral origins, the model includes measures for county-level religious church membership by the percentage of Roman Catholics and percentage of evangelical Christians.[52] The percentage of veterans in a county is also included in order to account for any residual political effects from the military tradition of the highland South. To ensure that the model controls for recent migration shifts, the model includes a "Born out of state" variable. It also includes a "Born out of the country" variable to control not only for migration patterns, but also for the level of consciousness in a community to immigrant roots. A variable for the week of the primary campaign has also been included, and a dichotomous variable for caucuses; caucuses tend to benefit the candidate who is best organized, or the best connected to the party apparatus. Neither describes Trump in 2016.

Of course, the key independent variables are those that are the focus of this research—the percentage of American ethnic identifiers in a county. Table 7.6 presents the results. Looking at the control variables, many behave in expected ways: *Median Income, Density*, and *Percent Graduate Degree* are all negative and significant. Trump's base was indeed among working-class, small-town voters in the primary. Other variables work in unexpected ways. *Percent Foreign Born* is negative and significant in the model. *Percent Evangelical* is also negative and significant, which fits with the 2016 pattern where Ted Cruz did the best with voters with high levels of religiosity.

Table 7.6: OLS Regression, 2016 Republican Presidential Nomination Contest, Demographic Variables.

Variable	Coefficient
Week	2.738*** (0.035)
Caucus	−3.219*** (0.503)
Percent American Ethnic Identifier	0.647*** (0.027)
Percent Black	0.250*** (0.012)

52 These two variables come from a study of the sizes of religious congregations by faith and county nationwide (Grammich et al. 2012). There are a very small number of counties where these data are unavailable, in which case the mean value of the contiguous counties' religious data was imposed.

Table 7.6 (continued)

Variable	Coefficient
Percent Latino	−0.159*** (0.018)
Percent Born Out of State	0.072*** (0.014)
Percent Foreign Born	0.569*** (0.048)
Percent Children	−0.522*** (0.065)
Percent Senior Citizen	0.035 (0.058)
Median Income	−1.164** (0.233)
Density (Logged)	−0.395** (0.121)
Percent Evangelical	−0.120*** (0.011)
Percent Catholic	0.110*** (0.013)
Percent Veteran	0.628*** (0.092)
Percent Graduate Degree	−1.360*** (0.101)
Constant	28.980*** (2.513)
R-Squared	.7983
Observations	2,779

Note: *** = $p < .001$; ** = $p < .01$; * = $p < .05$. Standard errors in parentheses. Dependent variable is Trump vote share at the county level. Data come from US Census Bureau. The variables on the size of religious congregations by county come from Grammich et al. (2012). Election results are not available from Alaska, Colorado, Kansas, Minnesota, North Dakota, and Wyoming. The Republican Party in these states did not report caucus results at the county level. Election results come from a dataset available at the Bucknell Digital Commons (Pirrman et al. 2016). Data on the date of primaries and caucuses in 2016 come from www.thegreenpapers.org.

Trump does better in counties that have higher shares of veterans and Catholics. He also did better as the share of residents born in another state increased, which is surprising, because Trump's small-town strength seemed to reflect support among those rooted in their communities. He does better as the share of African Americans in a county increases but worse as the share of Latinos increases.

The key variable is *Percent American Ethnic Identifier*, which is positive and significant. Having 1% more unhyphenated Americans in a county is associated with a 0.64% increase in Trump's vote share in the 2016 Republican primary. That finding is based on holding all else equal, which is quite important in a model. As noted, unhyphenated America is correlated with lower levels of educational attainment and median income and higher levels of evangelical faith and military service. Controlling for those factors does not take away the influence of American ethnic identifiers on Trump's vote share.

These data support the idea that unhyphenated America is a base for Trump. It has a positive effect on Trump's vote share once one accounts for the vote gains that Trump gets based on his campaign's momentum (the *Week* variable), and that effect holds even when one controls for correlated variables such as median income, professional degrees, and the share of evangelical Christians. In short, unhyphenated America is a base for Donald Trump. Of course, the results in Chapter 3 showed that is the case in general elections, but that is primarily because Donald Trump was the Republican nominee for president. Unhyphenated America was a base for Mitt Romney in November 2012 as well. These data show that unhyphenated America was a base for Donald Trump in the 2016 Republican nomination contest. He won a higher vote share in the region once one controls for the effects of momentum and winnowing. Trump was quite popular across the Republican Party in general, but he was especially popular in unhyphenated America.

6 The Unhyphenated Base Holds in 2024

Donald Trump did something in 2024 that had not been done since Theodore Roosevelt in 1912. He stood for election in primaries as a former president. While Roosevelt did well in the primaries, they were not decisive in determining the party nomination in 1912. Thanks to his advantages as incumbent president, William Howard Taft won slates of delegates from states that did not have primaries and easily secured the 1912 Republican nomination (Cowan 2016). In 2024, voters were the deciders, and they backed Trump. He won every primary but in Vermont and the District of Columbia to win the 2024 Republican nomination easily.

Trump's campaign in 2024 provides another opportunity to examine his standing among Republican voters, both inside and outside of unhyphenated America. Republican primary voters could evaluate Trump's four years in office, judging things like his ability to meet Republican priorities like regressive tax cuts and putting conservative judges on the Supreme Court and his inability to meet his own priorities such as building a wall at the Mexican border. They could evaluate his chaotic management style and inability to organize a response to the COVID-19 pandemic. And they could of course evaluate his attempts to steal the 2020 presidential election that he lost, including inspiring a violent mob to attack the US Capitol in an attempt to pressure Congress not to certify Joe Biden as the rightful winner of that election.

If ballots are the measure, then Republican voters approved of Trump's performance in office, and his campaign in the years since he lost in November 2020. Of the 21.4 million votes cast nationally in the 2024 Republican primary, Trump won 16.2 million of them.[53] That is 75.8%. But did unhyphenated America remain a base for Trump? Such a strong performance across the nation may indicate that Trump's current base is the entire Republican Party, as he won the entire primary by landslide margins. But as Table 7.7 shows, he won by an even larger landslide margin in unhyphenated America. There, he won 86.4% of the vote, as compared to the 74.8% that he won in the rest of the country. Nikki Haley, Trump's main opponent, won 21.7% of the vote in the rest of the country, but only 11.9% in counties with concentrations of American ethnic identifiers.[54]

Trump is thus dominant within the Republican Party as a whole, but he is especially dominant in unhyphenated America. Table 7.8 supports this conclusion. In the rest of the country, Trump won nearly every county, losing only thirty-four of the 2,212 counties where primary results were reported. But in unhyphenated concentrated counties, Trump ran the table. He won all 511 of the counties that voted in the 2024 primaries.

Further evidence of Trump's strong base in unhyphenated America in 2024 is provided by Figure 7.3, which is a scatterplot that shows Trump's vote share on the vertical axis and the percentage of unhyphenated by county on the horizontal

---

53 Popular vote results come from the website The Green Papers at https://www.thegreenpapers. com/P24/R.

54 Data are not available from eleven states, that is, those states where caucus results were not reported at the county level (Alaska, Missouri, New Mexico, North Dakota), where only Trump was on the ballot (Montana, New Jersey, Oregon, South Dakota), where Trump ran only in the caucuses but Haley ran only in the primary (Nevada), where the primary was canceled after Haley dropped out (Delaware), and Wyoming, where a statewide convention determined delegates.

Table 7.7: Republican Presidential Primary/Caucus Vote Share by Region, 2024.

	Trump	Haley
Unhyphenated Concentrated	86.4%	11.9%
	1,666,862	234,774
Rest of Country	74.8%	21.7%
	14,210,036	4,095,578

Note: Unhyphenated concentrated are defined as counties where 19.3% or more of the residents identify their heritage as "American." That value is the national mean at the county level plus one standard deviation. The data include both primary and caucus results, including for the District of Columbia. Election results are not available from Alaska, Delaware, Missouri, Montana, Nevada, New Jersey, North Dakota, Oregon, South Dakota, and Wyoming. Either these states did not provide caucus or convention results at the county level or the primary did not have a full slate of candidates.

Table 7.8: Counties Won by Region, 2024.

	Trump	Haley
Unhyphenated Concentrated	511	0
	100.0%	0.0%
Rest of Country	2,178	34
	98.4%	1.5%

Note: Unhyphenated concentrated are defined as counties where 19.3% or more of the residents identify their heritage as "American." That value is the national mean at the county level plus one standard deviation. The data include both primary and caucus results, including for the District of Columbia. Election results are not available from Alaska, Delaware, Missouri, Montana, Nevada, New Jersey, North Dakota, Oregon, South Dakota, and Wyoming. Either these states did not provide caucus or convention results at the county level or the primary did not have a full slate of candidates.

access. The scatterplot shows that as the share of unhyphenated Americans in a county rises, so does Trump's vote share.

In many ways, the scatterplot shows that concentrations of unhyphenated Americans provide a floor—a really high floor for Trump. In counties with low levels of American ethnic identifiers, there is great variation in Trump's vote share. He attains less than a third of the vote in places such as Washington, DC,

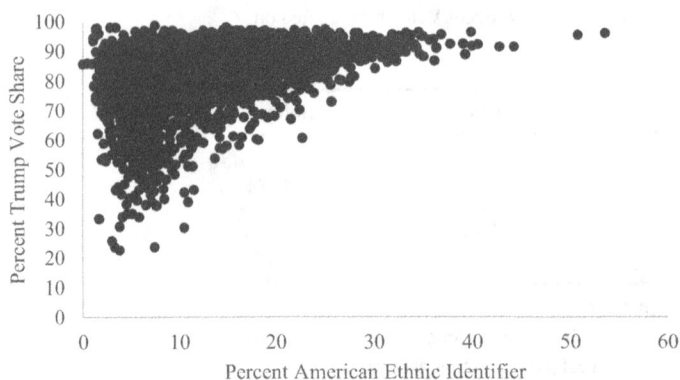

Figure 7.3: Scatterplot, Trump Vote Share by American Ethnicity, 2024 Republican Primary.
Note: County level data. "Percent American Ethnic Identifier" is the share of residents in each county who write "American" as their answer to the Census question "What is your ancestry or ethnic origin?" The "Percent Trump Vote Share" is the county-level vote for Trump in the 2024 Republican primaries and caucuses, including the District of Columbia. Election results are not available from Alaska, Delaware, Missouri, Montana, Nevada, New Jersey, North Dakota, Oregon, South Dakota, and Wyoming. Either these states did not provide caucus or convention results at the county level or the primary did not have a full slate of candidates.

Chittenden County, VT (Burlington), and Richmond, Charlottesville, and Arlington, VA. But there were plenty of counties with low levels of unhyphenated Americans where Trump romped home. For example, Trump won over 90% of the vote in places such as Benewah County, ID, Adams County, WI, and Richmond County (Staten Island), NY, all of which have less than 7% American ethnic identifiers. As Table 7.8 showed, Trump was dominant across the country. He lost only thirty-four counties to Nikki Haley. But the table also shows that he lost none in unhyphenated America, winning all 511 where a primary was held. In fact, in only fourteen of the 511 unhyphenated concentrated counties that voted in the 2024 primary did Trump earn less than the 75.8% of the vote he won nationally. A bivariate regression for the scatterplot shows that for every 1% greater the share of American ethnic identifiers in a county, Trump won an addition 0.58% of the vote in the 2024 Republican primary.

To show that unhyphenated America was a base for Trump in the 2016 Republican primary required all manner of analysis to control for Trump's momentum over the course of that race and the winnowing of the field. Such additional analysis is not needed for 2024. Trump has a base across the entire Republican Party, but his base is remarkably strong in unhyphenated America. Voters there chose Trump by even greater margins than their fellow Republicans in the rest of the country.

7 Unhyphenated America as Trump's Base

In this chapter, I tried to answer the question of whether unhyphenated America is Donald Trump's base within the Republican Party. Trump's performance in the 2016 West Virginia primary led some pundits to speculate that Trump had a base in small-town and rural areas in unhyphenated America. Other pundits noted that Trump's average voters had a higher income than the national average and voters for Democratic candidates in 2016, leading to questions about the location of Trump's base in the Republican Party.

The results here find that unhyphenated America was indeed a base for Trump in 2016 once the effects of momentum and winnowing are accounted for. Trump did better in unhyphenated concentrated counties on Super Tuesday and in the March primaries. This is when Trump built up a clear lead in the Republican nomination contest, and that led to higher vote totals later in the primary contest, often in states with lower shares of American ethnic identifiers. Trump ran up higher vote shares in these states due to his momentum.

Trump also seems to have another base within the Republican Party in the Northeast. The 2016 nomination contest was heavily focused in the Northeast in April with primaries in New York on April 19 and in Connecticut, Delaware, Maryland, Pennsylvania, and Rhode Island on April 26. Trump got a big boost in his vote share in this region, winning by at least twenty-five points in each of these contests. Some analysts found that Trump benefitted from higher vote shares from an ethnic group concentrated in the Northeast—Italian Americans (Aldhous and Singer-Vine 2016; Barone 2016; Grimaldi 2020).

I do not test whether Trump has a base in the Northeast in this chapter. Instead, I focus on unhyphenated America. In doing so, I join with much of the focus of media attention from the 2016 nomination contest on Trump's base in small towns and rural areas in Appalachia and the upper South.

For example, Neil Irwin and Josh Katz (2016) of the *New York Times* analyzed "hundreds of demographic and economic variables from census data, along with results from past elections," with the results of the first twenty-three states to hold primaries and caucuses in 2016. They examined what "factors predict a high level of Trump support" and identified variables such as the share of whites without a high school diploma, the percentage of voters living in mobile homes, the share of people holding "Old Economy" jobs,[55] and support for George Wallace in the 1968 presidential election as four of the strongest (and positive) correlations

---

[55] Irwin and Katz defined these as occupations in the Census Bureau categories for "agriculture, construction, manufacturing, and trade."

with support for Trump. The strongest negative correlation for Trump vote share was the labor participation rate—i.e. the fewer people that had a full-time job in a county, the better Trump did. This article, published on March 12, fit well with the conclusions that I reached based on fifty states' worth of results. Trump did well in places lower on the socioeconomic spectrum. I also find that Trump has a base in unhyphenated American. So did Irwin and Katz; the percentage of those identifying as American ethnic was the second highest correlation with Trump support that they found.

The Irwin and Katz article was published on March 12, which means that their results were preliminary, based on only about half of the country voting. While the Northeast would make a large contribution to Trump's nomination contest victory in 2016, only Massachusetts and Vermont had voted by the time the *Times* published Irwin and Katz's analysis.

Another reason that Trump's base in small-town unhyphenated America receives more attention than his base in the Northeast is the general election. Trump of course did very well in unhyphenated concentrated counties in the 2016 general election; he was the Republican nominee. As I have documented in the previous chapters, unhyphenated America has shifted to Republican candidates since the late 1990s. These trends in the general election seem stronger than just one candidate. But the combination of Trump's strength in this region in the primary and his increased vote share there in the general election made it the focus of a great deal of media attention, which described the region as "Trump Country" (Arbour 2018).

Further evidence that unhyphenated America is a base for Donald Trump within the Republican Party is provided by the results from the 2024 nomination contest. While Trump romped over all of his opposition, racking up three out of every four votes, he ran even stronger in counties with concentrations of unhyphenated Americans, where he won over 85% of the primary votes.

With that being said, the biggest conclusion from this chapter is one that has been obvious since Trump won the Republican nomination contest in 2016: Donald Trump has a base in the Republican Party as a whole. Trump may be seen as a factional candidate who drew the ire of the establishment and the traditional conservatives of his party, but one cannot tell that by his results over the course of the 2016 Republican presidential nomination contest. Trump gained vote share over the course of the campaign, showing all the traditional signs of campaign momentum. He did not seem to have a ceiling on his vote share among Republican voters but instead, took a proportionate share of the vote over the course of the campaign. The 2024 results show that Republicans broadly approved of Trump's actions as their party's most important and prominent member over the eight years before that. For all of his flaws—or possibly because of those flaws—Republican voters approve of Donald Trump.

In summing up the 2016 Republican primary race in June, Benjy Sarlin of *NBC News* wrote: "Over the course of the GOP race, Trump started with an enthusiastic base of blue-collar voters in downscale rural counties and only gradually expanded his appeal to bring in more affluent conservatives in suburbs and cities" (Sarlin and Petulla 2016). The results I present here fit well with Sarlin's conclusion. Trump had a small but important base in unhyphenated America that was helpful to him on Super Tuesday and in the other March primaries. But he expanded his base over the course of the campaign (and, of course, over the eight years between his 2016 and 2024 nominations) to the entirety of the Republican Party.

So yes, unhyphenated America is Trump's base.

Chapter 8
Unhyphenated America, Twenty-First-Century Politics, and the Republican Coalition

In 2024, Donald Trump named Ohio Senator J. D. Vance his running mate, and with Trump's election, Vance was inaugurated vice president the next year and will be a leading contender for the Republican presidential nomination when Trump leaves the political stage. Vance's political fate is, like all vice presidents, tied to the president who chose him for that job. But more than any other vice president, Vance's political fate—in fact, his entire rise—is tied quite specifically to Trump. Vance came to national prominence in 2016 when he published his memoir *Hillbilly Elegy*, describing his upbringing, his working-class family, his mother's addiction and multiple husbands, and his hometown's economic decline. Vance overcame those obstacles to serve in the Marines and graduate from Ohio State and Yale Law School. The book was a sensation, described by reviewers as "excellent," "beautiful," "starkly honest," "heartfelt," and "compelling and compassionate."[56] The book's popularity was not just based on the quality of the writing or the story, but in its connection to the upset victory of Donald Trump, a millionaire from New York who lived in a penthouse in a skyscraper, powered by his base among working-class whites, especially in unhyphenated American communities. In the *New York Times*, Jennifer Senior wrote that the book was a "discerning sociological analysis of the white underclass that has helped drive the . . . ascent of Trump" (Senior 2016). *The Economist* (2016a) wrote that "you will not read a more important book about America this year."

Another measure of the book's impact was that it was made into a Hollywood film with Glenn Close starring as Vance's MaMaw and Amy Adams as Vance's mother. Few political figures have been portrayed in film before they win election, but Vance was on screen in 2020 before winning election to the Senate in 2022 and to the vice presidency in 2024. By one definition—turning its author from an unknown into a statewide and national winner within eight years—*Hillbilly Elegy* is the most important political book ever written.

Vance's writing is relevant to this book because it is a deep probe of what might be called "Appalachian values." In telling the story of his upbringing, Vance attributes the economic struggles of communities of the white working class he grew up in not to issues of "equal opportunity" and the "hollowing out of the eco-

---

[56] Quotes are from Dolan 2016, Esfahani Smith 2016, The Economist 2016b, Simpson 2016, and Pitts 2016.

https://doi.org/10.1515/9783111615707-008

nomic core of working whites" in the industrial Midwest, but instead to a "culture that increasingly encourages social decay" and "a lack of agency" among blue-collar whites (Vance 2016, 7). In Vance's telling, the issue is not economics, but culture among those with Appalachian roots like himself. The subtitle of his book describes it as a "Culture in Crisis."

Vance did not grow up in unhyphenated America. Instead, he grew up in Middletown, Ohio. In 2021, only 12.2% of Butler County's residents identified their ethnicity as American. But Vance's roots are actually in Appalachia. His grandparents moved to Middletown seeking economic improvement through migration—Vance's grandfather worked at a steel mill in Middletown. Vance's grandparents grew up (and are buried) in Breathitt County, Kentucky, where 27.2% of residents are American ethnic identifiers. That is the 110th largest share of unhyphenated Americans out of the country's 3,114 counties. As such, Vance's story is a story of unhyphenated America, one he acknowledges when he writes that "there is an ethnic component lurking in the background of my story" (2016, 2–3).

As noted, Vance's book rose in popularity and acclaim in 2016 as a way to understand why the white working class gravitated to Trump. But Vance's book was written before Trump's general election victory and does not consider why a New York millionaire would appeal to Vance's fellow citizens of Middletown, Ohio. In fact, one could argue that Trump had no special appeal in Middletown. In 2016, Trump ran seven points behind the 69% of the vote that George H. W. Bush earned in Butler County, Ohio. Across twenty-eight years, what change there was in Middletown's political preferences were in the direction of the Democrats.

But Vance's book may be a better way to understand Vance's ancestral home of Breathitt County, Kentucky. Trump won 69% of the vote there in 2016, which was 30% higher than what Bush won in 1988. Like much of unhyphenated America, Breathitt has shifted strongly towards the Republicans and away from its ancestral Democratic roots. Vance tracks this shift in his grandparents, noting that his Democratic grandfather voted for Ronald Reagan in 1984 and never returned to voting for Democrats.

The success of Vance's book shows that there is a desire for more understanding about the culture, values, and thus politics of what Vance identifies as "hillbillies," and what I call unhyphenated America. The shift was meaningful enough to attract attention when Vance was just a memoirist in 2016, and its relevance is even more important now that Vance is vice president and a future presidential candidate.

It is notable that Vance never discusses Donald Trump in *Hillbilly Elegy*. In that, Vance's conclusions fit in with those of this book, which finds that most of the shift in unhyphenated America toward the Republicans happened well before

Donald Trump's surprise victory in 2016. Since our political media culture is focused on who wins, it was only after Trump won that there was a place to fully examine trends that had been in place for over twenty years by that point, and which had reached a plateau that year. But these trends had been occurring in places like Breathitt County, Kentucky and the rest of unhyphenated America since the 1994 midterm election.

The success of *Hillbilly Elegy* also indicates there is an appetite for explaining why the white working class in general and unhyphenated America specifically moved toward the Republicans. Vance offers his own explanation, focused heavily on the resentment he developed as a teenager working as a grocery store cashier of those who "gamed the welfare system" by selling their food stamp purchases for cash and then buying "beer, wine, and cigarettes" with that cash or due to a "drug-addict neighbor" (2016, 139) who would use food stamps to buy T-bone steaks that he was too poor to buy himself.

Vance feels his is a better explanation for "how Appalachia and the South went from staunchly Democratic to staunchly Republican in less than a generation" than the "millions of words" written by political scientists, focused on issues on topics such as "race relations" and "the hold that social conservatism has on that region" (2016, 140).

If Vance takes time away from reading national security briefings or polling reports on New Hampshire primary voters over the next several years to read this book, he will undoubtedly disagree with my conclusions. I am yet another political scientist attributing the shift of Appalachia and the upper South not to resentment over welfare policies, but to factors such as race and religiosity. In particular, I argue that an increase in salience of issues such as abortion and gay rights has played a pivotal role in pushing unhyphenated America to the right. In addition, the nationalization of racial views during the Obama and Trump administrations made the conservative views of unhyphenated America on these issues more relevant and helped to cement the region as not only a landslide Republican region, but a base for Donald Trump within the Republican Party.

Based on my conclusions, I am skeptical of Vance's culture and resentment-based argument for the white working class's affection for the Republicans of the twenty-first century, both those who came before and after Trump's rise in 2016. I also am skeptical of critics' conclusion that Vance's book is a guide to understanding Trump's appeal to voters in 2016. As noted, most of the shift of unhyphenated America to the Republicans had already happened before Trump announced his candidacy. In addition, Trump's signature issue is immigration, and Vance does not address the issue at all in the book. Does Vance's explanation of intra-class resentment explain why Trump's restrictionist stands on immigration appeal to residents of unhyphenated America? Based on the high employment rates of immigrants and the restrictions on their ability to access social welfare funds, it seems a stretch at best to make such claims.

Further, Vance attributes much of his own success to learning to work hard and strive, which he primarily credits to what he learned in the four years he spent in the Marines between high school graduation and enrolling at Ohio State. Among Trump's political talents is blaming others for the misfortunes he and those he ostensibly represents face. This is a useful political talent, but certainly not one associated with the ideals of working hard and striving to overcome obstacles. And of course, from the perspective of hindsight, we know that Trump's first presidency ended with his attempts to steal the 2020 election and the attack his supporters made on the US Capitol on January 6th to stop Congress from certifying Joe Biden as the rightful winner of the 2020 election. I guess one can make the argument that what the white working class needs is Trump to harm democracy, but I think that is a stretch.

Despite my criticism of the hype around the book and Vance's explanation of why he is a conservative, *Hillbilly Elegy* is an important book because without it, it seems impossible that Vance would be vice president right now. The popularity of the book in 2016 reflects the desire of many to understand better the move of the white working class toward the Republicans. The current book explores this topic as well by focusing geographically on the area of Vance's roots in unhyphenated America.

1 Partisan Shifts of Twenty-First-Century Politics

Throughout the book, I have documented the shift of unhyphenated America toward the Republicans over the most recent political generation. Republican gains in counties with a concentration of American ethnic identifiers is a large and important component of the broader national shift in politics to partisan cleavages around cultural issues. In twenty-first century politics, unhyphenated America and other rural areas have moved toward the Republicans. But there is a counter-movement to that in upscale suburbs, which have moved toward the Democrats. The national result of twenty-first century politics is that our national politics are exceedingly close and neither party has a large and sustained advantage. The results of presidential and US House elections often come down to a handful of votes in a handful of swing states or districts. Underlying the close national results are state and local results that became even more divergent, as Republicans ran up higher margins in places like unhyphenated America while Democrats made gains in suburban areas

The politics of the twenty-first century were shaped by decisions that the parties made to appeal to newly emergent policy demanders in the last third of the twentieth century. Much of my focus in this book has been on the decisions made by Democrats because they are the party that embraced the most *new* positions on *new* issues. For example, Democrats have embraced feminist principles and the interest groups that emerged in the wake of second-wave feminism. This has compelled Democrats to embrace positions favored by these feminist groups, most notably in their support of abortion rights. At one level, feminism and abortion are not *new* issues in American life. But for most of American history, concern for abortion and gender equality was a fringe position. As feminism and support for abortion rights emerged into the mainstream starting in the early 1970s, Democrats took up a *new* position for them, supporting abortion rights.

One can see a similar path on issues around gay rights. Gay rights groups moved into the mainstream after Stonewall and in response to the AIDS crisis in the 1980s. Democrats have since then embraced positions favorable to gay rights, a stance that would have been unthinkable in say the 1950s when homosexuality was so unacceptable that one could be arrested or fired for being gay.

On civil rights, Democrats did not take up a new position in American politics but took up a new position for the party of the Jim Crow South. With President Johnson's signature on the Civil Rights Act and Voting Rights Act, Democrats secured a supermajority of African American votes and set the party up to embrace the *new* immigrant populations of Hispanics and Asian Americans.

Republicans shifted less on these issues, maintaining a skepticism of abortion and gay rights that would not have been out of place before the feminist and gay rights movements. Yet the emphasis on these positions were meant to appeal to Christian conservative groups that emerged in the backlash to the *Roe v. Wade* decision and more societal acceptance of homosexuality. In taking up the cause of evangelical Christians, Republicans embraced traditional moralistic views, and, as seen in Chapter 5, benefitted from this stand in unhyphenated America.

Similarly, Republicans maintained a more skeptical view of immigration than Democrats before embracing a more restrictionist posture as Donald Trump became the party's dominant figure in recent years. Opposition to immigration fits well with the Republican skepticism of policies designed to promote civil rights. Many of these programs require an active government and as conservatives, Republicans are much more skeptical of government action in these spheres. That helped make the party more attractive to whites during the Southern Republican realignment. And as shown in Chapter 6, Republican skepticism of civil rights policies and immigration has made them more attractive to residents of unhyphenated concentrated counties in the twenty-first century.

The choice of the two parties to embrace different policy demands and positions on issues such as abortion and immigration have repelled some set of voters and attracted others. The Democratic embrace of abortion has repelled unhyphenated America with its traditionalistic views on sexuality. The Republican embrace of restrictionist positions on immigration has attracted voters in unhyphenated America.

This book has shown how these particular issue positions appealed to residents of unhyphenated America. But the trends identified in unhyphenated America are not isolated and are part of what Aistrup et al. (2023) identify as the geographic realignment. These authors build on the work of Lang and Pearson-Markowitz (2015, 124) who find that "there was a sharp change following the 1996 election. After 1996, the results suggest that on average counties began to polarize and this polarization increased in each election thereafter." Their findings fit well with the results presented here in Chapters 3 and 4, which show that the shift in unhyphenated America began in the 1994 congressional election and was first seen in presidential elections in 1996.

2 Unhyphenated America and National Politics

The choice made by the two parties to embrace conservative positions on non-material issues in the case of the Republicans and more liberal positions on these issues in the case of the Democrats helped create the large and durable Republican shift in unhyphenated America. I argue this shift happened as these non-material issues—such as abortion, gay rights, gun policy, and climate change—increased in salience starting in the 1990s, making them more relevant to voting decisions.

Changes in geographic voting patterns like the ones I identify in unhyphenated America are meaningful and worthy of deep study because the defining assumption of the study of American political behavior is that voters will follow their party identification (Campbell et al. 1960; Green et al. 2002; Huddy et al. 2015). As a result, voting decisions will primarily remain stable across time (Bartels 2000; Miller and Shanks 1996). One explanation of party identification describes it as a "standing decision" for voters and thus predicts that stability will reign (Key 1961). Obviously, this assumption presumes too much, as voters shift back and forth between different candidates and different states of party identification with great frequency. But overall, the prediction tends to hold true. Areas that vote for a Democrat in one election will tend to return a similar percentage for the next Democrat. And Republican areas will tend to vote the same for Republicans.

Big changes in voting patterns thus present an important puzzle for political scientists, not only to document but also to explain. This is why studies of realignment are so common and important in political science (Burnham 1970; Key 1955; Sundquist 1983) and why so much scholarship has focused on the Southern Republican realignment (cf. Chapter 2). That regions with concentrations of unhyphenated Americans are moving strongly and durably to the Republicans is important because it is another demonstration of shifting voting patterns that needs to be explained.

The shift of unhyphenated America to the right fits in with other shifts of rural areas toward the Republicans and a countervailing shift in urbane suburbs to the left. For all that unhyphenated America is shifting to the right and places like the suburban counties surrounding places such as Atlanta and Philadelphia are shifting to the left, the overall result in twenty-first-century politics is two party coalitions that are essentially the same size. Republican growth in rural areas is counterbalanced by Democratic growth in cities and suburbs.

The shifts in both rural areas and the suburbs seem to be driven primarily by non-material issues, such as abortion and gay rights. That non-material issues matter so much to voting decisions in the twenty-first century also goes against the expectation of political science, which holds that voters will primarily respond to the agenda presented to them by the news media and often (but not entirely) determined by the issues politicians choose to address (Ansolabehere and Puy 2018; Behr and Iyengar 1985; Hayes 2008; Zaller 1992). For most of the twenty-first century, the most commonly debated issues discussed in national politics have focused on material issues—the tax cuts sought by Presidents Bush and Trump, the health care reform backed by President Obama, the budget politics of Republican Congresses and the economic stimulus sought by President Obama after the Great Recession and Presidents Trump and Biden in response to the COVID-19 pandemic. On these issues, the parties have maintained their long-standing priorities—with Republicans favoring policies that help those toward the top of the income scale and Democrats prioritizing those lower down the scale. The most covered issues in national politics usually revolve around material concerns, yet non-material concerns have greatly increased in importance for vote choice decisions over this time period, with the move of unhyphenated America toward the Republicans one key component of this shift.

At one level, the focus on material issues should create tensions in both parties between the affluent and the economically struggling factions of each party (Kitschelt and Rehm 2019). Yet, one finds little resistance among working-class Republican voters to their party's support for regressive economic policies (Hacker and Pierson 2020) nor among upper-class Democratic voters to their party's support for redistributionist policies (Hacker et al. 2024). The relative acceptance of materialist policies designed to help the *other* economic class within each of the party coalitions suggests that ideology dominates policy making within each party. Unhyphenated Americans may not benefit from their party's economic policies, which tend to benefit communities higher up the socioeconomic ladder, but they accept conservative thinking that government redistribution programs are undesirable and that tax cuts are the most desirable economic policy, even if the lion's share of the benefits goes to the well-off.

Of course, the preferences of unhyphenated America are well represented in other forms of policy making by the contemporary Republican Party. As demonstrated in Chapter 5, unhyphenated America is notably conservative on abortion, and Republicans have responded by installing enough socially conservative Supreme Court justices to overturn the *Roe v. Wade* ruling. In addition, unhyphenated America supports restrictionist policies on immigration and Republicans have supported more and more of these policies in the Trump era. Thus far, the twenty-first-century Republican Party has been able to satisfy both the affluent and the working-class elements of its base by supporting different sets of policies to appeal to each group. Some tension may exist in these priorities, but Republicans have managed them to this point.

3 The Uniqueness of Unhyphenated America

While the shift of unhyphenated America toward the Republicans is part of a broader shift by rural voters to the Republicans in the twenty-first century, the evidence presented here highlights the uniqueness of the Appalachias and the upper South and their political views.

For one, the shift toward the Republicans is strongest in unhyphenated America. As shown in Chapter 3, the shift toward the Republicans in unhyphenated America is stronger than in other regions of the country. The shift among rural voters to the Republicans has happened for many reasons, but one important component of this broader shift in rural America is the strong move of unhyphenated America toward the Republicans. In unhyphenated America, Democrats lost seventeen points from their national vote share and nearly every US House seat they held in the region. This represents an outsized shift from one relatively small region of the country to the broader shift of rural America to the Republicans.

Further, the evidence presented here shows the shift in unhyphenated America beginning in the 1994 midterms and increasing in the 1996 presidential election when Bill Clinton's vote margin in the region declined from his 1992 margin. That stands in contrast to the conclusions of Lang and Pearson-Markowitz (2015,

124), who find that "this shift to polarization happens slightly earlier in urban areas . . . Thus, the results suggest that the polarizing trend spread from urban to rural density areas with some time lag." That time lag may be true for most rural and small-town America, but the shift happens sooner in unhyphenated America. Aistrup et al. (2023, 637) also find that a geographic realignment begins in 1996, but that a key moment is it "solidifying in 2008 when Democrat Barack Obama is elected." My results show that the shift in unhyphenated America crests in 2008 with Obama's election and Republican gains are more modest after the 2010 mid-term elections. Frankly, there was essentially no more ground for Republicans to win in House seats after 2010. The differences in my findings from the results of those who examined the geographic realignment in broader strokes help to show the uniqueness of the shift in unhyphenated America.

I also find that unhyphenated America has starkly more conservative opinions on a wide variety of issues than not just the rest of the country, but other regions selected based on their loyalty to the contemporary Republican Party. These include opinions on what are often called "social issues," such as abortion and gay rights. These views, combined with conservative views on race and immigration, were a key element in pushing unhyphenated America to the right. The conservatism of unhyphenated America on issues such as abortion also marks the region's distinctiveness. Nationally, views on abortion are similar across different community types. Notably, opinions on abortion are not that different between rural and suburban areas (Kaufman 2021b). In the small towns and rural areas of unhyphenated America though, abortion opinions are distinct and distinctly conservative.

While there is a clear broad national trend toward rural areas increasingly favoring Republicans (Brown and Mettler 2024; Aistrup et al. 2023), that broad statement overlooks much diversity in how much, when, and why rural areas moved toward the Republicans. Some small-town areas, especially ones with economies based on recreation activities, have resisted the Republican trend and moved left (Scala et al. 2015). Most others have moved right, but at different times and for different reasons.

Stephanie Ternullo (2024) studied three Midwestern small towns and found big differences in their political attitudes based primarily on the importance of local social institutions such as churches and labor unions. Applying this to unhyphenated America, one can see similarities to the community Ternullo identified that stayed Democratic through the Reagan and Bush years but moved right in more recent years. In some of the small towns Ternullo studied, social services were provided by extensive church networks or labor unions. But one town Ternullo studied had most of its social service provision provided by the government. The town stayed Democratic longer than the other two studies, but then moved quickly toward the Republicans in the twenty-first century. I see similar patterns in the social and voting patterns of unhyphenated America, where high values on independence and individuality reduce social cohesion. Of course, that is a generalization. The lesson of Ternullo's work and one that is backed up by the results presented here is that each area has its own individual story. There are connections between unhyphenated America and the rest of small-town America in its shift to the Republicans, but the rationales for these movements are distinct.

4 The Scots-Irish?

In quoting Vance earlier in this chapter talking about the "ethnic component" of his story, I did not include the part of his writing where he identifies his own ethnicity. He identifies as Scots-Irish. To quote Vance (2016, 3) more fully, he says "I may be white, but I do not identify with the WASPs of the Northeast. Instead, I identify with the millions of working-class white Americans of Scots-Irish descent who have no college degree . . . To understand me, you must understand that I am a Scots-Irish hillbilly at heart."

Vance's identification as Scots-Irish fits with the ethnic and historical analysis of Appalachia, which has identified the first white settlers of the region as descendants of Protestants who had first moved from Scotland to Ulster Ireland, and then across the Atlantic in the late colonial period. Crossing the Atlantic later than other colonial settlers compelled these Scots-Irish migrants to seek land and fortune in and beyond the Appalachian Mountains over the next century (Fischer 1989). Historical (Dobson 2004; Griffin 2012), ethnographic (Blaustein 2003; Hirschman et al. 2006), linguistic (Crozier 1984; Montgomery 1991), and musicological (Blethen 1994; Ritchie and Orr 2014) research has shown the close connections between Scotland, Ulster, and Appalachia.

Are unhyphenated Americans just Scots-Irish with a different name, or a lack of recognition of their own ethnic history? Quite possibly, as there are strong geographic, demographic, and attitudinal correlations between the two groups. Vance identifies himself as Scots-Irish, as does another former senator with deep family roots in Appalachia—Democrat Jim Webb of Virginia, who wrote a book about the Scots-Irish in America called *Born Fighting* (2004). Yet despite their personal identification as Scots-Irish, both have family roots in unhyphenated America. As noted, Vance's family is from Breathitt County, Kentucky and Webb's family roots are in Scott County, Virginia, where 29.7% of the population identifies their ethnicity as American.

My data do not allow me to provide direct evidence of the connection between Americans of Scots-Irish descent and unhyphenated Americans. My measure for unhyphenated America is individual responses to a census question. It is an open-ended question, and respondents can certainly choose Scots-Irish if they want. That they write American as the answer is meaningful by itself but does not disprove their Scots-Irish roots.

It is also not crucial to determine completely the full connection between the Scots-Irish and unhyphenated Americans. This is a study of geography and what I have shown clearly is that the geography of the Appalachias and upper South are politically meaningful, as voters there have moved strongly toward the Republicans over recent generations. Hints that the Scots-Irish are not very distinct in American culture exist across academic study of Appalachia. One historical examination of the Scots-Irish migration to the American colonies is titled *The People with No Name* (Griffin 2012), which sure sounds like an eighteenth-century term for the unhyphenated. From a more contemporary standpoint, I will add the thoughts of famed Southern sociologist John Shelton Reed, who said that if you "ask people what their ethnicity is, and a lot of Scots-Irish people either don't know or if they know it they just [don't] acknowledge it. It's not something they really identify with. They're just plain old Americans, plain vanilla" (quoted in Joseph 2009).

5 A Force of Populism and Trumpism

Whether one calls residents of areas with concentrations of American ethnic identifiers Scots-Irish, unhyphenated Americans, the people with no name, or anything else, what is clear from the results of this book is that they are an important and growing part of the contemporary Republican coalition. The share of the national population in unhyphenated America is about one in twenty, but about one in seven of the additional votes Donald Trump won in 2024 over George H. W. Bush in 1988 came from the region.

Certainly, the demographic characteristics of unhyphenated America—low levels of income, education, and wealth—are similar to those in other rural and small-town areas across the country where Republicans have gained a greater vote share over the last political generation. Broadly, the growth of a large working-class faction within the Republican Party is at odds with the Republicans' traditional base among the upper middle class. As discussed above, while Republicans have maintained their preference for economic policies that appeal to their donor class, downscale voters have had great influence in pushing the Republican coalition to support their priorities.

This is apparent in the Republican push to restrict abortion rights, but the clearest indication of the impact of unhyphenated America on the Republican coalition has been around the issue of immigration. In recent years, the Republicans have more fully adopted a restrictionist policy on issues of immigration. This has happened in large part due to takeover of the party by Donald Trump, who has propelled himself to the top of the Republican Party through his support of these restrictionist policies. As seen in Chapter 6, these views were popular in unhyphenated America and were part of why, as shown in Chapter 7, unhyphenated America responded so strongly to Trump in the 2016 Republican primary. For years, the Republican Party's position on immigration was unsettled between a restrictionist wing and a business wing that favored liberalizing immigration policy to increase the quality and size of the pool of potential employees. Trump's domination of the Republican Party has settled this conflict primarily—though not wholly—in favor of the restrictionist side. And as one of Trump's bases within the Republican Party, unhyphenated America provided key support for the victory of not only Trump, but also the restrictionist position within the party. In promoting restrictionist views over business-friendly policies, unhyphenated America has shown that it can be a force for populism in the Republican Party.

This examination of immigration policy helps to demonstrate that unhyphenated America is a force for Trumpism within the Republican coalition. As shown in Chapter 7, counties with concentrations of unhyphenated Americans gave Trump higher vote shares in the 2016 nomination contest once the effects of momentum and winnowing are controlled. They also gave Trump a higher vote share than other counties in 2024, full stop. No controls for momentum are needed.

In addition, unhyphenated America has strongly conservative opinions on issues of race, as shown in Chapter 6. Donald Trump is distinct from most other politicians and one demonstration of that distinctiveness is Trump's ability to credibly make openly racist appeals to voters. Trump's willingness to engage in racist rhetoric appeals directly to voters with racist views but seems, in my opinion, to work more as an appeal to voters frustrated with the status quo and who see Trump's willingness to violate social norms as a positive. Regardless of the reason, Trump's racially charged rhetoric appears to work in unhyphenated America and is part of why the region is a force for Trumpism.

An obvious question about Trumpism at the time of publication is, what is the future for Trumpism in the Republican coalition after Donald Trump himself leaves the stage? Obviously, to answer this question, one must understand what Trumpism is, and that is a slippery concept. For as much as one can identify Trump with a single signature issue—immigration—or connect him with specific and unique ideas—such as election denial—Trump's political success—even more than most modern politicians—seems intimately tied to his personality.

Others can call for restrictionist policies on immigration, make racially resentful appeals, hold big rallies, or vote to overturn the actual results of the 2020 election, but that does not make one a Trump. From my perspective, Trump seems to succeed not just through policy stands or soaring rhetoric, but by making his appeals in an entertaining and compelling way. Most people know that Trump is insulting people and lies with great frequency; but among his supporters, they think he is doing this on their behalf and against those they do not like. That different supporters of Trump with different priorities and different opponents can think Trump is lying and insulting people on their behalf seems a feature, not a bug, of Trump's political appeal.

Trump's personality and ability to connect with his audience makes it difficult for other Republican politicians to replicate Trump's success. To date, none has done so successfully on a large scale. Other Republican politicians have adopted Trump's confrontational style, his restrictionist policies on immigration, and his resistance to acceptance of the country's diversification, yet no one came close to defeating Trump in the 2024 primaries. Trumpist candidates have often fared poorly in statewide races, even in places were Trump himself won that year (cf. the Nevada Senate race in 2024). Trump ran ahead of every swing-state Republican Senate candidate in 2024, showing both his personal popularity, and demonstrating the issue for other Republicans of matching Trump's appeal once he leaves the political stage.

Due to the Electoral College, unhyphenated America plays a relatively small role in determining which presidential candidate wins the general election. Of states with large concentrations of unhyphenated Americans, only North Carolina was a swing state in the 2024 presidential election. But in Republican nomination contests, unhyphenated America might play a pivotal role. The region provided a base for Donald Trump in the highly contested 2016 nomination contest and again in the less contentious 2024 contest. Its stronger vote for Trump differentiates unhyphenated America from more urban and suburban parts of the Republican coalition, even inside states like Tennessee with a large number of counties in unhyphenated America. Trump was able to build a coalition beyond his base in unhyphenated America in both 2016 and in the years since then. This will be a challenge for subsequent Republican presidential candidates.

Of course, part of the challenge for such candidates is identifying what part of Trump appeals to different sets of Republican voters—including those in unhyphenated America—and adapting that to one's one personality and political style as well as new sets of concerns that develop over the course of the second Trump Administration.

This analysis brings us back to Vance. Vance will have the advantage in future Republican primaries of having been vice president in the second Trump Administration. Being the sitting vice president proved advantageous for George H. W. Bush and Al Gore in their quest for their party's nomination. However, the vice presidency does not automatically confer those advantages on its occupant, as Dan Quayle and Joe Biden in 2016 can attest. Vance must work through a party with lots of ambitious presidential aspirants such as himself, low favorability ratings from the 2024 campaign, and the fact that Donald Trump takes up so much of the spotlight that no member of his administration seems likely to get out of his shadow. One way Vance is likely to try to overcome those drawbacks is by highlighting his Appalachian and small-town roots.

Highlighting one's biography and humble background is of course standard fare for politicians, who want to connect with voters who are less accomplished, less wealthy, and less educated than the candidate. For Vance, this strategy has advantages beyond those for an average politician. Vance came to some degree of political fame through writing a memoir of his and his family's struggle and the role that his unhyphenated American roots played in that story. Vance has already highlighted his roots in Appalachia to a national audience. In his acceptance speech at the 2024 Republican Convention, Vance talked about his family's "cemetery plot on a mountainside in Eastern Kentucky . . . near my family's ancestral home" (Vance 2024). Vance then talked about the generations of his relatives buried in Breathitt County. "Seven generations of people who have fought for this country. Who have built this country. Who have made things in this country. And who would fight and die to protect this country if they were asked to. That is our homeland. People will not fight for abstractions, but they will fight for their home" (Vance 2024).

In writing about unhyphenated America, I have identified a political region that is worth studying because it has shifted strongly toward the Republicans over the most recent political generation, defying expectations that party identification leads to geographically stable voting patterns. I have identified a political region that has moved politically in large part due to its conservative positions on non-material issues and the increase in salience of these issues in the politics of the twenty-first century. It is worthwhile studying the region for these historical and political science reasons. But the region is going to matter politically in the future—as an important part of the contemporary Republican coalition and as a key potential voting block in future Republican nomination contests. Specifically, it will be a locus of rhetoric and used in attempts to strive for authenticity by one of those future Republican presidential candidates in J. D. Vance. For all of those reasons, unhyphenated America has mattered in American politics over the last political generation. And for all of those reasons, it will continue to matter into the future.

Works Cited

ABC News. 2016. "Tracking Appalachia's Swing from Hillary Clinton to Donald Trump Country: Clinton Faces an Uphill Battle in Appalachia, a Growing Base for Trump." ABCNews.com, May 4. Accessed March 22, 2024 from https://abcnews.go.com/Politics/tracking-appalachias-swing-hillary-clinton-donald-trump-country/story?id=38868590

Abramowitz, Alan I. 1989. "Viability, Electability, and Candidate Choice in a Presidential Primary Election: A Test of Competing Hypotheses." *Journal of Politics* 51(4): 977–992.

Abramowitz, Alan I. 2022. "The Polarized American Electorate: The Rise of Partisan-Ideological Consistency and Its Consequences." *Political Science Quarterly* 137(4): 645–674.

Abramowitz, Alan, and Jennifer McCoy. 2019. "Racial Resentment, Negative Partisanship, and Polarization in Trump's America." *The ANNALS of the American Academy of Political and Social Science* 681(1): 137–156.

Abramowitz, Alan I., and Steven Webster. 2016. "The Rise of Negative Partisanship and the Nationalization of US Elections in the 21st Century." *Electoral Studies* 41(1): 12–22.

Acharya, Avidit, Matthew Blackwell, and Maya Sen. 2016. "The Political Legacy of American Slavery." *The Journal of Politics* 78(3), 621–641.

Acharya, Avidit, Matthew Blackwell, and Maya Sen. 2018. *Deep Roots: How Slavery Still Shapes Southern Politics*. Princeton, NJ: Princeton University Press.

Adams, Greg D. 1997. "Abortion: Evidence of an Issue Evolution." *American Journal of Political Science* 41(3): 718–737.

Adler, Ben. 2010. "Democrat Joe Manchin's Republican TV Commercial." Newsweek.com, October 12. Accessed October 23, 2023 from https://www.newsweek.com/democrat-joe-manchins-republican-tv-commercial-214504

Aistrup, Joseph A. 1996. *The Southern Strategy Revisited: Republican Top Down Advancement in the South*. Lexington, KY: University of Kentucky Press.

Aistrup, Joseph A., Binita Mahato, and John C. Morris. 2023. "The 1990s Party Realignment of US Presidential Elections: Geographic Sorting of Counties by Blue or Red." *Social Science Quarterly* 104(4): 636–668.

Alba, Richard D. 1990. *Ethnic Identity: The Transformation of White America*. New Haven, CT: Yale University Press.

Alba, Richard D., and Victor Nee. 1997. "Rethinking Assimilation Theory for a New Era of Immigration." *International Migration Review* 31(4): 826–874.

Albrecht, Don E. 2019. "The Nonmetro Vote and the Election of Donald Trump." *Journal of Rural Social Sciences* 34(1): Article 3.

Aldhous, Peter, and Jeremy Singer-Vine. 2016. "Which White People Support Trump?" Buzzfeed, October 9. Accessed January 12, 2025 from https://www.buzzfeednews.com/article/peterald hous/trump-and-the-white-vote

All Things Considered. 2000. "Tennessee Voters Speculate About Why Gore Didn't Win Their State." *National Public Radio*, November 13. Accessed July 14, 2024 via Nexis Uni (LexisNexis).

Allen, Jonathan. 2002. "A Big-Spending Rematch in West Virginia Goes on the Air." *Congressional Quarterly Daily Monitor*. November 1. Accessed November 11, 2024 via Nexis Uni (LexisNexis).

Ansolabehere, Stephen, and M. Socorro Puy. 2018. "Measuring Issue-Salience in Voters Preferences." *Electoral Studies* 51(1): 103–114.

Arbour, Brian K. 2011. "Unhyphenated Americans in the 2010 U.S. House Election." *The Forum* 9(2): Article 4.

https://doi.org/10.1515/9783111615707-009

Arbour, Brian. 2018. "'This Is Trump Country: Donald Trump's Base and Partisan Change in Unhyphenated America." In *American Political Parties Under Press: Strategic Adaptations for a Changing Electorate*, edited by Chapman Rackaway and Laurie Rice, 15–42. Cham: Palgrave Macmillan.

Arbour, Brian K., and Jeremy M. Teigen. 2011. "Barack Obama's 'American' Problem: Unhyphenated Americans in the 2008 Elections." *Social Science Quarterly* 92(3): 563–587.

Arbour, Brian, and Jeremy M. Teigen. 2016. "The Two Maps Are Incredibly Revealing about Who Is Voting for Trump, and Why." The Monkey Cage (Washington Post.com), April 5. Accessed January 3, 2020 from https://www.washingtonpost.com/news/monkey-cage/wp/2016/04/05/these-two-maps-are-incredibly-revealing-about-whos-voting-for-trump-and-why/

Arsenault, Raymond. 1984. "The End of the Long Hot Summer: The Air Conditioner and Southern Culture." *The Journal of Southern History* 50(4): 597–628.

Astor, Aaron. 2008. "Speak Your Piece: Inspecting the McCain Belt." *The Daily Yonder*, November 15. Accessed December 5, 2004 from https://dailyyonder.com/speak-your-piece-inspecting-mccain-belt/2008/11/15/

Ayers, John W., C. Richard Hofstetter, Keith Schnakenberg, and Bohdan Kolody. 2009. "Is Immigration a Racial Issue? Anglo Attitudes on Immigration Policies in a Border County." *Social Science Quarterly* 90(3): 593–610.

Azari, Julia. 2016. "A for Effort? Republican Elites Tried to Coordinate but Never Quite Got There." *Vox*, May 19. www.vox.com/mischiefs-of-faction/2016/5/19/1171261/republican-elites-coordination

Barone, Michael. 2016. "Ethnicity Still Matters in the Politics of 2016." *Washington Examiner* (published at AEI.org), April 25. Accessed January 12, 2025 from https://www.aei.org/articles/ethnicity-still-matters-in-the-politics-of-2016/

Barone, Michael, and Chuck McCutcheon. 2011. *The Almanac of American Politics 2012*. Chicago, IL: University of Chicago Press.

Barone, Michael, Chuck McCutcheon, Sean Trende, and Josh Kraushaar. 2013. *The Almanac of American Politics 2013*. Chicago, IL: University of Chicago Press.

Barone, Michael, and Grant Ujifusa. 1995. *The Almanac of American Politics 1996*. Washington, DC: National Journal.

Barone, Michael, and Grant Ujifusa. 1999. *The Almanac of American Politics 2000*. Washington, DC: National Journal.

Barreto, Matt A., Claudia Alegre, J. Isaiah Bailey, Alexandria Davis, Joshua Ferrer, Joyce Nguy, Christopher Palmisano, and Crystal Robertson. 2024. "Black Lives Matter and the Racialized Support for the January 6th Insurrection." *The ANNALS of the American Academy of Political and Social Science* 708(1): 64–82.

Bartels, Larry M. 1988. *Presidential Primaries and the Dynamics of Public Choice*. Princeton, NJ: Princeton University Press.

Bartels, Larry M. 2000. "Partisanship and Voting Behavior, 1952–1996." *American Journal of Political Science* 44(1): 35–50.

Bartels, Larry M. 2020. "Ethnic Antagonism Erodes Republicans' Commitment to Democracy." *Proceedings of the National Academy of Sciences* 117(22): 22752–22759.

Bartley, Numan V., and Hugh D. Graham. 1978. *Southern Elections, County and Precinct Data 1950–1972*. Baton Rouge, LA: Louisiana State University Press.

Bass, Jack, and Walter de Vries. 1976. *The Transformation of the Southern Electorate*. New York: Basic Books.

Baumgardner, James L. 2004. "Civil Rights, Culture Wars, Voting and the Downfall of the Democratic Party in the South." *American Review of Politics* 25(Spring): 6–23.

Baylor, Christopher. 2017. *First to the Party: The Group Origins of Political Transformation*. Philadelphia, PA: University of Pennsylvania Press, 2017.

Beck, Paul Allen. 1977. "Partisan Dealignment in the Postwar South." *American Political Science Review* 71(2): 477–496.

Behr, Roy L., and Shanto Iyengar. 1985. "Television News, Real-World Cues, and Changes in the Public Agenda." *Public Opinion Quarterly* 49(1): 38–57.

Bell, Shannon Elizabeth, and Richard York. 2010. "Community Economic Identity: The Coal Industry and Ideology Construction in West Virginia." *Rural Sociology* 75(1): 111–143.

Benegal, Sahil E. 2018. "The Spillover of Race and Racial Attitudes into Public Opinion about Climate Change." *Environmental Politics* 27(4): 733–756.

Berg, Justin Allen. 2013. "Opposition to Pro-Immigrant Public Policy: Symbolic Racism and Group Threat." *Sociological Inquiry* 83(1): 1–31.

Berke, Richard L. 1994. "Democrats Rediscover Knack of Losing." *New York Times*, May 29. D5.

Berman, Russell. 2016. "Can Clinton Win Back Appalachia?" TheAtlantic.com, May 3. Accessed March 22, 2024 from https://www.theatlantic.com/politics/archive/2016/05/can-clinton-win-back-appalachia/480900/

Bishin, Benjamin G., and Casey A. Klofstad. 2012. "The Political Incorporation of Cuban Americans: Why Won't Little Havana Turn Blue?" *Political Research Quarterly* 65(3): 586–599.

Bishop, Bill with Robert Cushing. 2008. *The Big Sort: Why the Clustering of Like-Minded America Is Tearing Us Apart*. New York: Houghton Mifflin.

Black, Earl, and Merle Black. 1973. "The Wallace Vote in Alabama: A Multiple Regression Analysis." *Journal of Politics* 35(3): 730–736.

Black, Earl, and Merle Black. 1987. *Politics and Society in the South*. Cambridge, MA: Harvard University Press.

Black, Earl, and Merle Black. 1992. *The Vital South*. Cambridge, MA: Harvard University Press.

Black, Earl, and Merle Black. 2002. *The Rise of Southern Republicans*. Cambridge, MA: Harvard University Press.

Blaustein, Richard. 2023. *The Thistle and the Brier: Historical Links and Cultural Parallels between Scotland and Appalachia*. Contributions to Southern Appalachian Studies, vol. 7. New York: McFarland.

Blethen, H. Tyler. 1994. "The Transmission of Scottish Culture to the Southern Back Country." *Journal of the Appalachian Studies Association* 6: 59–72.

Bobo, Lawrence, and James R. Kluegel. 1997. "Status, Ideology, and Dimensions of Whites' Racist Beliefs and Attitudes: Progress and Stagnation." In *Racial Attitudes in the 1990s: Continuity and Change*, edited by Steven A. Tuch and Jack K. Martin, 93–120. Westport, CT: Praeger.

Bobo, Lawrence, James R. Kluegel, and Ryan A. Smith. 1997. "Laissez-faire Racism: The Crystallization of a Kinder, Gentler, Antiblack Ideology." In *Racial Attitudes in the 1990s: Continuity and Change*, edited by Steven A. Tuch and Jack K. Martin, 15–42. Westport, CT: Praeger.

Brown, Jacob R., and Ryan D. Enos. 2021. "The Measurement of Partisan Sorting for 180 Million Voters." *Nature Human Behavior* 5: 998–1008.

Brown, Trevor E., and Suzanne Mettler. 2024 "Sequential Polarization: The Development of the Rural-Urban Political Divide, 1976–2020." *Perspectives on Politics* 22(3): 630–658.

Bullock, Charles S., III. 1985. "Congressional Roll Call Voting in a Two-Party South." *Social Science Quarterly* 66(4): 789–804.

Burnham, Walter Dean. 1970. *Critical Elections and the Mainsprings of American Politics*. New York: W.W. Norton.

Burnham, Walter Dean. 1999. "Constitutional Moments and Punctuated Equilibria: A Political Scientist Confronts Bruce Ackerman's 'We the People'." *Yale Law Journal* 108(8): 2237–2277.

Burns, Peter, and James Gimpel. 2000. "Economic Insecurity, Prejudicial Stereotypes, and Public Opinion on Immigration Policy." *Political Science Quarterly* 115(2): 201–225.

Cain, Bruce E., John A. Ferejohn, and Morris P. Fiorina. 1987. *The Personal Vote: Constituency Service and Electoral Independence.* Cambridge, MA: Harvard University Press.

Campbell, Angus, Philip E. Converse, Warren E. Miller, and Donald E. Stokes. 1960. *The American Voter.* New York: John Wiley & Sons.

Campbell, Bruce A. 1977. "Patterns of Change in the Partisan Loyalties of Native Southerners: 1952–1972." *Journal of Politics* 39(3): 730–761.

Carmines, Edward G., and James A. Stimson. 1989. *Issue Evolution: Race and the Transformation of American Politics.* Princeton, NJ: Princeton University Press.

Carmines, Edward G., and James Woods. 2002. "The Role of Party Activists in the Evolution of the Abortion Issue." *Political Behavior* 24(2): 361–377.

Carter, Shan, Jonathan Corum, Amanda Cox, Farhanna Hossain, and Xaquin G. V. 2011. "Electoral Shifts." *New York Times*, April 14. Accessed December 5, 2024 from https://archive.nytimes.com/www.nytimes.com/interactive/2008/11/05/us/politics/20081104_ELECTION_RECAP.html

Casellas, Jason P., and Sonia Jordan Wallace. 2020. "Sanctuary Cities: Public Attitudes toward Enforcement Collaboration between Local Police and Federal Immigration Authorities." *Urban Affairs Review* 56(1): 32–64.

Census Reporter. n.d. "Ancestry." Accessed January 2, 2025 from https://censusreporter.org/topics/ancestry/

Chen, Philip, and Ruchika Mohanty. 2017. "Obama's Economy: Conditional Racial Spillover into Evaluations of the Economy." *International Journal of Public Opinion Research* 30(3): 365–391.

Clerk of the US House of Representatives. 1945. "Statistics of the Presidential and Congressional Election of November 7, 1944." March 1, 1945. Washington, DC: Government Printing Office. Accessed October 8, 2024 from https://clerk.house.gov/member_info/electionInfo/1944election.pdf

Clymer, Adam. 2002. "Turning Phrase to Wrest Social Security Issue from Democrats." *New York Times*, October 16. Accessed October 30, 2024 via Nexis Uni (LexisNexis).

Cohen, Richard E. 2002. "The GOP's Social Security Blanket." *National Journal*, October 5. Accessed October 30, 2024 via Nexis Uni (LexisNexis).

Confessore, Nicholas, and Karen Yourish. 2016. "$2 Billion Worth of Free Media for Donald Trump." *New York Times*, March 15. https://www.nytimes.com/2016/03/16/upshot/measuring-donald-trumps-mammoth-advantage-in-free-media.html

Cook Political Report. 2000. "The Cook Political Report: Dec. 20, 2000." Accessed October 30, 2024 from https://www.cookpolitical.com/analysis/national/cpr-archives/cook-political-report-december-20-2000

Cook Political Report. 2001. "The Cook Political Report: Dec. 20, 2021." Accessed October 30, 2024 from https://www.cookpolitical.com/analysis/national/cpr-archives/cook-political-report-december-20-2001

Cook Political Report. 2002. "The Cook Political Report: Feb, 25, 2002." Accessed November 11, 2024 from https://www.cookpolitical.com/analysis/national/cpr-archives/cook-political-report-february-25-2002

Coombs, Michael W., John R. Hibbing, and Susan Welch. 1984. "Black Constituents and Congressional Roll Call Votes." *Western Political Quarterly* 37(3): 424–434.

Cooper, Christopher A., Scott H. Huffmon, Gibbs H. Knotts, and Seth C. McKee. 2024. "Population Change, Racial Settlement Patterns, and the Newest Southern Electorate." *Politics, Groups, and Identities*, 1–17. https://doi.org/10.1080/21565503.2024.2328559

Cosman, Bernard. 1966. *Five States for Goldwater: Continuity and Change in Southern Presidential Voting Patterns*. Tuscaloosa, AL: University of Alabama Press.

Cowan, Geoffrey. 2016. *Let the People Rule: Theodore Roosevelt and the Birth of the Presidential Primary*. New York: W.W. Norton.

Cramer, Katherine J. 2016. *The Politics of Resentment: Rural Consciousness in Wisconsin and the Rise of Scott Walker*. Chicago, IL: University of Chicago Press.

Crespi, Irving. 1971. "Structural Sources of the George Wallace Constituency." *Social Science Quarterly* 52(1): 115–132.

Cross, Al. 1994a. "KY 02: Natcher Is Remembered, Prather Likely Successor?" *The Hotline*, March 31. Accessed October 23, 2024 via Nexis Uni (LexisNexis).

Cross, Al. 1994b. "May Races: National GOP Money Makes KY 02 a 'Race.'" *The Hotline*, May 18. Accessed October 23, 2024 via Nexis Uni (LexisNexis).

Cross, Al. 1994c. "KY 02: Dems Lose Another One, Lewis Defeats Prather." *The Hotline*, May 25. Accessed October 23, 2024 via Nexis Uni (LexisNexis).

Crozier, Alan. 1984. "The Scotch-Irish Influence on American English." *American Speech* 59(4): 310–331.

Dahl, Robert Alan. 1961. *Who Governs? Democracy and Power in an American City*. New Haven, CT: Yale University Press.

Davis, Darren W., and David C. Wilson. 2023. "'Stop the Steal': Racial Resentment, Affective Partisanship, and Investigating the January 6th Insurrection." *The ANNALS of the American Academy of Political and Social Science* 708(1): 83–101.

Dobson, David. 2004. *Scottish Emigration to Colonial America, 1607–1785*. Atlanta, GA: University of Georgia Press.

Dolan, Jon. 2016. "Review: Drive-By-Truckers' 'American Band' Is Election-Year Evaluation." *Rolling Stone*, September 30. Accessed January 12, 2025 from https://www.rollingstone.com/music/music-album-reviews/review-drive-by-truckers-american-band-is-election-year-evalution-103194/

Douthat, Ross. 2010. "How We Got Here." *New York Times*, November 1. Accessed October 29, 2024 via Nexis Uni (LexisNexis).

Eller, Ronald D. *Uneven Ground: Appalachia since 1945*. Lexington, KY: University Press of Kentucky.

Enders, Adam M., and Jamil S. Scott, 2019. "The Increasing Racialization of American Electoral Politics, 1988–2016." *American Politics Research* 47(2): 275–303.

Enders, Adam M., and Judd R. Thornton. 2022 "Racial Resentment, Electoral Loss, and Satisfaction with Democracy among Whites in the United States: 2004–2016." *Political Behavior* 44(1): 389–410.

Enns, Peter K., and Ashley Jardina. 2021. "Complicating the Role of White Racial Attitudes and Anti-Immigrant Sentiment in the 2016 US Presidential Election." *Public Opinion Quarterly* 85(2): 539–570.

Erikson, Robert S., and Gerald C. Wright. 2000. "Representation of Constituency Ideology in Congress." In *Continuity and Change in House Elections*, edited by David W. Brady, John F. Cogan, and Morris P. Fiorina, 149–177. Stanford, CA: Stanford University Press.

Esfahani Smith, Emily. 2016. "The Forgotten Americans." *Wall Street Journal*, July 27. Accessed January 12, 2025 from https://www.wsj.com/articles/the-forgotten-americans-1469660992

Farley, Reynolds. 1991. "The New Census Question about Ancestry: What Did It Tell Us?" *Demography* 28(3): 411–429.

Feigenbaum, James, and Cameron A. Shelton. 2013. "The Vicious Cycle: Fundraising and Perceived Visibility in US Presidential Primaries." *Quarterly Journal of Political Science* 8(1): 1–40.

Filindra, Alexandra, Noah J. Kaplan, and Andrea Manning, 2024. "Who Buys the 'Big Lie'? White Racial Grievance and Confidence in the Fairness of American Elections." *The Journal of Race, Ethnicity, and Politics* 9(1): 182–203.

Fiorina, Morris P. 1977. "The Case of the Vanishing Margins: The Bureaucracy Did It." *The American Political Science Review* 71(2): 177–181.

Fischer, David Hackett. 1989. *Albion's Seed: Four British Folkways in America*. New York: Oxford University Press.

Gans, Herbert J. 1979. "Symbolic Ethnicity: The Future of Ethnic Groups and Cultures in America." *Ethnic and Racial Studies* 2(1): 1–20.

Garand, James C., Dan Qi, and Max Magaña. 2022 "Perceptions of Immigrant Threat, American Identity, and Vote Choice in the 2016 U.S. Presidential Election." *Political Behavior* 44(2): 877–893.

Garretson, Jeremiah J. 2018. *The Path to Gay Rights: How Activism and Coming Out Changed Public Opinion*. New York: New York University Press.

Gelman, Andrew. 2010. *Red State, Blue State, Rich State, Poor State: Why Americans Vote the Way They Do*. Princeton, NJ: Princeton University Press.

Giles, Michael W. 1977. "Percent Black and Racial Hostility: An Old Assumption Revisited." *Social Science Quarterly* 58(3): 412–417.

Giles, Michael W., and Melanie A. Buckner. 1993. "David Duke and Black Threat: An Old Hypothesis Revisited." *Journal of Politics* 55(3): 702–713.

Giles, Michael W., and Arthur Evans. 1986. "The Power Approach to Intergroup Hostility." *Journal of Conflict Resolution* 30(3): 460–485.

Giles, Michael W., and Kaenen Hertz. 1994. "Racial Threat and Partisan Identification." *American Political Science Review* 88(2): 317–326.

Gimpel, James G. 2017. "Immigration Policy Opinion and the 2016 Presidential Vote." December 4. Washington, DC: Center for Immigration Studies. Accessed May 18, 2020 from https://cis.org/Report/Immigration-Policy-Opinion-and-2016-Presidential-Vote

Gimpel, James G., and Wendy K. Tam Cho. 2004. "The Persistence of White Ethnicity in New England Politics." *Political Geography* 23(8): 987–1008.

Glaser, James M. 1994. "Back to the Black Belt: Racial Environment and White Racial Attitudes in the South." *Journal of Politics* 56(1): 21–41.

Glaser, James M. 1996. *Race, Campaign Politics, and the Realignment in the South*. New Haven, CT: Yale University Press.

Glaser, James M. 2005. *The Hand of the Past in Contemporary Southern Politics*. New Haven, CT: Yale University Press.

Glaser, James M., and Martin Gilens. 1997. "Interregional Migration and Political Resocialization: A Study of Racial Attitudes under Pressure." *The Public Opinion Quarterly* 61(1): 72–86.

Glazer, Nathan, and Daniel P. Moynihan. 1963. *Beyond the Melting Pot: The Negroes, Puerto Ricans, Jews, Italians, and Irish of New York City*. Cambridge, MA: MIT Press.

Goetz, Stephan J., Meri Davlasheridze, Yicheol Han, and David A. Fleming-Muñoz. 2019. "Explaining the 2016 Vote for President Trump across US Counties." *Applied Economic Perspectives and Policy* 41(4): 703–722.

Grammich, Clifford, Kirk Hadaway, Richard Houseal, Dale E. Jones, Alexei Krindatch, Richie Stanley, and Richard H. Taylor. 2012. *2010 U.S. Religion Census: Religious Congregations & Membership Study*. Association of Statisticians of American Religious Bodies.

Greeley, Andrew M. 1972. "Political Attitudes among American White Ethnics." *Public Opinion Quarterly* 36(2): 213–220.

Green, Donald, Bradley Palmquist, and Eric Schickler. 2002. *Partisan Hearts and Minds: Political Parties and the Social Identity of Voters*. New Haven, CT: Yale University Press.

Green, John C., Lyman A. Kellstedt, Corwin E. Smith, and James L. Guth. 2010. "The Soul of the South: Religion and Southern Politics in the New Millennium." In *The New Politics of the Old South*. 4th ed. Charles S. Bullock III and Mark J. Rozell, eds. New York: Rowman and Littlefield Publishers, 283–303.

Griffin, Patrick. 2012. *The People with No Name: Ireland's Ulster Scots, America's Scots Irish, and the Creation of a British Atlantic World, 1689–1764*. Princeton, NJ: Princeton University Press.

Grimaldi, Christine. 2020. "The Paesano of Shame: Trump's Italian American Consiglieres." *Los Angeles Review of Books*, November 2. Accessed January 12, 2025 from https://lareviewofbooks.org/article/the-paesano-of-shame-trumps-italian-american-consiglieres/

Grofman, Bernard, Lisa Handley, and Richard G. Niemi. 1992. *Minority Representation and the Quest for Voting Equality*. Cambridge: Cambridge University Press.

Grogan, Colleen M., and Sunggeum Ethan Park. 2017. "The Racial Divide in State Medicaid Expansions." *Journal of Health Politics, Policy, and Law* 42(3): 539–572.

Grossman, Matt, and David A. Hopkins. 2024. *Polarized by Degrees: How the Diploma Divide and the Culture War Transformed American Politics*. New York: Cambridge University Press.

Guber, Deborah Lynn. 2013. "A Cooling Climate for Change? Party Polarization and the Politics of Global Warming." *American Behavioral Scientist* 57(1): 93–115.

Gutman, David. 2016a. "GOP Candidate Cole Endorses Trump Bid." *Charleston Gazette-Mail*, May 4. Accessed March 8, 2024 via Nexis Uni (LexisNexis).

Gutman, David. 2016b. "'Save Your Vote' for Fall, Trump Says; Trump Praises Miners, Hits All Campaign Themes for Civic Center Crowd." *Charleston Gazette-Mail*. May 6. Accessed March 8, 2024 via Nexis Uni (LexisNexis).

Hacker, Jacob S., Amelia Malpas, Paul Pierson, and Sam Zacher. 2024. "Bridging the Blue Divide: The Democrats' New Metro Coalition and the Unexpected Prominence of Redistribution." *Perspectives on Politics* 22(3): 609–629.

Hacker, Jacob S., and Paul Pierson. 2020. *Let Them Eat Tweets: How the Right Rules in an Age of Extreme Inequality*. New York: Liveright.

Haider-Markel, Donald P., and Kenneth J. Meier. 1996. "The Politics of Gay and Lesbian Rights: Expanding the Scope of the Conflict." *Journal of Politics* 58(2): 332–349.

Hajnal, Zoltan, and Michael U. Rivera. 2014. "Immigration, Latinos, and White Partisan Politics: The New Democratic Defection." *American Journal of Political Science* 58(4): 773–789.

Hassell, Hans J. G. 2017. *The Party's Primary: Control of Congressional Nominations*. Cambridge: Cambridge University Press.

Havard, William C. 1972. *The Changing Politics of the South*. Baton Rouge, LA: Louisiana State University Press.

Hayes, Danny. 2008. "Does the Messenger Matter? Candidate-Media Agenda Convergence and Its Effects on Voter Issue Salience." *Political Research Quarterly* 61(1): 134–146.

Hayes, Danny, and Seth C. McKee. 2008. "Toward a One-Party South?" *American Politics Research* 36(1): 3–32.

Haynes, Audrey A., Paul-Henri Gurian, Michael H. Crespin, and Christopher Zorn. 2004. "The Calculus of Concession: Media Coverage and the Dynamics of Winnowing in Presidential Nominations." *American Politics Research* 32(3): 310–337.

Heard, Alexander. 1952. *A Two-Party South?* Chapel Hill, NC: University of North Carolina Press.

Henderson, Michael, and D. Sunshine Hillygus. 2011. "The Dynamics of Health Care Opinion, 2008–2010: Partisanship, Self-Interest, and Racial Resentment." *Journal of Health Politics, Policy and Law* 36(6): 945–960.

Hernandez, Raymond. 2002. "Bush Swings through 3 States to Build Support for the G.O.P." *New York Times*, November 1. Accessed October 30, 2024 via Nexis Uni (LexisNexis).

Herrnson, Paul. S., and James G. Gimpel. 1995. "District Conditions and Primary Divisiveness in Congressional Elections." *Political Research Quarterly* 48(1): 117–134.

Hester, Wesley P. 2010. "Greenhouse-Gas Claim Questioned: GOP's Griffith Said Democrat Boucher Had Key Cap-and-Trade Role." *Richmond Times Dispatch*, October 29. Accessed October 28, 2024 via Nexis Uni (LexisNexis).

Hetherington, Marc J. 2001. "Resurgent Mass Partisanship: The Role of Elite Polarization." *American Political Science Review* 95(3): 619–631.

Hetherington, Marc J. 2009. "Putting Polarization in Perspective." *British Journal of Political Science* 39(2): 413–448.

Hill, Seth J., and Chris Tausanovitch. 2018. "Southern Realignment, Party Sorting, and the Polarization of American Primary Electorates, 1958–2012." *Public Choice* 176: 107–132.

Hillygus, D. Sunshine, Seth C. McKee, and McKenzie Young. 2017. "Reversal of Fortune: The Political Behavior of White Migrants to the South." *Presidential Studies Quarterly* 47(2): 354–364.

Hirschman, Elizabeth, Stephen Brown, and Pauline MacLaran. 2006. *Two Continents, One Culture: The Scotch-Irish in Southern Appalachia*. Johnson City, TN: The Overmountain Press.

Hood, M. V., III, and Seth C. McKee. 2010. "What Made Carolina Blue? In-migration and the 2008 North Carolina Presidential Vote." *American Politics Research* 38(2): 266–302.

Hood, M. V., III, and Seth C. McKee. 2022. *Rural Republican Realignment in the Modern South: The Untold Story*. Columbia, SC: University of South Carolina Press.

Hood, M. V., III, Quentin Kidd, and Irwin L. Morris. 2012. *The Rational Southerner: Black Mobilization, Republican Growth and the Partisan Transformation of the American South*. New York: Oxford University Press.

Hood, M. V., III, and Irwin Morris. 1997. "¿Amigo o Enemigo?: Context, Attitudes, and Anglo Public Opinion toward Immigration." *Social Science Quarterly* 78(2): 309–323.

Hooghe, Marc, and Ruth Dassonneville. 2018. "Explaining the Trump Vote: The Effect of Racist Resentment and Anti-Immigrant Sentiments." *PS: Political Science & Politics* 51(3): 528–534.

Hopkins, Daniel J. 2018. *The Increasingly United States: How and Why American Political Behavior Nationalized*. Chicago, IL: University of Chicago Press.

Hout, Michael. 1999. "Abortion Politics in the United States, 1972–1994: From Single Issue to Ideology." *Gender Issues* 17(2): 3–34.

Howell, Susan E. 1994. "Race, Cynicism, Economics and David Duke." *American Politics Quarterly* 22(2): 190–207.

Huddy, Leonie, Lilliana Mason, and Lene Aarøe. 2015. "Expressive Partisanship: Campaign Involvement, Political Emotion, and Partisan Identity." *American Political Science Review* 109(1): 1–17.

Hunt, Charles. 2022. *Home Field Advantage: Roots, Reelection, and Representation in Modern Congress*. Ann Arbor, MI: University of Michigan Press.

Irwin, Neil, and Josh Katz. 2016. "The Geography of Trumpism." *New York Times*, March 12. Accessed January 3, 2020 from https://www.nytimes.com/2016/03/13/upshot/the-geography-of-trumpism.html?ref=politics&_r=1

Iyengar, Shanto, Yphtach Lelkes, Matthew Levendusky, Neil Malhotra, and Sean J. Westwood. 2019. "The Origins and Consequences of Affective Polarization in the United States." *Annual Review of Political Science* 22(1): 129–146.

Iyengar, Shanto, Gaurav Sood, and Yphtach Lelkes. 2012. "Affect, Not Ideology: A Social Identity Perspective on Polarization." *Public Opinion Quarterly* 76(3): 405–431.

Jacobs, Nicholas F., and B. Kal Munis. 2019. "Place-Based Imagery and Voter Evaluations: Experimental Evidence on the Politics of Place." *Political Research Quarterly* 72(2): 263–277.

Jacobson, Gary C. 2015. "It's Nothing Personal: The Decline of the Incumbency Advantage in US House Elections." *The Journal of Politics* 77(3): 861–873.

Jacobson, Gary C., and Samuel Kernell. 1983. *Strategy and Choice in Congressional Elections*. New Haven, CT: Yale University Press.

Jacobson, Louis. 2010. "A Witch and 'Demon Sheep': Ads That Mattered." NPR.org, November 4. Accessed October 23, 2023 from https://www.npr.org/2010/11/04/131074946/a-witch-and-demon-sheep-ads-that-mattered

Jardina, Ashley. 2019. *White Identity Politics*. New York: Cambridge University Press.

Jardina, Ashley, and Robert P. Mickey. 2022. "White Racial Solidarity and Opposition to American Democracy." *The Annals of the American Academy of Political and Social Science* 699(1): 79–89.

Johnston, Ron, David Manley, and Kelvyn Jones. 2016. "Spatial Polarization of Presidential Voting in the United States, 1992–2012: The 'Big Sort' Revisited." *Annals of the Association of American Geographers* 106(5): 1047–1062.

Joseph, Cameron. 2009. "The Scots-Irish Vote." *Atlantic Online*. Accessed April 27, 2025 from http://www.theatlantic.com/politics/archive/2009/10/the-scots-irish-vote/27853i

Kam, Cindy D., and Camille D. Burge. 2018. "Uncovering Reactions to the Racial Resentment Scale across the Racial Divide." *Journal of Politics* 80(1): 314–320.

Kam, Cindy D., and Camille D. Burge. 2019. "Racial Resentment and Public Opinion across the Racial Divide." *Political Research Quarterly* 72(4): 767–784.

Kamarck, Elaine. 2018. *Primary Politics: Everything You Need to Know About How American Nominates Its Presidential Candidates*. Washington, DC: Brookings Institute Press.

Karol, David. 2023. "How Does Party Position Change Happen? The Case of LGBT Rights in the US." *Political Research Quarterly* 76(4): 1736–1750.

Kaufman, Chelsea N. 2021a. "Where Are the Values Voters? Ideological Constraint and Stability among Rural, Suburban, and Urban Populations in the United States." *Journal of Rural Studies* 88: 169–180.

Kaufman, Chelsea. 2021b. "Clinging to Guns and Religion? Issue Opinions and Ideology in Rural, Suburban, and Urban America." Paper Presented at the Annual Meeting of the Midwest Political Science Association, April 14–18, 2021.

Keith, Bruce E., David B. Magelby, Candice J. Nelson, Elizabeth A. Orr, Mark C. Westlye, and Raymond E. Wolfinger. 1992. *The Myth of the Independent Voter*. Berkeley, CA: University of California Press.

Kenney, Patrick J., and Thomas W. Rice. 1994. "The Psychology of Political Momentum." *Political Research Quarterly* 47(4): 923–938.

Kenny, Christopher, Michael McBurnett, and David Bordua. 2004. "The Impact of Political Interests in the 1994 and 1996 Congressional Elections: The Role of the National Rifle Association." *British Journal of Political Science* 34(2): 331–344.

Kercheval, Hoppy. 2016. "Clinton Popularity Fades in Coalfields; W.Va. Once Was a Clinton Stronghold, but Hillary Faces a Tough Election Battle." *Charleston Gazette-Mail*, May 4. Accessed March 28, 2024 via Nexis Uni (LexisNexis).

Kersey, Lori, and Andrew Brown. 2016. "Peaceful Crowd Includes Miners, Teachers, Jobless." *Charleston Gazette-Mail*, May 6. Accessed March 28, 2024 via Nexis Uni (LexisNexis).

Key, V. O., Jr. 1949. *Southern Politics in State and Nation*. New York: A. A. Knopf.

Key, V. O., Jr. 1955. "A Theory of Critical Elections." *The Journal of Politics* 17(1): 3–18.

Key, V. O., Jr. 1961. *Public Opinion and American Democracy*. New York: Alfred A. Knopf.

Kinder, Donald R. 2013. "Prejudice and Politics." In *The Oxford Handbook of Political Psychology*, 2nd ed., edited by Leonie Huddy, David O. Sears, and Jack Levy, 812–851. Oxford: Oxford University Press.

Kinder, Donald R., and Lynn M. Sanders. 1996. *Divided by Color: Racial Politics and Democratic Ideals*. Chicago, IL: University of Chicago Press.

Kinder, Donald R., and David O. Sears. 1981. "Prejudice and Politics: Symbolic Racism versus Racial Threats to the Good Life." *Journal of Personality and Social Psychology* 40(3): 414–431.

Kinsella, Chad, Colleen McTague, and Kevin N. Raleigh. 2015. "Unmasking Geographic Polarization and Clustering: A Micro-scalar Analysis of Partisan Voting Behavior." *Applied Geography* 62: 404–419.

Kitschelt, Herbert P., and Philipp Rehm. 2019. "Secular Partisan Realignment in the United States: The Socioeconomic Reconfiguration of White Partisan Support since the New Deal Era." *Politics & Society* 47(3): 425–479.

Knowles, Eric D., Brian S. Lowery, and Rebecca L. Schaumberg. 2010. "Racial Prejudice Predicts Opposition to Obama and His Health Care Reform Plan." *Journal of Experimental Social Psychology* 46(2): 420–423.

Knuckey, Jonathan. 2005a. "A New Front in the Culture War? Moral Traditionalism and Voting Behavior in US House Elections." *American Politics Research* 33(5): 645–671.

Knuckey, Jonathan. 2005b. "Racial Resentment and the Changing Partisanship of Southern Whites." *Party Politics* 11(1): 5–28.

Knuckey, Jonathan. 2011. "Racial Resentment and Vote Choice in the 2008 U.S. Presidential Election." *Politics & Policy* 39(4): 559–582.

Knuckey, Jonathan. 2017. "The Myth of the 'Two Souths?' Racial Resentment and White Party Identification in the Deep South and Rim South." *Social Science Quarterly* 98(2): 728–749.

Knuckey, Jonathan, and Myunghee Kim. 2015. "Racial Resentment, Old-Fashioned Racism, and the Vote Choice of Southern and Nonsouthern Whites in the 2012 U.S. Presidential Election." *Social Science Quarterly* 96(4): 905–922.

Knuckey, Jonathan, and Myunghee Kim. 2016. "Evaluations of Michelle Obama as First Lady: The Role of Racial Resentment." *Presidential Studies Quarterly* 46(2): 365–386.

Knuckey, Jonathan, and Myunghee Kim. 2020. "The Politics of White Racial Identity and Vote Choice in the 2018 Midterm Elections." *Social Science Quarterly* 101(4): 1584–1599.

Kousser, J. Morgan. 1974. *The Shaping of Southern Politics*. New Haven, CT: Yale University Press.

Kousser, J. Morgan. 2010. "The Immutability of Categories and the Reshaping of Southern Politics." *Annual Review of Political Science* 13(1): 365–383.

Krauthammer, Charles. 2010. "GOP Mandate? Just a Return to the Norm." *Chicago Tribune*, November 2010. Accessed October 28, 2024 via Nexis Uni (LexisNexis).

Kroom, Chris. 2008. "Election 2008: The McCain Belt – It's Not 'the South.'" Institute for Southern Studies (FacingSouth.org). Accessed December 5, 2024 from https://www.facingsouth.org/2008/11/election-2008-the-mccain-belt-its-not-the-south.html

Kuriwaki, Shiro. 2022. "Cumulative CCES Common Content." https://doi.org/10.7910/DVN/II2DB6, Harvard Dataverse, V7.

Kuziemko, Ilyana, and Ebonya Washington. 2018. "Why Did the Democrats Lose the South? Bringing New Data to an Old Debate." *American Economic Review* 108(10): 2830–2867.

Lacombe, Matthew. 2021. *Firepower: How the NRA Turned Gun Owners into a Political Force*. Princeton, NJ: Princeton University Press.

Lamis, Alexander P. 1988. *The Two-Party South*. Oxford: Oxford University Press.

Lanford, Daniel, and Jill Quadagno. 2016. "Implementing ObamaCare: The Politics of Medicaid Expansion under the Affordable Care Act of 2010." *Sociological Perspectives* 59(3): 619–639.

Lang, Corey, and Shanna Pearson-Merkowitz. 2015. "Partisan Sorting in the United States, 1972–2012: New Evidence from a Dynamic Analysis." *Political Geography* 48: 119–129.

Lassiter, Matthew D. 2007. *The Silent Majority: Suburban Politics in the Sunbelt South*. Princeton, NJ: Princeton University Press.

Lax, Jeffrey R., and Justin H. Phillips. 2009. "Gay Rights in the States: Public Opinion and Policy Responsiveness." *American Political Science Review* 103(3): 367–386.

Lazarus, Jeff. 2005. "Unintended Consequences: Anticipation of General Election Outcomes and Primary Election Divisiveness." *Legislative Studies Quarterly* 30(3): 435–461.

Lee, Frances E. 2016. *Insecure Majorities: Congress and the Perpetual Campaign*. Chicago, IL: University of Chicago Press.

Levendusky, Matthew S., and Neil Malhotra. 2016a. "(Mis) Perceptions of Partisan Polarization in the American Public." *Public Opinion Quarterly* 80(1): 378–391.

Levendusky, Matthew S., and Neil Malhotra. 2016b. "Does Media Coverage of Partisan Polarization Affect Political Attitudes?" *Political Communication* 33(2): 283–301.

Lewin, Philip G. 2019. "'Coal Is Not Just a Job, It's a Way of Life': The Cultural Politics of Coal Production in Central Appalachia." *Social Problems* 66(1): 51–68.

Lieberson, Stanley. 1985. "Unhyphenated Whites in the United States." *Ethnic and Racial Studies* 8(1): 159–180.

Lieberson, Stanley, and Mary C. Waters. 1986. "Ethnic Groups in Flux: The Changing Ethnic Responses of American Whites." *Annals of the American Academy of Political and Social Science* 487: 79–91.

Lieberson, Stanley, and Mary C. Waters. 1989. "The Rise of a New Ethnic Group: The 'Unhyphenated American'." *Social Science Research Council Items* 43: 7–10.

Lieberson, Stanley, and Mary C. Waters. 1993. "The Ethnic Responses of Whites: What Causes Thier Instability, Simplification, and Inconsistency?" *Social Forces* 72(2): 421–450.

Lippard, Cameron D. 2016. "Playing the 'Immigrant Card': Reflections of Color-Blind Rhetoric within Southern Attitudes on Immigration." *Social Currents* 3(1): 24–42.

Lopez, German. 2020. "Donald Trump's Long History of Racism, from the 1970s to 2020." Vox.com, August 13. Accessed February 15, 2022 from https://www.vox.com/2016/7/25/12270880/donald-trump-racist-racism-history

Lublin, David. 2004. *The Republican South: Democratization and Partisan Change*. Princeton, NJ: Princeton University Press.

Luo, Michael, and Griff Palmer. 2010. "Outside Groups on the Right Flexed Muscles in House Races." *New York Times*, November 4. Accessed October 28, 2024 via Nexis Uni (LexisNexis).

Luttig, Matthew D., and Matthew Motta. 2017. "President Obama on the Ballot: Referendum Voting and Racial Spillover in the 2014 Midterm Elections." *Electoral Studies* 50: 80–90.

Lyons, Jeffrey, and Stephen M. Utych. 2023. "You're Not from Here!: The Consequences of Urban and Rural Identities." *Political Behavior* 45(1): 75–101.

Mansfield, Duncan. 2000. "Gore's Roots Little Effect in Home State." *Associated Press State and Local Wire*, November 8. Accessed July 14, 2024 via Nexis Uni (LexisNexis).

Marcus, Ruth. 2010. "Clueless on a Shellacking." *Washington Post*, November 10. Accessed October 29, 2024 via Nexis Uni (LexisNexis).

Martin, Gregory J., and Steven W. Webster. 2020. "Does Residential Sorting Explain Geographic Polarization?" *Political Science Research and Methods* 8(2): 215–231.

Maskin, Eric, and Amartya Sen. 2016. "How Majority Rule Might Have Stopped Donald Trump." *New York Times*, May 1. Accessed March 14, 2024 from www.nytimes.com/2016/05/01/opinion/sunday/how-majority-rule-might-have-stopped-donald-trump.html

Mason, Liliana. 2015. "I Disrespectfully Agree: The Differential Effects of Partisan Sorting on Social and Issue Polarization." *American Journal of Political Science* 59(1): 128–145.

Mason, Liliana. 2018. *Uncivil Agreement: How Politics Became Our Identity*. Chicago, IL: University of Chicago Press.

Mason, Liliana, Julie Wronski, and John V. Kane. 2021. "Activating Animus: The Uniquely Social Roots of Trump Support." *American Political Science Review* 115(4): 1508–1516.

Maxwell, Angie, and Todd G. Shields. 2014. "The Fate of Obamacare: Racial Resentment, Ethnocentrism and Attitudes about Healthcare Reform." *Race and Social Problems* 6(4): 293–304.

Maxwell, Angie, and Todd G. Shields. 2019. *The Long Southern Strategy: How Chasing White Voters in the South Changed American Politics*. New York: Oxford University Press.

Mayhew, David. 1974. *Congress: The Electoral Connection*. New Haven, CT and London: Yale University Press.

McConahay, John B. 1986. "Modern Racism, Ambivalence, and the Modern Racism Scale." In *Prejudice, Discrimination, and Racism*, edited by John F. Dovidio and Samuel L. Gaertner, 91–125. Orlando, FL: Academic Press.

McCright, Aaron M., and Riley E. Dunlap. 2011. "The Politicization of Climate Change and Polarization in the American Public's Views of Global Warming, 2001–2010." *The Sociological Quarterly* 52(1): 155–194.

McCright, Aaron M., Chenyang Xiao, and Riley E. Dunlap. 2014. "Political Polarization on Support for Government Spending on Environmental Protection in the USA, 1974–2012." *Social Science Research* 48(2): 251–260.

McGhee, Eric, and Daniel Krimm. 2009. "Party Registration and the Geography of Party Polarization." *Polity* 41(3): 345–367.

McGowen, Ernest. 2017. *African Americans in White Suburbia: Social Networks and Political Behavior*. Lawrence, KS: University Press of Kansas.

McKee, Seth C. 2010. *Republican Ascendancy in Southern US Elections*. Boulder, CO: Westview Press.

McKee, Seth C., and Jeremy M. Teigen. 2016. "The New Blue: Northern In-Migration in Southern Presidential Elections." *PS: Political Science & Politics* 49(2): 228–233.

McKee, Seth C., and Antoine Yoshinaka. 2015. "Late to the Parade: Party Switchers in Contemporary US Southern Legislatures." *Party Politics* 21(6): 957–969.

Meckler, Laura, and Colleen McCain Nelson. 2016. "Hillary Clinton Is Taking Fire from Two Rivals; Democrat Is Trying to Turn Her Focus to Donald Trump but Has Yet to Fend Off Bernie Sanders." *Wall Street Journal* (Online), May 4. Accessed March 28, 2024 from: https://www.wsj.com/articles/hillary-clinton-is-taking-fire-from-two-rivals-1462406215

Mendelberg, Tali. 2001. *The Race Card: Campaign Strategy, Implicit Messages, and the Norm of Equality*. Princeton, NJ: Princeton University Press.

Meola, Olympia. 2010a. "Perriello and Hunt Stockpile Cash; GOP Rivals in 5th District Reports Raising More Than $900,000 in 3rd Quarter." *Richmond Times Dispatch*, October 10. Accessed October 28, 2024 via Nexis Uni (LexisNexis).

Meola, Olympia. 2010b. "McDonnell Surprised by Size of Win in 9th; 'No One Really Saw That Coming,' He Says of Griffith's 5-Point Upset." *Richmond Times Dispatch*, November 5. Accessed October 28, 2024 via Nexis Uni (LexisNexis).

Miller, Warren E, and J. Merrill Shanks. 1996. *The New American Voter*. Cambridge, MA: Harvard University Press.

Montgomery, Michael. 1991. "The Roots of Appalachian English: Scotch-Irish or British Southern?" *Journal of the Appalachian Studies Association* 3: 177–191.

Morris, Irwin L. 2021. *Movers and Stayers: The Partisan Transformation of 21st Century Southern Politics*. New York: Oxford University Press.

Morris, Irwin L. 2022. "Partisan Politics in the 21st Century South: The Fading Impact of Antebellum Slavery." *American Politics Research* 50(6): 743–751.

Mummolo, Jonathan, and Clayton Nall. 2017. "Why Partisans Do Not Sort: The Constraints on Political Segregation." *Journal of Politics* 79(1): 45–59.

Mutz, Diana C. 1997. "Mechanics of Momentum: Does Thinking Make It So?" *Journal of Politics* 59(1): 104–125.

Mutz, Diana C. 2018. "Status Threat, Not Economic Hardship, Explains the 2016 President Vote." *Proceedings of the National Academy of Sciences* 115(19): E4330–E4339.

Myers, Adam S. 2013. "Secular Geographical Polarization in the American South: The Case of Texas, 1996–2010." *Electoral Studies* 32(1): 48–62.

National Journal. 1994a. "Ky. Special Election Tightening amid Influx of GOP Money." *National Journal*, May 19. Accessed October 23, 2024 via Nexis Uni (LexisNexis).

National Journal. 1994b. "Dole Campaigns in Kentucky Race." *National Journal*, May 23. Accessed October 23, 2024 via Nexis Uni (LexisNexis).

Neidert, Lisa J., and Reynolds Farley. 1985. "Assimilation in the United States: An Analysis of Ethnic and Generation Differences in Status and Achievement." *American Sociological Review* 50(6): 840–850.

Newsweek. 2000. "Face to Face Combat." *Newsweek*, November 20. Accessed July 14, 2024 via Nexis Uni (LexisNexis).

Nolan, Jim. 2010. "Boucher, Griffith Hold Debate; Cap and Trade Is Most Heated Topic at Face-Off in 9th." *Richmond Times Dispatch*, October 22. Accessed October 28, 2024 via Nexis Uni (LexisNexis).

Norrander, Barbara. 2006. "The Attrition Game: Initial Resources, Initial Contests and the Exit of Candidates during the US Presidential Primary Season." *British Journal of Political Science* 36(3): 487–507.

Norris, Pippa, and Ronald Inglehart. 2006. "God, Guns, and Gays: The Supply and Demand for Religion in the US and Western Europe." *Public Policy Research* 12(4): 224–233.

Nyden, Paul J. 2000. "NRA May Have Helped Bush Carry W.Va." *Charleston Gazette*, November 8. 18A. Accessed July 14, 2024 via Nexis Uni (LexisNexis).

Oliver, Eric. 2008. "Eric Oliver on the 'Bigot Belt.'" Freakonomics (blog), November 19. Accessed October 4, 2019 from https://freakonomics.com/2008/11/eric-oliver-on-the-bigot-belt/

Omi, Michael A. 2001. "The Changing Meaning of Race." In *America Becoming: Racial Trends and Their Consequences*, ed. N. J. Smelser, W. J. Wilson and F. Mitchell. Washington, DC: National Academy Press. 243–263.

Omi, Michael A., and Howard Winant. 2014. *Racial Formation in the United States*. 3rd ed. New York: Routledge.

Patterson, Thomas E. 2016. "News Coverage of the 2016 Presidential Primaries: Horse Race Reporting Has Its Consequences." Shorenstein Center on Media, Politics, and Public Policy (Harvard).

July 11. Accessed March 12, 2024 from: https://shorensteincenter.org/news-coverage-2016-presidential-primaries/

Perez, Anthony Daniel, and Charles Hirschman. 2009. "The Changing Racial and Ethnic Composition of the US Population: Emerging American Identities." *Population and Development Review* 35(1): 1–51.

Perez-Pena, Richard. 2000. "Loss in Home State Leaves Gore Depending on Florida." *New York Times*, November 9. B1. Accessed July 14, 2024 via Nexis Uni (LexisNexis).

Pershing, Ben. 2010. "Sink-or-Swim Time for Democrats in 4 Congressional Races in Va." *Washington Post*, November 1. Accessed October 29, 2024 via Nexis Uni (LexisNexis).

Pirrman, Carrie M., Emily Sherwood, and Emily Tevebaugh. 2016. "2016 Primary Election and Caucus Data." Bucknell Digital Common. Downloaded January 5, 2024 from https://digitalcommons.bucknell.edu/election_data/1/

Pitts, Leonard, Jr. 2016. "The Forgotten Americans Who Love Trump." *Miami Herald*, August 26. Accessed January 12, 2025 from https://www.miamiherald.com/opinion/opn-columns-blogs/leonard-pitts-jr/article98142422.html

Portes, Alejandro, and Rafael Mozo. 1985. "The Political Adaptation Process of Cubans and Other Ethnic Minorities in the United States: A Preliminary Analysis." *International Migration Review* 19(1): 35–63.

Rastogi, Ankit, and Michael Jones-Correa. 2023. "Not Just White Soccer Moms: Voting in Suburbia in the 2016 and 2020 Elections." *RSF: The Russell Sage Foundation Journal of the Social Sciences* 9(2): 184–203.

Reny, Tyler T., Loren Collingwood, and Ali A. Valenzuela. 2019. "Vote Switching in the 2016 Election: How Racial and Immigration Attitudes, Not Economics, Explain Shifts in White Voting." *Public Opinion Quarterly* 83(1): 91–113.

Reny, Tyler T., Ali A. Valenzuela, and Loren Collingwood. 2020. "'No, You're Playing the Race Card': Testing the Effects of Anti-Black, Anti-Latino, and Anti-Immigrant Appeals in the Post-Obama Era." *Political Psychology* 41(2): 283–302.

Rhodes, Jesse H., and Tatishe M. Nteta. 2024. "The New Racial Spillover: Donald Trump, Racial Attitudes, and Public Opinion toward Accountability for Perpetrators and Planners of the January 6 Capitol Attack." *Political Science Quarterly* 139(2): 159–176.

Risen, Clay. 2008. "The Mind of the South." New Republic (blog), November 11. Accessed December 5, 2024 from https://newrepublic.com/article/45957/the-mind-the-south

Ritchie, Fiona, and Doug Orr. 2014. *Wayfaring Strangers: The Musical Voyage from Scotland and Ulster to Appalachia*. Chapel Hill, NC: University of North Carolina Press.

Roccas, Sonia, and Marilynn B. Brewer. 2002. "Social Identity Complexity." *Personality and Social Psychology Review* 6(2): 88–106.

Rodgers, Harrell R., Jr., and Charles S. Bullock III. 1972. *Law and Social Change: Civil Rights Laws and Their Consequences*. New York: McGraw-Hill.

Rohla, Ryne, Ron Johnston, Kelvyn Jones, and David Manley. 2018. "Spatial Scale and Geographic Polarization of the American Electorate." *Political Geography* 65: 117–122.

Rozell, Mark J., and Clyde Wilcox. 1995. "Virginia: God, Guns, and Oliver North." In *God at the Grass Roots: The Christian Right in the 1994 Elections*, edited by Mark J. Rozell and Clyde Wilcox, 109–131. Lanham, MD: Rowman & Littlefield.

Rozell, Mark J., and Clyde Wilcox. 1996. "Second Coming: The Strategies of the New Christian Right." *Political Science Quarterly* 111(2): 271–294.

Rozell, Mark J., Clyde Wilcox, and John C. Green. 1998. "Religious Constituencies and Support for the Christian Right in the 1990s." *Social Science Quarterly* 79(4): 815–827.

Sabato, Larry. 2006. "Election Exceptions." *Sabato's Crystal Ball* (The Center for Politics), June 15. Accessed October 23, 2024 from https://centerforpolitics.org/crystalball/ljs2006061501/

Sarlin, Benjy, and Sam Petulla. 2016. "United States of Trump." NBCNews.com, June 20. Accessed March 22, 2024 from https://www.nbcnews.com/specials/donald-trump-republican-party/

Scala, Dante J. 2020. "The Skeptical Faithful: How Trump Gained Momentum among Evangelicals." *Presidential Studies Quarterly* 50(4): 927–947.

Scala, Dante J., and Kenneth M. Johnson. 2017. "Political Polarization along the Rural-Urban Continuum? The Geography of the Presidential Vote, 2000–2016." *The ANNALS of the American Academy of Political and Social Science* 672(1): 162–184.

Scala, Dante J., Kenneth M. Johnson, and Luke T. Rogers. 2015. "Red Rural, Blue Rural? Presidential Voting Patterns in a Changing Rural America." *Political Geography* 48: 108–118.

Schaffner, Brian F., and Kaitlyn Gaus. 2023. "Donald Trump and the Democratic Shift among College-Educated Suburban White Voters." *The Forum* 21(1): 75–96.

Schaffner, Brian F., Matthew MacWilliams, and Tatishe Nteta. 2018. "Understanding White Polarization in the 2016 Vote for President: The Sobering Role of Racism and Sexism." *Political Science Quarterly* 133(1): 9–34.

Scher, Richard K. 1997. *Politics in the New South: Republicanism, Race and Leadership in the Twentieth Century.* 2nd ed. Armonk, NY: M.E. Sharpe.

Schildkraut, Deborah J. 2003. "American Identity and Attitudes toward Official-English Policies." *Political Psychology* 24(3): 469–499.

Schuman, Howard, Charlotte Steeh, and Lawrence Bobo. 1985. *Racial Attitudes in America: Trends and Interpretations.* Cambridge, MA and London: Harvard University Press.

Schuman, Howard, Charlotte Steeh, Lawrence Bobo, and Maria Krysan. 1997. *Racial Attitudes in America: Trends and Interpretations.* Revised ed. Cambridge, MA: Harvard University Press.

Sears, David O. 1988. "Symbolic Racism." In *Eliminating Racism: Profiles in Controversy*, edited by Phyllis A. Katz and Dalmas A. Taylor, 53–84. New York: Plenum Press.

Sears, David O., Colette Van Laar, Mary Carrillo, and Rick Kosterman. 1997. "Is It Really Racism? The Origins of White Americans' Opposition to Race-Targeted Policies." *Public Opinion Quarterly* 61(1): 16–53.

Seelye, Katharine. 1994. "The Iron Man of Congress Ends a Streak in Absentia." *New York Times*, March 4. A24.

Seiler, Fanny. 2000. "How Bush Won West Virginia." *Charleston Gazette*, November 14. 9A. Accessed July 14, 2024 via Nexis Uni (LexisNexis).

Senior, Jennifer. 2016. "Review: In 'Hillbilly Elegy,' A Tough Love Analysis of the Poor Who Back Trump." *New York Times*, August 10. Accessed January 3, 2025 from https://www.nytimes.com/2016/08/11/books/review-in-hillbilly-elegy-a-compassionate-analysis-of-the-poor-who-love-trump.html

Shafer, Byron E., and Richard G. C. Johnston. 2001. "The Transformation of Southern Politics Revisited: The House of Representatives as a Window." *British Journal of Political Science* 31(4): 601–625.

Shafer, Byron E., and Richard G. C. Johnston. 2006. *The End of Southern Exceptionalism: Class, Race, and Partisan Change in the Postwar South.* Cambridge, MA: Harvard University Press.

Shapiro, Robert Y., John T. Young, Kelly D. Patterson, Jill E. Blumenfeld, Douglas A. Cifu, Sara M. Offenhartz, and Ted E. Tsekerides. 1991, "Media Influence on Support for Presidential Candidates in Primary Elections: Theory, Method, and Evidence." *International Journal of Public Opinion Research* 3(4): 340–365.

Shea, Daniel M., and Nicholas F. Jacobs. 2024. *The Rural Voter: The Politics of Place and the Disuniting of America*. New York: Columbia University Press.

Sheagley, Geoffrey. Philip Chen, and Christina Farhart. 2017. "Racial Resentment, Hurricane Sandy, and the Spillover of Racial Attitudes into Evaluations of Government Organizations." *Analyses of Social Issues and Public Policy* 17(1): 105–131.

Sides, John. 2008. "The Bigot Belt." Good Authority (blog), November 19. Accessed December 5, 2024 from https://goodauthority.org/news/the-bigot-belt/

Sides, John, and Kalev Leetaru. 2016. "A Deep Dive into the News Media's Role in the Rise of Donald J. Trump." Monkey Cage (WashingtonPost.com), June 24. Accessed March 15, 2024 from https://www.washingtonpost.com/news/monkey-cage/wp/2016/06/24/a-deep-dive-into-the-news-medias-role-in-the-rise-of-donald-j-trump/

Sides, John, Chris Tausanovitch, and Lynn Vavreck. 2022. *The Bitter End: The 2020 Presidential Campaign and the Challenge to American Democracy*. Princeton, NJ: Princeton University Press.

Sides, John, and Lynn Vavreck. 2013. *The Gamble: Choice and Chance in the 2012 Presidential Election*. Princeton, NJ: Princeton University Press.

Silver, Nate. 2016. "The Mythology of Trump's 'Working Class' Support." FiveThirtyEight.com, May 3. Accessed March 22, 2024 from https://fivethirtyeight.com/features/the-mythology-of-trumps-working-class-support/

Simpson, Dan. 2016. "One Man's Harrowing Journey from the Hollers." *Pittsburgh Post-Gazette*, July 12. Accessed January 12, 2025 from https://www.post-gazette.com/ae/books/2016/08/21/Book-review-Hillbilly-Elegy-by-J-D-Vance/stories/201608210058

Singer, Nora. 2018. "What the History of Gun Rights in Appalachia Tells Us About the Current Gun Debate." A Contest of Ideas (blog), November 6. Accessed January 10, 2019 from https://www.acontestideas.com/new-blog/2018/11/6/what-the-history-of-gun-rights-in-appalachia-tells-us-about-the-current-gun-debate

Smith, Ben. 2008. "Real America?" Ben Smith Blog (Politico.com), November 6. Accessed October 4, 2019 from https://www.politico.com/blogs/ben-smith/2008/11/real-america-014013

Sonenshein, Raphael J., and Nicholas A. Valentino. 2000. "The Distinctiveness of Jewish Voting." *Urban Affairs Review* 35(3): 358–389.

Sosna, Morton. 1987. "More Important Than the Civil War? The Impact of World War II on the South." In *Perspectives on the American South: An Annual Review of Society, Politics, and Culture*, vol. 4, edited by James C. Cobb and Charles R. Wilson, 145–161. New York: Gordon and Breach.

Springer, Melanie J. 2019. "Where Is 'the South'? Assessing the Meaning of Geography in Politics." *American Politics Research* 47(5): 1100–1134.

Stanley, Harold W. 1987. *Voter Mobilization and the Politics of Race: The South and Universal Suffrage, 1952–1984*. New York: Praeger.

Stanley, Harold W., and David S. Castle. 1988. "Partisan Changes in the South: Making Sense of Scholarly Dissonance." In *The South's New Politics: Realignment and Dealignment*, edited by Robert Swansbrough and David Brodsky, 238–252. Columbia, SC: University of South Carolina Press.

Steger, Wayne P., John J. Hickman, and Ken Yohn. 2002. "Candidate Competition and Attrition in Presidential Primaries, 1912–2000." *American Politics Research* 30(5): 528–554.

Stewart, Martina. 2016. "Emotional Unemployed W.Va. Coal Worker Confronts Hillary Clinton over Comment about Putting Coal 'Out of Business.'" *Washington Post*, May 3. Accessed March 8, 2024 from https://www.washingtonpost.com/news/morning-mix/wp/2016/05/03/unemployed-w-va-coal-worker-confronts-clinton-over-comment-about-putting-coal-out-of-business/

Stokols, Eli. 2016. "GOP Elites Line Up behind Ted Cruz." *Politico*, March 23. Accessed March 15, 2024 from www.politico.com/story/2016/03/ted-cruz-republican-establishment-elites-221174

Sullivan, Andrew. 2008. "The McCain Belt." The Daily Dish (TheAtlantic.com), November 5. Accessed March 18, 2017 from https://www.theatlantic.com/daily-dish/archive/2008/11/the-mccain-belt/208968/

Sundquist, James L. 1983. *Dynamics of the Party System: Alignment and Realignment of Political Parties in the United States*. Washington, DC: The Brookings Institution.

Sutton, David. 2009. "The 2008 Presidential Election in Appalachia: Reading from the Margins." *Appalachian Journal* 36(3/4): 188–198.

Ternullo, Stephanie. 2024. *How the Heartland Went Red: Why Local Forces Matter in an Age of Nationalized Politics*. Princeton, NJ: Princeton University Press.

Tesler, Michael. 2012a. "The Spillover of Racialization into Health Care: How President Obama Polarized Public Opinion by Racial Attitudes and Race." *American Journal of Political Science* 56(3): 690–704.

Tesler, Michael. 2012b. "The Spillover of Racialization into Same-Sex Marriage." YouGov.com, May 22. Accessed January 3, 2020 from https://today.yougov.com/topics/politics/articles-reports/2012/05/22/spillover-racialization-same-sex-marriage

Tesler, Michael. 2012c. "The Spillover of Racialization into Evaluations of Bo Obama." YouGov.com, April 10. Accessed January 3, 2020 from https://today.yougov.com/topics/politics/articles-reports/2012/04/10/spillover-racialization-evaluations-bo-obama

Tesler, Michael. 2015. "The Conditions Ripe for Racial Spillover Effects." *Political Psychology* 36(S1): 101–117.

Tesler, Michael. 2016. *Post-Racial or Most-Racial? Race and Politics in the Obama Era*. Chicago, IL: University of Chicago Press.

The Economist. 2016a. "Books of the Year 2016." *The Economist*, December 10. Accessed January 12, 2025 from https://www.economist.com/books-and-arts/2016/12/10/books-of-the-year-2016

The Economist. 2016b. "Promises, Promises; American Memoirs." *The Economist*, August 13. (Via Gale in Context).

The Hotline. 2010. "Fun with Numbers." *National Journal's House Race Hotline*, October 4. Accessed October 28, 2024 via Nexis Uni (LexisNexis).

Thompson, Derek. 2016. "Donald Trump and the Twilight of White America." TheAtlantic.com, May 13. Accessed March 22, 2024 from https://www.theatlantic.com/politics/archive/2016/05/donald-trump-and-the-twilight-of-white-america/482655/

Timpone, Richard J. 1995. "Mass Mobilization or Government Intervention? The Growth of Black Registration in the South." *Journal of Politics*. 57(2): 425–442.

Tracy, Tennille. 2010. "In Virginia House Race, Cap and Trade Matters." *Wall Street Journal*, October 25. Accessed October 29, 2024 via Nexis Uni (LexisNexis).

Trubowitz, Peter. 1992. "Sectionalism and American Foreign Policy: The Political Geography of Consensus and Conflict." *International Studies Quarterly* 36(2): 173–190.

Trujillo, Kristin Lunz, and Zack Crowley. 2022. "Symbolic versus Material Concerns of Rural Consciousness in the United States." *Political Geography* 96: 102658.

US Census Bureau. 2023. "Ancestor Appreciate Day: September 27, 2023." September 27. Accessed January 7, 2025 from https://www.census.gov/newsroom/stories/ancestor-appreciation-day.html

US Census Bureau. n.d. "Why We Ask About Ancestry." Accessed January 2, 2025 from https://www.census.gov/acs/www/about/why-we-ask-each-question/ancestry/

Valentino, Nicholas A., and David O. Sears. 2005. "Old Times There Are Not Forgotten: Race and Partisan Realignment in the Contemporary South." *American Journal of Political Science* 49(3): 672–688.

Vance, J. D. 2016. *Hillbilly Elegy: A Memoir of a Family and Culture in Crisis*. New York: Harper.

Vance, J. D. 2024. "Read the Transcript of J.D. Vance's Convention Speech." *New York Times*, July 18. Accessed January 3, 2025 from https://www.nytimes.com/2024/07/17/us/politics/read-the-transcript-of-jd-vances-convention-speech.html

Vavreck, Lynn, and Ryan D. Enos. 2012. "Recent Changes in Support for Same-Sex Marriage: Is There a Difference across Races?" YouGov.com, May 19. Accessed January 3, 2020 from https://today.yougov.com/topics/politics/articles-reports/2012/05/19/recent-changes-support-same-sex-marriage-there-dif

Voss, D. Stephen. 1996. "Beyond Racial Threat: Failure of an Old Hypothesis in the New South." *The Journal of Politics* 58(4): 1156–1170.

Wasserman, Dave. 2010. "House: Ratings Changes in 15 Districts Explained." *The Cook Political Report* (cookpolitical.com), January 28, 2010. Accessed November 13, 2024 from https://www.cookpolitical.com/analysis/house/house-overview/house-ratings-changes-15-districts-explained

Waters, Mary C. 1990. *Ethnic Options: Choosing Identities in America*. Berkeley, CA: University of California Press.

Webb, James H. 2004. *Born Fighting: How the Scots-Irish Shaped America*. New York: Broadway Books.

Weigel, David. 2016. "Nine Amazing Numbers from the May 10 Primaries." *Washington Post*, May 11. Accessed March 8, 2024 from https://www.washingtonpost.com/news/post-politics/wp/2016/05/11/nine-amazing-numbers-from-the-may-10-primaries/

White, Steven. 2019. "Race, Religion, and Obama in Appalachia." *Social Science Quarterly* 100(1): 38–59.

Whitley, Tyler, and Olympia Meola. 2010. "Congressional Races Flush with Cash in Va." *Richmond Times-Dispatch*, October 24. Accessed October 28, 2024 via Nexis Uni (LexisNexis).

Wilson, David C., and Paul R. Brewer. 2013. "The Foundations of Public Opinion on Voter ID Laws: Political Predispositions, Racial Resentment, and Information Effects." *Public Opinion Quarterly* 77(4): 962–984.

Wilson, David C., and Darren W. Davis. 2018. "Appraisals of President Obama's Economic Performance: Racial Resentment and Attributional Responsibility." *Electoral Studies* 55: 62–72.

Wilson, James Q., and Edward C. Banfield. 1964. "Public-Regardingness as a Value Premise in Voting Behavior." *American Political Science Review* 58(4): 876–887.

Wilson, Thomas C. 1986. "Interregional Migration and Racial Attitudes." *Social Forces* 65(1): 177–186.

Wines, Michael. 1994. "William H. Natcher Dies at 84; Held Voting Record in Congress." *New York Times*, March 31. B10.

Wing, Ian Sue, and Joan L. Walker. 2010. "The Geographic Dimensions of Electoral Polarization in the 2004 US Presidential Vote." In *Progress in Spatial Analysis: Methods and Applications*, edited by Antonio Paez, Julie Gallo, Ron N. Buliung, and Sandy Dall'erba, 253–285. Berlin: Springer Nature.

Wolfinger, Raymond E. 1965. "The Development and Persistence of Ethnic Voting." *American Political Science Review* 59(4): 896–908.

Woon, Jonathan, Sean Craig, Amanda Leifson, and Matthew Tarpey. 2020. "Trump Is Not a (Condorcet) Loser! Primary Voters' Preferences and the 2016 Republican Presidential Nomination." *PS: Political Science & Politics* 53(3): 407–412.

Wright, Gerald C. 1977. "Contextual Models of Electoral Behavior: The Southern Wallace Vote." *American Political Science Review* 71(2): 497–508.

Wuest, Joanna. 2023. *Born This Way: Science, Citizenship and Inequality in the American LGBTQ+ Movement*. Chicago, IL: University of Chicago Press.

Yglesias, Matt. 2008. "The McCain Belt." Center for American Progress (ThinkProgress.org). November 5. Accessed March 18, 2017 from http://yglesias.thinkprogress.org/archives/2008/11/the_mccain_belt.php

Yglesias, Matthew. 2016. "You Can't Talk about Trump's Rise without Talking about Racism." Vox.com, May 9. Accessed March 22, 2024 from https://www.vox.com/2016/5/9/11635426/donald-trump-rise-racism

Zaller, John R. 1992. *The Nature and Origin of Mass Opinion*. New York: Cambridge University Press.

Zingher, Joshua N. 2022a. "Diploma Divide: Educational Attainment and the Realignment of the American Electorate." *Political Research Quarterly* 75(2): 263–277.

Zingher, Joshua N. 2022b. *Political Choice in a Polarized America: How Elite Polarization Shapes Mass Behavior*. New York: Oxford University Press.

Zuckerbrod, Nancy. 2000. "Tennessee, Arkansas Wins Would Have Meant Victory for Gore." *Associated Press State and Local Wire*, November 8. Accessed July 14, 2024 via Nexis Uni (LexisNexis).

Index

https://doi.org/10.1515/9783111615707-010

www.ingramcontent.com/pod-product-compliance
Lightning Source LLC
Chambersburg PA
CBHW050650280326
41932CB00015B/2852

* 9 7 8 3 1 1 1 6 1 5 4 5 5 *